ART IN FEDERAL BUILDINGS

AN ILLUSTRATED RECORD OF THE TREASURY DEPARTMENT'S NEW PROGRAM IN PAINTING AND SCULPTURE

VOLUME I

MURAL DESIGNS, 1934-1936

TEXT BY

EDWARD BRUCE AND FORBES WATSON

ART IN FEDERAL BUILDINGS INCORPORATED

WASHINGTON, D. C.

1936

COPYRIGHT, 1936, BY

ART IN FEDERAL BUILDINGS INCORPORATED

15294

FORMAT BY HARRY ROBERTS, JR.

PRINTING BY THE JOHN D. LUCAS PRINTING COMPANY, BALTIMORE, MARYLAND

ENGRAVINGS BY THE STANDARD ENGRAVING COMPANY, WASHINGTON, D. C.

THIS WORK IS DEDICATED TO

THE HONORABLE, THE SECRETARY OF THE TREASURY

HENRY MORGENTHAU, JR.

BECAUSE OF HIS FAR-SIGHTED OFFICIAL ACTS FOR THE ADVANCEMENT OF

ARCHITECTURE, SCULPTURE & PAINTING

AND TO

MRS. MORGENTHAU

BECAUSE OF HER UNFAILING ENCOURAGEMENT

& SYMPATHETIC UNDERSTANDING OF

AMERICAN ART AND ARTISTS

SPONSORS' STATEMENT

ALTHOUGH THE series of volumes to be published under the general title, *Art in Federal Buildings*, will deal exclusively with painting and sculpture carried out under the Treasury Department, the Department has no funds which legally can be devoted to a publication of this nature. However, there are many reasons why such volumes should be compiled. In the belief that the new program, which has brought about the cooperation of painting and sculpture with architecture under the Supervising Architect's Office, is of outstanding creative and social significance, the undersigned have raised the funds from private sources for the production cost of publishing Volume I.

The work done by American painters and sculptors for Federal buildings constructed by the Treasury will be permanently placed in widely separated regions throughout the country. To see it completely would necessitate becoming a most persistent traveller. In order that the public may gauge its meaning as a whole, *Art in Federal Buildings* proposes to make a complete illustrative record of the work. Beginning with the mural designs approved since the inception of the new program it plans to publish further volumes which shall fully illustrate sculpture models, installed sculpture, completed and installed murals and all other work in the fine arts created for the decoration of Federal buildings. Justice to the artists demands the publication of their work.

The undersigned believe that such publication, by bringing the artists of the country to a wider public, will win for them private commissions. This is a primary purpose of these volumes. It is hoped that they will come to the attention of manufacturers, industrialists, financiers, architects and others directly or indirectly concerned with the construction of large and small buildings, and that their reproductions will induce the employment of painters and sculptors. Quite aside from any benefits derived by the artists, and by society in general, through such employment, there is no more direct and far-reaching way to make a building and those concerned with it famous than by introducing into it the work of first-rate painters and sculptors. As a matter of record business always profits by associating with art.

In a period of economic emergency when social conscience is spurred by need, both artists and administrators are beneficially stimulated. This is evident through the fact that the Government and the artists have proved their ability to cooperate to the end that our public buildings shall be more interesting, more beautiful and more educational. The undersigned hold the firm conviction, on the other hand, that governmental stimulus, by itself, is not all that the artists of our country require in order to achieve their own highest aims.

Nor is it all that the Government requires in order that it may secure the best art for the people. To continue its high efforts under the easier conditions of prosperity the rivalry of private initiative, in giving commissions to our painters and sculptors, is necessary. The Government cannot for long have things its own way—cannot be the one and only client, without an inevitable slump. Similarly it is not enough for the artists to rest in the conviction that a government in which they have the same voice as other citizens, will inevitably continue an expansive painting and sculpture program. Within themselves the artists must enjoy the stimulus of knowing that their fellow men have a direct need for their art. Otherwise, with emergency stimulus removed, the average, the moderate, the correct will take complete command while enterprise, inspiration and high quality go unsupported.

EDWARD BRUCE   CECIL H. JONES
OLIN DOWS   HENRY LA FARGE
MARIA EALAND   EDWARD ROWAN
INSLEE HOPPER   FORBES WATSON

PREFACE

MY EXPERIENCE as director of the former Public Works of Art Project and as one of the workers in the Treasury Department Art Projects has given me a close-up of how the Government has worked in carrying out the plan to secure "the best available American art for public buildings" and at the same time to "give encouragement to the American artist." The Government has recognized that the value of this work depends upon its quality; therefore it has placed its main emphasis on quality.

On December 8, 1933, a meeting was held of the Advisory Committee to the Treasury on Fine Arts, to which were invited artists, museum directors and other qualified leaders in the world of art from many regions of the country. The purpose of the meeting was to ascertain ways and means of carrying forward the work of encouraging the fine arts as a function of the Federal Government. This meeting resulted in the organization of the Public Works of Art Project. A nation wide system of voluntary regional chairmen was immediately begun. These in turn formed committees in their own regions with sub-chairmen of state committees for every state in the Union.

The money to carry on this work was allocated by the then existing Civil Works Administration to the Treasury Department, to be administered by that department. The Public Works of Art Project began, without delay, to function. On December 12th, the first artists were already on the payroll. The rate of pay was determined by the "going rates" of the Civil Works Administration for skilled craftsmen.

The idea of paying salaries to artists, and allowing them to work in a medium selected by them, to create paintings, prints, sculpture, wood carving, pottery, iron work—allowing them, in fact, complete liberty to express themselves, with the single provision that their work, in the broadest sense, should be appropriate in design and quality for the adornment of public buildings—that idea certainly was a new conception of the relationship between the artist and his client.

The files of the Public Works of Art Project contain many letters by artists written to explain what seems to me a most interesting point in the Government's adventure into the field of art. The artists wrote that the certainty of a regular check gave them a sense of security which enabled them to work without the distraction of financial uncertainty.

This was only one point in the new adventure. Previously the artist carried on his creative efforts under his own solitary guidance. What other people might come to think of his work, what support the public might give him, how quickly he might become well enough known to obtain support, were matters of chance.

On the other hand the receipt of a check from the United States Government meant much more than the amount for which it was drawn. It brought to the artist for the first time in America the realization that he was not a solitary worker. It symbolized a people's interest in his achievement. It gave him a sense of powerful encouragement, which inspired in him both a broader and a more realistic conception. No longer was he, so to speak, talking to himself. No longer was he limited in his appeal to a group of fellow artists or to pleasing a small minority of specialists. Symbolically he had become the spokesman of his community. His statement was unconsciously directed to the understanding of a much larger, less specialized public.

The Public Works of Art Project was an emergency agency, a selective employment plan in which over 3,600 artists participated, producing over 16,000 works in various mediums. It would be folly to maintain that 16,000 masterpieces were produced. However, it is not an exaggeration to say that a sufficient number of vigorous, original works of art were produced to give satisfaction and stimulation to the Government and to all those who had faith in the high civilizing influence of what a disinterested government could accomplish through cooperation with the artists of the country.

When this project closed on June 30th, 1934, the Secretary of the Treasury, Mr. Henry Morgenthau, Jr., became, as a result of its success, personally interested in the formation of a permanent section of the Government which would devote itself to the securing of "the best available American art" for those Federal buildings (the great majority of Federal buildings, in fact) constructed under the Supervising Architect's office of the Treasury Department Procurement Division.

Careful study of organization possibilities, in which Messrs. Henry Morgenthau, Jr., C. J. Peoples, Director of Procurement, and Louis A. Simon, Supervising Architect, cooperated with other members of the Treasury Department, resulted in the organization on October 16th,

1934, of the Section of Painting and Sculpture. This Section did not follow the plan of the Public Works of Art Project, but there is no doubt that its existence resulted from the success of the former undertaking.

It was decided that the time had come when the decoration of public buildings with painting and sculpture should be planned in such a way that artists in every portion of the country would feel the stimulating influence of the Government's recognition of quality and of its desire to secure quality. No longer could the more or less hit or miss system that previously prevailed be continued in the light of what the Government had learned about the needs and potentialities of American artists.

In his Departmental Order, the Secretary of the Treasury stressed two points: first, the acquisition of the best available American art, and, second, the encouragement of those talents which, although known to exist in the country, had not had a reasonable opportunity to bring themselves to the public attention until after the Government had become a serious client of the artists.

After the Treasury's permanent section devoted to painting and sculpture had been in operation for some time, an allocation was made by the Works Progress Administration to the Treasury to pay for the employment of artists on relief who were able to meet the standard established by the Supervising Architect's Office for painting and sculpture to be placed in Federal buildings. A detailed description of this project will be found in later pages of this volume.

Up to the time when the Government entered the field of art, painters and sculptors had found it necessary to concentrate in the great financial centers. Roughly speaking, men who were not known in New York, Chicago, San Francisco, or some other great city, found it almost impossible to make a living. The former speculative relationship between the public and the artist made the life of the painter and sculptor a gamble. The star system prevailed in painting and sculpture, if not as obviously at least as effectively as in the case of musicians and actors.

One of the first steps taken by the Treasury Department Art Projects was to initiate a series of competitions which artists could enter anonymously. Indeed they were obliged to enter them anonymously. Mural designs, sculpture models, all were submitted unsigned. The name of the entrant was not disclosed until after the award was made. This method of course was a powerful blow at the star system. For the first time America purchased art on a large scale regardless of the fame of the artists, the purchasing being based entirely on the quality of the work.

The volumes which we are now bringing out tell the story visually. As a painter I can't help envying the younger artists who are lucky enough to be growing up under a system of art promotion which has such healthy similarities to the periods in which some of the greatest art in the world was produced. We have found that great art has developed under various conditions, but rarely did the best appear unless the community was back of it. Once more the community is behind the artist. My inference, I hope, is sufficiently obvious.

I have added, in the appendix, the dry statistics of our procedure. These are not necessary here. My pleasure in this work has been to realize once more the value of the artists to their country. Given the opportunity to work in, with, and for, their communities, how well our artists have taken advantage of their unprecedented chances to give their best. Disinterested administration, together with the realization that the civilization of a country reaches its highest development through an encouraged freedom of expression, justify faith. My faith is that as long as the artists of this country can utilize their best powers, without materialistic or petty hindrance, progress, in the highest sense of the word, is our inevitable destiny.

EDWARD BRUCE

CONTENTS

CONTENTS

CONTENTS

*Buildings have been constructed during the tenure of office of three Supervising Architects: James Knox Taylor, James A. Wetmore, Acting Supervising Architect, and Louis A. Simon, the present incumbent. The initials of the architect in office are given after each notation of the Supervising Architect's Office.

CONTENTS

A PERSPECTIVE OF AMERICAN MURALS
BY FORBES WATSON

The Ascension BY JOHN LA FARGE

Church of The Ascension, New York

A PERSPECTIVE OF AMERICAN MURALS
BY FORBES WATSON

THE ART of painting murals is necessarily less intimate than the art of painting individual pictures. Paintings commissioned for particular spaces, set up, in the mind of the artist, considerations and ideas extending beyond the personal. His freedom is qualified by a whole series of relationships. Fixed dimensions, the architectural setting, the uses of the building, the appropriateness of subject-matter, create new esthetic, technical and social problems which the artist is called upon to solve. At the outset he is brought face to face with the test of the true mural painter. If legitimate external limitations to his freedom rouse his imagination to greater efforts, he has found his calling. If they thwart his imagination, dilute his efforts (which they may do without invalidating him as an artist) he might better return to his own domain there to create works conceived and completed without thought of architectural surroundings or structural distractions. Painting for the exclusive purpose of interpreting his own unhindered idea, he may achieve an intimacy of expression more satisfying and pertinent to his special gifts than he could achieve under the social obligations inherent in the mural. One of his consolations will be his happy freedom from the architect's tender solicitation for the subservience of painting to architecture.

Aside from the architect's efforts to hold painting down to what he considers its functions as a handmaiden to his supposedly nobler art; and aside from the occasionally limited sense of appropriateness of subject-matter manifested by the private or public owner of the building, there arises, to affect the mural painter's point of view, the feeling that he has escaped from a limited audience to a public extending far beyond the narrower circles of specialized art appreciation. This does not mean in the least that he will be overcome by a desire to paint "down." It may mean, however, that logic will demand the use of symbols which are both simpler and broader in appeal. His goal then would become less consciously individual. Something less egotistical, and bigger than the protection of his own personal statement, might imbue his work. That, I suppose, will depend on the force and humanity of his imagination, and very much on whether mural painting, aside from its present tempting opportunities, is his real calling. If it is, he will not degenerate into being a mere glorified pedestrian enlarger.

If he inherently prefers the implicit rights of unthwarted individualism, resenting either social or architectural cooperation, his murals, if he does them, will lack enthusiasm. Not everyone who paints on walls, even habitually, is a mural painter, although he may insist upon that title. Some wearying practitioners of this noble art are inclined to think that quality and size are interchangeable terms. Yet, in the last analysis, both the mural and the now humble easel painting depend for their validity on the creative vitality of the artist who does them. It is as true that the mediocrity cannot increase his stature as an artist by diligently painting large walls as it is that all great painting is not necessarily attached to walls. Size and quantity and prominence of position impress the naive, but in art quality will continue to reign supreme. I recall these elementary axioms in an effort to discover whether a more just idea will not be gained of our significant mural movement if we remember that easel paintings often represent the highest realms of art and that the mural is not, in and by itself, sacrosanct.

Even under the present great mural stimulus which the future may consider the strongest civilizing force of modern times, there will continue to be, as in the past, artists whose gifts are curtailed by the obligations and the implications of the mural. Especially is this true in a country like our own in which, for so long a time, the leading artists have been in the habit of painting uncommissioned pictures. To understand the full significance of the collaboration of the artist and the Government in the decorating of Federal buildings, let us look for a moment to a past long antedating America's mural history, to a time when the leaders of art did not find the limitations imposed upon them by appointed spaces and architectural settings, or by the obligation to glorify the Church or the State, subversive to their genius. At that time the fairy tale of the mythical wedding between architecture and painting was not current among painters wishing to secure work from architects, or among architects wishing to keep painting in a humble relationship. When mural painting was healthiest, the mural was considered more important than the architectural setting. The doctrine of innocuous harmonization was unestablished and murals were not considered improper if they rose above or overcame a perfect state of flat-

Wall Painting from "Marmion"
Metropolitan Museum of Art

cal story which it was designed to illustrate. But this is a very different limitation in its nature. It is not based on an esthetic artifice but grows out of the logical function of the church mural. It is not a limitation intended to dilute one art under the misconception that thereby it will better set off another art. Faith being of the essence of the mural, the strong personalities in the history of art often found their most powerful inspiration under conditions which would crush the smaller and more petted egos of an age without faith.

Back of all great mural painting is a belief. The painter shares this belief with his audience. The belief may be religious as in the thirteenth century in Italy, or it may be social as in the twentieth century in America. The Government has afforded the artists an incredible opportunity to express in terms of art our social faith. And on the richness and reality of that faith will depend the quality of the artists' ultimate achievements exactly as, in the thirteenth century, they depended on the richness and reality of a religious faith. In different ages the mural painter has been the exponent of a great religious faith, of a great civic pride, of the glories of the state, of the noble deeds of prince and monarch, of conquering heroes, of courtly gallantries and pastorals. He has depicted biblical themes with the powerful simplicity of the unquestioning primitive. And as originally he served the church so did he later serve the conquering monarch by glorifying the pomp and panoply of fabulous ceremonies in which, often enough, actual heroes were flatteringly translated into the heroes of mythology. The innocence of an early day, in which the tribute was to a divine faith, was lost in the gorgeous unrestraint of a tribute far more temporal.

The rise and fall of faith did not literally parallel the rise and fall of mural painting. Otherwise every country where faith grew great would have produced an equally great body of art. Incidentally, every country, as we know, does not naturally turn to painting or to sculpture for the expression of its beliefs. Some turn more naturally to music or to literature. Yet some relation we can trace through the fact that in those places where mural painting rose to its greatest height, religious faith reigned unchallenged, and through the correlative fact that it has not reached the same height in epochs of questioning and doubt. This is certainly true of a mural art largely devoted to biblical themes. Whether Giotto, Masaccio, Piero della Francesca, and other impressive artists devoted their genius to the service of the Church, or whether, in more worldly mood, Veronese, Rubens and later men devoted their genius to the glorification of a pageantry extolling the gorgeousness of

ness. That emasculated theory is the invalid relative of the handmaiden theory containing the same germs of timidity, the same acceptance of an inferiority imposed from without. The depth of faith necessary to the creation of a great mural is as far removed from scholastic theories of subservience as reality is from make-believe.

These pallid latter day compromises drove the more vital spirits in painting away from the walls, whereas the masters of the past were not in the least discouraged either by the demands of liturgical accuracy or by the requirement to make their divine or earthly story telling clear to multitudes incapable of understanding art. It is inconceivable that an altarpiece could have been acceptable to church or other patron if, for instance, it exemplified so highly specialized a field of untraditional abstraction that the humble worshipper could not recognize the bibli-

earthly triumphs, the general thesis is not destroyed that all great mural painting is a form of social communication as distinguished from the more purely personal communication of an art which is projected and completed in the solitude of the studio.

The claim that in the Renaissance, early and late, the noblest painting was a servant of architecture, satisfies the wishful thinking of the archaeologically inclined architect. A short morning stroll in Florence upsets the claim. The murals in Santa Maria Novella, Santa Croce, or Santa Maria del Carmine are certainly not placed in obedience to a self-conscious architecturally decorative plan. The sacred story was so much more important than ideals of conscious decoration that many churches had a random arrangement of panels. And no doctrine of flatness then prevailed. The flat decorative fashion started by Puvis de Chavannes actually flies in the face of classic painting. Giotto, Piero and Masaccio achieved the utmost relief and richness of color of which the medium of fresco as then used was capable. When mural painters began to use the medium of oil, three dimensional form went still further. In a comparatively plain room, the refectory at San Rocco's, Tintoretto has filled the walls with great swirling and mysterious paintings in which the power of color and form remain a permanent contradiction of the infallibility of the flat mural, and in which the theory of subservient painting is thrown to the winds. Is Tintoretto less traditional than the discreet decorators who a few centuries later tactfully accepted their right to be inferior?

By the time that the art of mural painting had left the Church far behind and had passed through various monarchical feats, it arrived in a somewhat uncertain state of health to offer its services to a heterogeneous public and a republican form of government which for some decades had thought much more about a great many other things than it had thought about art. We had ideals and a faith which found expression in literature, but although many a good Bostonian has died in Florence and many a Raphael and Botticelli reproduction has hung on many a nice New England wall, our Protestant tradition was opposed to the expression of our religious beliefs in pictorial form as being, if not heretical, at least a touch Papist. However, no taint of Popery could be attached to such impersonal abstractions as Justice, the Law, Ideal Government, Democracy, the Wedding of the Atlantic and the Pacific. An element of earnest righteousness, of the uplifting and the ennobling, a sense of the rightness of being out of, and consequently above, the world, began to appear in mural painting in America in those conceptions which immediately preceded our present era of much-

propounded social consciousness. They convey a faint aroma of a half-recalled transcendentalism delicately flavored with a nostalgic deference to our all too good forbears. Yet in the best of these, if they are good at all, appears a faith, however gently modulated.

The declining of a common religion did not necessarily mean that each individual lost his faith in the universe or in his fellow man. Art teaches us that the lack of a mass faith occasionally produced an individual belief all the more obstinate for its lack of community support. In this process faith became more individualized. Art followed a similar course until by the time painting had reached the nineteenth and twentieth centuries it had become increasingly a means whereby the artist expressed his own personal wonder rather than a wonder shared by the community. As the current of a highly individualized

L. C. Handy Studies

Detail of Fresco, Dome of Capitol, Washington, D. C. BY CONSTANTINO BRUMIDI

Washington Resigning His Commission BY JOHN TRUMBULL   The Capitol, Washington, D. C.

expression grew stronger, the current of mural painting dried up until it was a pale outsider in a world devoted to the unattached and framed picture. Despite Delacroix, famous in both fields, despite Chassériau, Puvis, La Farge, and others, painting in the nineteenth century did not celebrate the glories of the mural. Its greatness depended upon a rich succession of powerful individuals who had each his own faith, and not upon a productive common faith. So it is not surprising to find that the number of distinguished murals within the past hundred years, compared with the number of distinguished easel paintings, is insignificant.

Although, as I have so gently hinted, some architects, before the present period of their greater cooperation, liked to imagine that painting was the handmaiden of architecture, few painters have been willing to accept this quaint phrase as a fitting description either of the aim or of the relative position of their art. It is a phrase that makes the average individualistic painter's temperature rise slightly above normal. The theory, somewhat shopworn now, attracted its most insistent adherents and its fiercest opponents at a time when our architecture was devoted to learned adaptation and our painting at its best to original

The Feast of Belshazzar BY WASHINGTON ALLSTON

Courtesy of The Boston Museum of Fine Arts

7

Westward the Course of Empire Takes Its Way BY EMANUEL LEUTZE   The Capitol, Washington, D. C.

native creation. When Stanford White was passing about the office details of famous Italian buildings and a Herald Building or a Madison Square Garden or a Union Club was duly born out of the process, Winslow Homer was painting the Maine coast and its characters, and Eakins was painting boating and prize fight scenes in the neighborhood of Philadelphia. To be sure we had plenty of painters who were rather tame followers, but the ideal of painting was far less scholastic than the ideal of architecture. The artist and the architect were then much further apart than they are to-day. The growing cooperation of the architects has become invaluable and in matters both of scale and de-

sign they have helped many a painter of to-day to improve his mural.

Since I have mentioned Stanford White, it is only fair to his memory to record the fact that he did much more about artists than perhaps any other architect of his period. He knew and helped many painters and sculptors outside of the field of the professional decorators. The extent of the separation of the artist and the architect, which I dwell on solely because of its effect on our mural painting, is suggested by the fact that in the past several decades, before the Government combined architecture and painting, if we except the names of Richardson and White, we do not need the fingers of one hand in order to count the American architects who have dared to risk collaboration with first rate painters. By no means the least of the possibilities of the present system under which many artists are being given opportunities to paint murals, is the evidence already present of the architect's relearning that good painting will add more to the interest of his building, to its fame and to his own fame, than will mere safety-first make-believe painting and sculpture. The more the architect of the learned adaptation type pushed original painting away from him, the more he embraced the gentle sanities of scrap-book painting, the further apart painting and architecture drifted. McKim tried to repair the rift by creating the American Academy at Rome and thereby making our painters and sculptors as learned in adapting as our architects. But very few painters have been able to survive the deadening influence of the Academy at Rome. So the drift apart continued until in the natural course of events the architect himself grew tired of the only type of painting he would use. The first rate painters deserted the field entirely, and the architect tried by all devices to save his own purisms from a mural art gone dowdy and phlegmatic. There was no general movement toward mural painting, and with the smaller expanse of a canvas over which he was the sole arbiter, the painter inevitably approached a condition of affairs in which he could undertake radical experiments. The architect, on the other hand, is proud to claim that he has never been "burdened by the weight of too much freedom." Compared with painting experimentation, architectural experimentation is necessarily very slow. It is far more expensive and in many ways far more difficult, since before the architect can effectively experiment he must win a client to his ideas.

The painter can continue constantly experimenting and constantly exhibiting his experiments. Like Picasso, he may eventually win a public which will absorb experiments that for years were not acceptable to the same public. A great many unsold paintings can be stored in a comparatively small space, but a great many unsold buildings are an assessment which no individual would create voluntarily. The recent history of so-called modern architecture is full of evidence of the immense amount of propaganda that had to be sent forth to prepare the public's mind before commissions to execute untraditional buildings were sufficient to tempt more than the most determined architectural experimenters. Yet newly imported architecture in America had the added advantage of the years of propaganda that had been carried on for the kind of newly imported art which used to be called modern. Its hasty victories produced an army of virtually forgotten imitators.

To make clear the effects of the thinly disguised war that went on for so many years between painting and architecture, it is not enough to attempt to clarify the architect's general attitude toward painting. One has also to realize a few of his difficulties because, if we are to assist in bringing about the cooperation between the art of building and the art of murals which is happiest for the production of both, there has to be as sympathetic an approach by the painter toward the problems of the architect as by the latter toward the former.

Although the American architect in general has received volumes of praise for his achievements, his personal fame, with certain outstanding

Thomas E. Marr & Son

Christ and Nicodemus BY JOHN LA FARGE   Trinity Church, Boston

Study for *The Flight of Night*—Detail BY WILLIAM MORRIS HUNT
Courtesy of The Metropolitan Museum of Art

they have received from him. During the late period of the extreme individuality of statement in the pictorial arts, most painters criticized buildings freely without taking the trouble to consider the architect's problems. There was fabulous inconsistency in their implied demand that the architect should experiment with a building designed to meet both working requirements and financial limitations, with the same fine, free audacity with which the painter experimented on a picture which, far from meeting the terms of a contract, had only to satisfy the artist himself and to entertain an audience quite as avid for painting novelties as it was for painting realities.

The late Bertram Goodhue occasionally told me what he thought of the average painter's knowledge of architecture. This is not the place in which to register his untamed epithets. Nor is it the place to repeat what some distinguished painters have said about the architect's knowledge of painting. I refer to such personalities only as additional proof of a lack of coordination between the practitioners of two arts which can do so much for each other. If it is true that the majority of painters, through a trend, which possibly they themselves only felt without analyzing, were dedicated to the concealment of all obvious reminders of a tradition, it may be equally true that the majority of architects were limited by a practical world, the only world which could pay the bills, to tactful variations of a tradition. That being the case, the ideal moment certainly had not arrived for the rebirth of that fortunate cooperation between architect and painter which existed in the periods when mural painting really flourished. It is a commonplace today that before mural painting can win its deserved victories, the idea of the need for vital murals must be ''sold'' to the architects. On them accordingly rests a definite responsibility.

How long building and art would have drifted apart if the starved painters and the starved architects had been able to live with economic happiness in their separated spheres, must remain a question of academic speculation. The fact is that the Government art projects, made possible by an economic emergency, have already stimulated the production of art, and are laying the foundation for a highly valuable collaboration. This mural stimulus has been accepted by many, actively engaged in producing public buildings, with a spirit of cooperation. Out of the new social consciousness and the objective point of view which has replaced, in so many of our painters, their complete belief in a purely individualistic expression, and out of the cooperation of the less traditionally prejudiced architects, who can tell what may evolve?

exceptions, has been limited compared with the painter's. Richardson is probably as famous as La Farge, yet many people who know in what churches the painter's work may be seen are entirely unaware of the names of the architects of those churches. The architect has received a good deal of unreasonable criticism from painters, almost as much as

The illustrations in the main body of this volume are of work selected by committees whose memberships included the architect of the building for which each design was made. They have been passed upon by the Government's Supervising Architect and accepted by the Director of Procurement for Federal buildings. Many an architect whose building calculations seldom, if ever, included the thought of murals, is now seeing them installed in his building. In initiating a much closer affiliation between architecture and painting than has heretofore existed—at least in modern times— the Government has obviously helped the artist. But it has done much more. It has helped the architect to escape from his own timidities in judging painting and sculpture. And ever since the architect took the first cold plunge, he has been swimming nobly side by side with the painters and the sculptors. He has felt the humanizing influence of a more native and less frightened decorative plan. He has come to realize that in many cases his community's interest in his building has been greatly increased. Architects who a short two years ago were very shy about submitting the purities of a blank wall to the eager brushes of interpreters of native subject-matter (for which there were no traditional molds, smoothed by over-use) now ask for murals. Even in so formal an array of buildings as the "Triangle" in Washington, the Post Office Department and the Justice Department Buildings are emerging as the most famous of the group on account of the murals already installed in them. These offer concrete examples of the benefit to painting and architecture to be expected when architects and artists actively cooperate. If the lack of cooperation on which I have dwelled, has retarded the development of a strong native school of mural painters, has encouraged the use of worn-out recipes and "swiping" from this European and that, a growing cooperation may be expected to advance our mural painting to its full natural growth. That growth depends upon the reality and depth of our social beliefs and upon the genuine capacities of our artists. Non-political intelligent governmental encouragement and the sympathetic cooperation of the architects remove hindrances and prepare the way, but eventual progress depends on how the artists use their fortunate opportunities, on the quality of their gifts, and the strength of their faith.

, , , , ,

In the light of this general discussion let us look back for a moment on the history of American mural painting.

In Colonial days and in the days of the early Republic, American wall paintings aimed to be delightful, to add charm and enlivenment to

Study for *The Flight of Night*—Detail BY WILLIAM MORRIS HUNT
Courtesy of The Metropolitan Museum of Art

graceful living. The oldest examples of this type of work are wainscot panels in the Clark house, Boston, and in "Marmion," Virginia. As the visitor to the Metropolitan Museum can see, by examining the room from "Marmion" which is now installed there, the decorations increase the charm of an already pleasing interior. "Marmion," a plan-

Religion BY CHARLES SPRAGUE PEARCE

L. C. Handy Studios

Library of Congress, Washington, D.C.

tation in Stafford County, Virginia, was built in 1674 by William Fitzhugh, and was purchased from his heirs by George Lewis, a nephew of Washington. The wood panels of the wall were painted about the middle of the 18th Century. Edward B. Allen, in his illustrated book, *Early American Wall Paintings*, published by the Yale University Press, 1926, repeats in a note the legend that, according to family tradition, the "Marmion" paintings were done by a Hessian soldier who was rescued from starvation by the great-grandfather of the present owner. The landscapes are now dim reminders of their original charm, but the flowers are still completely delightful. However correct the installation in the Metropolitan Museum, those who are more sentimental than acquisitive will regret, in seeing the bare room now in "Marmion," that enough local interest could not be aroused to keep such houses maintained in their original loveliness. However, that is a point which might reward insistence but is outside of our discussion.

One of the most famous names connected with the early wall painting is that of Michele Felice Cornè. He came to America about 1799. His method of painting murals, according to Mason's *Reminiscences of Newport* was: "not to paint directly upon the wall, but to cover the whole surface of the wall with wide strips of white paper, joining the edges neatly, and putting it on like ordinary wall paper. On this he first sketched his subject in charcoal and lead pencil and then washed it in with water colors, using in the foreground opaque colors laid on with size, which gave his work more body than he could secure in any other way."

The names of the various houses made famous by wall paintings between the time when the more or less legendary Hessian soldier was

painting at "Marmion" and the frescoes were done in the Alsop house in Middletown, Connecticut, are given in Mr. Allen's book from which this account is culled. There are panels and details that will be recalled by those who have explored the pleasant resources of this engaging field of art. To cite a few, there is in the house of Mrs. Philip Wells near Middletown, Connecticut, built in 1742, an overmantel on wood, in the style of Claude Lorraine, supposed to have been done by an Italian artist at about the time that the house was built. Mr. Allen suggests that it may have been done later by Cornè, about 1812. There is a very attractive panel done in oil on wood in the Alexander King house, Suffield, Connecticut, a wide flat landscape with coach, and in the Allen house, Brooklyn, Connecticut, there is the ever-enchanting "Garden of Eden" panel suggesting Henri Rousseau, with a leopard in a tree and an antelope on the ground. These and many other panels have done much to spread the reputation of the modest beginnings of our mural tradition and to create sources to which many an interior decorator has since returned to refill his teaspoonful of inspiration.

Apollo in His Chariot with the Hours BY JOHN SINGER SARGENT
Courtesy of the Boston Museum of Fine Arts

The earliest frescoes are those in the Warner house built about 1716, in Portsmouth, New Hampshire. The artist is unknown. Other early frescoes are in Plymouth, Massachusetts, and Marlboro, Vermont, in Saco, Maine, in Bernardston and Deerfield, Massachusetts, in Washington and Old Lyme, Connecticut, and among other houses, in the Jaynes house, East Setauket, Long Island. These were all attributed to the years between 1782 and 1820. In the Mather house in Marlboro, Vermont, the decorative quality of the frescoes must appeal greatly to some of our sophisticated contemporary decorators in their quest for a lost innocence. Later frescoes, anonymous landscapes, are found in the Colburn house in Westwood, Massachusetts, in the Sumner and Baker houses, in the Cobb Inn, Groton, Massachusetts, and in the Priest house, in the Norman Street house, Salem, in the Winthrop, Knowlton, Hanson and Stevens houses in Maine and also in "Quillcote," Hollis, Maine. Mr. Allen considers the Alsop frescoes "unique and apart." Pompeian in derivation they are considered by some students to be the work of Constantino Brumidi who executed the frescoes in the National Capitol. The latter might be called our first Federal frescoes. Brumidi came to America in 1849. In 1852 he worked in Philadelphia, decorating churches and later went to Mexico City. Mr. Allen suggests that if he did the Alsop frescoes they were done between 1849 and 1852. Our earliest wall paintings had in common the aim to lend charm to their surroundings. They are never pretentious or heavy-handed, often naive and always entertaining. For both the artist and the antiquarian they have great fascination. Since these modest paintings have spread the fame of their dwelling places throughout the land, it might not be amiss to whisper once more that painting has a way of adding to the fame of architecture.

Peace and Prosperity BY ELIHU VEDDER   Library of Congress, Washington, D. C.

Although American mural paintings, in the larger and more public sense, began with the work of John La Farge, in 1876, in Trinity Church, Boston, a good deal of work had been previously done which was touched with the social purpose of the mural, although technically it was not mural painting. Brumidi had painted the dome of the Capitol twenty years before, but he was pure Italian. He was employed in the Government for many years at a fixed salary of: "Ten Dollars per day with occasional extra allowances." He represented the Italian tradition of mural painting at the "lowest level of its decay." Yet so much more skillful was he than any native painter in the craft of mural painting, that it is doubtful if any American could have done the work with equal efficiency. As Isham explains, the native school of American decorators, or at least the school from which they might have been expected to graduate, had had practice in painting signs and coaches. They rarely attempted mural work. When we think of them submerged by such painters as Brumidi, more sophisticated of course and less provincial, one cannot help wondering what might have happened in the history of American mural painting if native innocence had been given an equal opportunity with foreign sophistication.

President Buchanan appointed an art commission in 1859, consisting of H. K. Brown, sculptor, James R. Lambkin and John F. Kensett, painters. They criticized the work of Brumidi and recommended the employment of native artists. Certainly one might prefer to possess a landscape by Kensett, although he was not outstanding, than a dome by Brumidi. Yet the fact remains that there was no one in America then who knew the technical problems of decorating a dome. Samuel Isham, in his *American Painting* (The MacMillan Company, New York, 1910)

Sight BY ROBERT REID   Library of Congress, Washington, D. C.

gives a most amusing account of Brumidi's equipment. There will always be, of course, people who believe that experience in mural painting is more important than talent. The following passage from Isham is submitted for what it may be worth to expose the sham of hollow facility.

"Brumidi was a decorative painter. Not only did he know the technical side of the craft, how to draw and paint large figures in distemper on the curved plaster surfaces, but he was the inheritor of the great Italian traditions which started with Raphael and Corregio and were harmonized and codified by the later Italian school. He knew all the gods and goddesses of classical antiquity, their attributes and accessories, their floating formless draperies, the way in which they should be grouped together, the scale on which they should be drawn to fit a given space, the architectural details necessary to bind the whole together, and when to paint in color and when to give variety in monotint." One can know a lot, it appears, and still be second-rate. And Isham continues . . . . "The 'frescoing' of the Italian journeyman painter was the only style of mural decoration recognized in the country at this time, and furnished what Goddesses of Liberty, figures of Justice, sporting cupids or flowery garlands were needed for public buildings or for private parlors."

I especially like in that passage the last sentence. A painter himself, Isham was the friend of practically all of our mural painters from La Farge to men now active and he probably intended a quiet dig when he wrote: "what figures of Justice, sporting cupids," etc., "were needed for our public buildings." Discounting the formalities thought to be desirable in depicting the nobility of grandiose ladies representing Justice, the Law, or whatever had to be represented, this phrase constitutes rather a handy measuring rod to estimate exactly how much inspiration a dogged handmaiden may develop through experience.

The literal history of formal American mural painting should begin chronologically with Benjamin West, but the decorations which he actually did for specific places were executed in England. However, he painted some large decorative canvases for itinerant exhibitions. His "Christ Healing the Sick" was done as a subscription to the building fund of the Pennsylvania Hospital. It was first exhibited in London and the British Institution offered him three thousand guineas for it. He accepted the guineas and painted a replica for the benefit of the hospital. The replica was exhibited in Philadelphia with an admission charge and earned $4,000 for the hospital in the first year. Of course, this happened in days when the country was not flooded with exhibitions and the simple act of going to see a picture was not considered proof of a supreme virtue nor thought to be a satisfactory, if intangible, support of art. It happened before the uplifters had taken art to their bosoms and determined that the sweetness and light of the exhibition visitor were more important than the very existence of the artist. People bought pictures then without expecting thereby to win immortality.

Benjamin West believed in the "grand style" and inspired many of his pupils to carry out "noble conceptions." His studio, from the be-

The Apotheosis of the Family BY N. C. WYETH
Wilmington Savings Fund Society, Wilmington, Delaware

Law BY EDWIN BLASHFIELD   Court Room of the Federal Building, Cleveland, Ohio   *Peter Juley*

ginning, was the resort in London of American students to whom he was always helpful. C. W. Peale, John Trumbull, Gilbert Stuart, Washington Allston, Ralph Earle, Robert Fulton and Rembrandt Peale were among the pupils of Benjamin West. Many of his pupils emulated their master in attempting what Frank Jewett Mather so wittily decribes as "the grand style, which Sir Joshua Reynolds, ever too wise to practice himself, most eloquently and persuasively preached to his students. West did the practicing—the Bible, ancient poets, history." West was described in England as a great painter and brought American painting into the English tradition. There was not much chance in America at that time for the grand style, and the returning American artists trained by West found little encouragement at home.

The first opportunity which American artists received to carry out mural decorations was in the rotunda of the Capitol at Washington,

but this was not technically mural painting, since the order was for eight panels, which are framed pictures hanging as flat surfaces against the concave wall of the rotunda. They are simply pictures in frames and there was no effort to fit them to the architectural setting. They approximate exhibition paintings rather than murals.

Four of these are by Trumbull. He had political influence and his commission to do this work caused a great deal of jealousy. Vanderlyn especially developed a great antipathy to Trumbull. He not only considered himself a better painter, but he said so quite frankly. The four panels by Trumbull in the Capitol are: "Signing the Declaration," "Surrender of General Burgoyne," "Surrender of Lord Cornwallis," and "Washington Resigning His Commission." These are larger replicas of better paintings by Trumbull which are now in the Yale Museum. Vanderlyn was commissioned to do one of the paintings: "The Landing

Erato BY WILLIAM SIMMONS
L. C. Handy Studios
Library of Congress, Washington

of Columbus.'' William Powell did ''The Discovery of the Mississippi.'' John Chapin: ''Baptism of Pocahontas,'' and Robert Weir: ''The Embarkation of the Pilgrims.''

The order for the original eight panels was as near as Congress came at that time to voting money for mural art. Isham points out that a portrait of Washington or a landscape by Bierstadt was more likely to be ordered. Congress did vote money for ''Westward the Course of Empire Takes Its Way'' by Emanuel Leutze. Leutze went to Germany to study technical methods and to the Rocky Mountains to lend verisimilitude to his landscape. Apparently he learned his technical problems, since the painting has lasted very well, but it can hardly be called good decoration. Leutze was a typical exponent of the Düsseldorf school and his ''Washington Crossing the Delaware'' has probably enjoyed as much popular acclaim as any painting in America. He was born in Wurtemberg in 1816, and came to America in his early youth. He painted a great many historical compositions during his stay in Düsseldorf, where he remained nearly twenty years.

Leutze was essentially a German, not only by birth, but also by tradition. Whether or not it was due to the quality of his work as a painter that his influence did not continue, the fact remains that for the most part the painters of large exhibition canvases were at this time affected by the English tradition which ''Sir Joshua Reynolds preached and Benjamin West practiced.'' It is only necessary to refer to these artists as occupying a middle ground between the early wall painters and the later professional mural painters. We reproduce the works of several of the artists represented by paintings in the rotunda of the

Capitol which may be said to be characteristic of this type of work.

In some ways the most naturally gifted practitioner of the half-pretentious exhibition style was Washington Allston. He had great social attractiveness and in early youth inspired his friends with belief in his genius. Unquestionably gifted, his production did not fulfill his natural equipment. He was found delightful by artists, writers and other distinguished people wherever he traveled. His social activities probably were an interruption to his work. In any case he left behind him, among his larger exhibition canvases, works like ''The Feast of Belshazzar'' which have in them more actual feeling, whatever the technical errors, than many of the large paintings designed to impress visitors to itinerant exhibitions and thereby win fame.

Washington Allston once made the remark that: ''No woman ever lost any beauty from his hand.'' This sentence may be taken as suggestive of the spirit in which the large decorative paintings of West and his followers, were carried out. In other words, there was more than a

L. C. Handy Studios
Thalia BY FRANK BENSON   Library of Congress, Washington

touch of artificiality in the point of view. The object was to idealize and, it is probably fair to say, it was therefore to exaggerate. But by the time we come to La Farge the purpose is both more knowing and more serious, the point of view more cultivated. La Farge is quoted as saying in reference to his decorations in Trinity Church:

"I have always been impressed by one great quality never failing in the works of the past that we care for. It may be bungling like some of the Romanesque, for instance, or it may be extremely refined like the Greek; but it is never like our usual modern work, which suggests machinery, that is to say, the absence of personality. I knew that our work at Trinity would have to be faulty, but this much I was able to accomplish, that almost every bit of it would be living, would be impossible to duplicate." A revealing statement.

John La Farge was not only the first of the American mural painters. In his own field he stands alone. A scholar, a Catholic, quietly serious, a man whose social manner resembled that of a benevolent, wise, and experienced priest, he had the air, even when he was charming a group

Lyric Poetry BY H. O. WALKER

Library of Congress, Washington

at the club, of living a life apart and of arriving at estimates too subtle and complex to waste upon ordinary mortals. His field, although he did other work, was religious decoration. And his "Ascension" justly ranks as the greatest of our religious murals. With the aid of his confirmed Catholicism and his painting scholarship, he was able, in an age lacking in religious vitality, to lift religious subject matter in painting out of the slough into which it had sunk. Unlike Edwin Blashfield, who unfailingly advocated the idea that experience is the great need of mural painting, La Farge stated that talent is the greatest need. Blashfield quotes La Farge as having said to him:

"In the arts one thing is born of another as surely as man is born of woman." And he added severely: "If a pupil tells me that he has done something wholly original, I do not want to see it."

Addressing an audience of architects, La Farge once said:

"It will always be difficult, for instance, to have a mere architect understand that the placing of stained glass windows in a building must largely modify color, so that the hue which is violent in out-of-door light may become very quiet within, as we know, for instance, in the red colors used for painting brick work. I do not believe that you young architects study the use of colors in decoration in any strict manner, so that my point of view would not be obvious to you as it would have been long ages ago. But the use of color in architectural decoration, as we can trace it in the older works—the Greek, let us say, or even the Pompeian—is not a mere arrangement of pleasing tints. It is a matter of construction by color."

Although the fame of La Farge rests so largely on his church murals, such as those which he did in Trinity Church, Boston, in 1876, "The Resurrection" painted in 1882 for the old St. Thomas' Church, New York, and destroyed by fire, "The Ascension" painted in 1895 for the

Building the Grand Central BY FREDERIC DANA MARSH
Engineers' Club, New York

Church of the Ascension, New York, and "The Nativity" and "The Magi" painted for the Church of the Incarnation, New York, in 1897, he also carried out distinguished murals for public buildings. In 1904 and 1905 he decorated the courtroom of the St. Paul, Minnesota, Capitol, and about the last work in this field that he achieved were the six

ing. For, together with Hunt, he stands as one of the artists who turned the minds of Americans toward the cultivating powers of French art.

It was not until two years after the commission given to La Farge for his work in Trinity Church that William Morris Hunt received the commission to decorate the Capitol at Albany. He painted with oil

The Judicial Virtues BY KENYON COX   Wilkes-Barre Court House, Pennsylvania

spandrels of the great lawgivers: Numa Pompilius, Mohammed, Lycurgus, Confucius, Emperor Justinian. These were unveiled in 1907 in the Baltimore Court House. La Farge was an important civilizing influence in American art. He was an outstanding force in cutting the softness of American taste in his time with the acid of good French paint-

colors directly on the stone, and it is reported: "The stones had to be braced to support the straining roof, so that in ten years after Hunt's murals were finished, they vanished from sight, owing to the changes that were absolutely necessary to preserve the building." Unfortunately, also, when dampness attacked his work it flaked very badly.

The Manuscript by JOHN W. ALEXANDER   Library of Congress, Washington

They are now known only from the studies, two details of which are herewith reproduced. These are from the "Flight of Night." It appears that when Hunt's decorations were installed, they were received with great enthusiasm. A plan was initiated which, had it been carried out, would have given Hunt a magnificent opportunity in decorating the Assembly Chamber at Albany. The Legislature voted $100,000 for the purpose and Hunt had already begun an immense plan when Governor Robinson vetoed the bill, not knowing, when he did so, that his veto would be his one lasting claim to fame. The stupidity of the Governor's act was a terrible blow to Hunt and he died soon after.

After Hunt and La Farge had made the beginnings, there was a lapse in opportunities for artists to secure mural commissions. To be sure, decorations in private houses, clubs, and hotels were carried out by such artists as Edwin Blashfield, Frederick Crowninshield, Edwin Austin Abbey, and Thomas Dewing. But when the World's Fair in Chicago was planned, there was great excitement among the painters and sculptors. Augustus Saint Gaudens had supervising charge of the sculpture and Frank D. Millet supervised the mural painting. Millet chose J. Alden Weir, Edwin H. Blashfield, George W. Maynard, Robert Reid, Carroll Beckwith, C. S. Reinhart, Kenyon Cox, Gari Melchers, De Leftwich Dodge, and Walter McEwen. With the exception of Blashfield and Maynard they were all novices in the field of mural painting. There was also in the Chicago Fair a Woman's Building, with ceiling and wall decorations done by Mary MacMonnies and Mary Cassatt, and panels by Amanda Brewster Sewall, Lucia Fairchild Fuller, Rosina Emmet Sherwood, Lydia Field Emmet, and Dora Wheeler Keith.

The World's Fair in 1893 in Chicago has often been cited as a historic event in American painting. That it did much to stimulate mural painting and to bring the work of American painters, sculptors, and architects to the knowledge of a far wider public can hardly be questioned. Perhaps the next most important opportunity for mural painters was that which opened to them through plans to decorate the Boston Public Library. In this connection there is the interesting story of Saint Gaudens having recommended to Stanford White, Winslow Homer. Saint Gaudens had heard from Abbey of the decorations which Homer did for the old offices of Harper's. These have since disappeared and are, I believe, the only decorations that Homer ever made. Whistler was also offered a commission but evidently preferred not to accept it.

Fashiongraph, Inc.

Detail of Mural by BARRY FAULKNER   Archives Building, Washington

19

In the Boston Public Library, the mural projects which created the greatest excitement were the panels in the entrance hall by Puvis de Chavannes. The late Mrs. "Jack" Gardner is said to have been mainly instrumental in securing this commission for the celebrated French artist. There is much talk, some of it bordering on twaddle, of the impossibility of a painter doing a good mural without complete collaboration between himself and the architect of the building. Aside from the fact that this over-labored scholasticism presupposes that no buildings, however loudly their walls might cry for murals, could possibly be ade-

War BY GARI MELCHERS   Library of Congress, Washington

quately decorated after the architect's death, there is, among many other cases throughout the long history of mural painting, the case of Puvis and the Boston Library. His murals, among all the murals in the building, fit most harmoniously their architectural setting. Yet Puvis never saw the library. His sole guides were plans and elevations and a specimen of the yellow marble in the entrance hall which was sent to him from Boston. No doubt had Puvis seen the hall which he decorated, his work might have been still more in keeping with it. He might have allowed more for the slightly insistent color, as compared with the colors which he employed in his murals, of the Sienese marble surroundings. These apparently he could not accurately visualize with an ocean between him and the room. He did not come to America to oversee the installation of his murals and he never saw them in place.

But granted that Puvis might have improved upon his work by using a tonality somewhat more aggressive, he did actually succeed in a finer harmony than Sargent who worked for a long time in Boston and knew the proportions of the room which he decorated and every detail of its architectural character. While it is obviously advisable for the painter and the architect to collaborate on work which concerns them both, the fact remains in the case of Puvis that he produced decorations better adapted to the position in which they found themselves than the complex scheme which Sargent executed after years of study within walking distance of the interior architecture. The immense labors which the intricate plans of Sargent's decorations demanded and received have resulted in a body of criticism, which extends on the one hand from something very like idolatry to something like vituperation at the other extreme.

In addition to the work by Sargent and Puvis, the most widely discussed murals in the Boston Library are those by Edwin Austin Abbey —romantic illustrations of the Arthurian legends which are still very popular. Robert Reid, Edward Simmons, Henry O. Walker, John Elliott, Elmer Garnsey and Joseph Lindon Smith, also worked there.

Detail of Mural for Swimming Pool BY ROBERT CHANLER

20

The tradition of La Farge and Hunt, who were, as I have said, more responsible than any other single artists for the predominance of French influence in America, continued through the period dominated by Cox, Blashfield, and in large part by the graduates of the American Academy in Rome, that now famous institution through which McKim hoped to insure first rate professional painting and sculpture.

The decorating of the Boston Public Library, left in its wake an added enthusiasm for mural painting. A public competition was held by the Municipal Art Society for the decoration of the Criminal Court Building in New York. Edward Simmons won the competition. Among the private enterprises at this time were the murals done by Robert Blum for the Mendelssohn Glee Club and the decorations by Cox, Thayer, Vedder and La Farge for the Walker Art Gallery of Bowdoin College. Finally the new Library of Congress at Washington again brought together a group of artists who had begun their work as decorators at the Chicago World's Fair in 1893. From these decorations we reproduce examples by H. O. Walker, Frank Benson, John Alexander, Robert Reid, Elihu Vedder, Gari Melchers and Charles Sprague Pearce.

Interrupting the historical sequence of our story, an interesting practical fact was brought out when the Library of Congress was completed. It was then discovered that mural paintings are really cheaper than costly interior fittings so often placed in great public buildings, and contrary to either expectations or precedent, at that time at least, the Library of Congress cost no more than the estimates called for. The habit of relying upon marbles, inlaid woods, gilded bronzes and other expensive items, to add impressiveness to public interiors, has greatly developed in modern times. Yet good mural paintings which add far more distinction to a room and have greater educational value are both more helpful to the artist and may be less expensive.

The result of the decorating of the Library of Congress was that both private and public orders for mural paintings increased. In New York City the great hotels employed leading artists of the day. The old Waldorf-Astoria was decorated by Blashfield, Low and Simmons; and the Hotel Manhattan was decorated by J. M. W. Turner. Decorations were ordered for private houses, banks and the great insurance companies. The demand spread to other parts of the country. When Boston enlarged its State House, Simmons, Walker and Reid were given commissions. The Appellate Courts Building in New York, the Baltimore Court House, the Capitol at Harrisburg, St. Paul and Des Moines gave orders to painters to decorate their new State Houses.

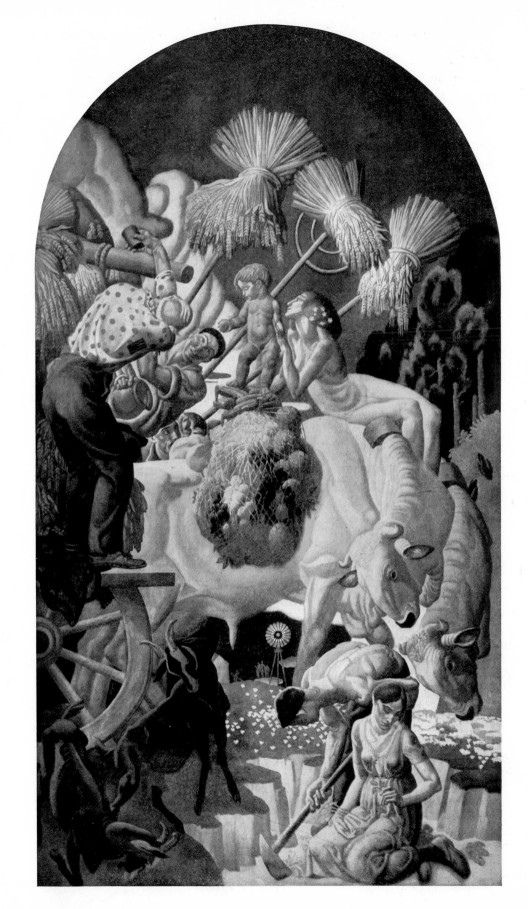

(Right) *Peace* BY EUGENE SAVAGE Courtesy Elks National Memorial Bldg., Chicago

Mural Panels BY ARTHUR B. DAVIES   International House, New York

Mural painting in America came to depend very much upon the architects because, generally speaking, it was to them that the client turned for advice on painters and sculptors. As was stated in the early part of this introduction, the architects were, on the whole, more conservative in their outlook than were the leading painters of individual pictures. Therefore, for the most part, they confined their encouragement to men who had had experience in mural painting. They followed the maxim of Blashfield that experience is the greatest necessity for good mural painting rather than that of La Farge, which was that talent is the greatest necessity. Those painters who were not "in" with the architects, yet whose pictures indicated their ability to do a good mural, were nevertheless left without commissions, and the spirit of unrest between the more vigorous painters and the architects grew apace.

Perhaps the first man to scale the Chinese wall that was being buil[t] around the profession of decorating buildings, was Arthur B. Davies in his decorations for International House, New York. The language o[f] Davies, directed against architects, was much more heretical than one might suspect from his painting, for even in his decorations for Mis[s] Lizzie Bliss the abstractions are more pleasing than aggressive. The surprising thing is that he was not selected long before he was to do murals because his work had many of the qualities that the architects of the day claimed to like. The next two painters after Davies, who were considered to be revolutionary, in comparison with the official professional mural painters most favored by the architects, were Thomas Benton and Boardman Robinson.

Benton has for some years now been an ardent champion of the mural and has executed more murals than any of his American contemporaries, including those for the New School for Social Research and the

Ceiling Painting BY EZRA WINTER
Industrial Trust Savings Bank, Providence, Rhode Island

22

The Great Wall of China BY FREDERIC CLAY BARTLETT
Art Institute of Chicago

Whitney Museum of American Art in New York. Robinson, originally one of the foremost cartoonists of America, has been devoting himself to mural painting for a number of years. His murals, for a large department store in Pittsburgh, were exhibited at the Art Students' League and were received most favorably by his fellow artists.

Whether the impetus to employ the more liberal painters in America would ever have made the progress that it has without the great awakening which was brought to us from Mexico is doubtful. The story of what was happening in Mexico, of the mural work that was being done by Diego Rivera, by José Clemente Orozco and others, came across the border with a progressive sense of its militant social importance. Reproductions were sent to America, articles began to pour into the editorial rooms of the art magazines hailing the Mexicans. These drew to Mexico a large number of our artists, some of whom stayed and worked there, and eventually Rivera himself came to this country and set off all the fireworks of modern publicity. Mean-

while Orozco making his entry, less noisily, won a more solid if a less forcibly publicized fame. His position with the artists is stronger.

Supported by the more daring commissions that were being carried out in Mexico and following in the wake of the great propaganda for what was once called modern art, the opportunities for less conventional mural painting began to appear. It was discovered that the field of mural art, lying open for cultivation in this country, could be developed more richly if it were not limited to the conventional, the archeological, the stylistic and the rather tepidly idealistic. Some adventure, some discovery, some reflection of our new social faith might better be given at least a share of the mural opportunities.

In the midst of this movement toward a more courageous development of mural painting, the United States Government organized in the Treasury Department a permanent Section of Painting and Sculpture, devoted to the decoration of Federal buildings. The details of procedure will be found in the appendix to this volume. We are here only concerned with the meaning of this extraordinary governmental act and the potentialities of the Government's direct entrance into the field of mural painting. The mural painting has one advantage over the unattached individual canvas. As great cities draw so many of the large fortunes to their gates, there has been an increasing tendency to centralize the distribution of movable works of art. One tendency against this has been the growth of traveling exhibitions. But although many small cities and small towns have accepted, with pleasure, whatever benefits these exhibitions have given, the purchasing of pictures has been largely a business carried on in the great cities. The cultivating and educational forces of art have disproportionately remained there. To a certain extent this will always be true, but the mural shows us at least that it is possible to have not only a Rome with its Vatican, but an Assisi. So in America, as we encourage and develop our artists in the craft of mural painting, the walls of more and more public buildings outside of the great centers will be found adorned with paintings which to be seen must be visited. This is an important educational fact. Good contemporary art, spread through the country and always visible to the inhabitants of town and hamlet and city, is almost certainly destined to have results in educating the artists and the layman.

We live in a heterogeneous country. Many people from many different races are more intimately acquainted with their inherited traditions than they are with the traditions of their adopted environment. But when the farmer, the laborer, the village children and the storekeepers

The Arts of the City BY THOMAS H. BENTON
Detail of Mural, Courtesy of The Whitney Museum of American Art

go to the nearest Post Office and see there, for example, a distinguished work of contemporary art depicting the main activities, or some notable events in the history of the town, is it too exaggerated to suggest that their interest will be increased and their imaginations stirred?

The pessimist may ask how we know that any such ideal situation can or will exist. How do we know that the small and medium sized court houses and post offices and other Federal buildings will contain distinguished works of art in the form of mural paintings or of sculpture. The answer, of course, is that we don't know until they are actually in place. We do know, however, that in the past it was possible to build a Chartres Cathedral in a comparatively small city and we know that other architectural masterpieces adorned with masterpieces of sculpture or painting, or both, carried their expression of a great faith beyond the limits of metropolitan centers. What has been done can be done again. If America has faith it can, with certain material obstacles overcome, produce an art that will say as much.

I look upon the illustrations in this book as promising evidence,— that talents, too fine to be submerged by a materialistic world, have been brought out through governmental response to our spiritual needs.

Yet it cannot be repeated too often that by the breaking down of the conventional obstacles which a materialistic world sets up against the achievements of art, literature, poetry, music and the higher exercises of man's spirit, everything is not thereby already accomplished. The country is prepared by this civilizing activity to give to its artists a position of greater genuine social significance than that which the artists would possess if they worked apart. But after everything is ready, after numerous walls have been thrown open to artists, after a method whereby they can be supported in their profession has been evolved, there is still much to do. That much depends entirely upon the artist. If the people's faith is deep, rich and genuine, and if the artists apprehend this faith, to that extent are they lifted out of themselves by a desire to express something greater than themselves.

The richest country in the world, the finest organizers could not create one square inch of art without the artists. They can, however, make it easier for the artists to find themselves and they can encourage the development of painters and sculptors who without such encouragement might not fulfill their natural gifts, although the quality of the results depends finally and inevitably on the artists themselves.

MURAL DESIGNS

THE REPRODUCTIONS OF THE

APPROVED MURAL DESIGNS ARE IN

ALPHABETICAL ORDER ACCORDING TO THE NAMES OF

THE ARTISTS. FLOOR PLANS AND WALL ELEVATIONS, SHOWING THE

PROPORTIONS OF THE ROOMS BEING DECORATED AND THE POSITIONS OF THE MURALS,

IMMEDIATELY FOLLOW THE REPRODUCTIONS OF THE MURAL DESIGNS

AND ARE IN ALPHABETICAL ORDER ACCORDING TO THE

CITIES AND TOWNS IN WHICH THE

BUILDINGS ARE LOCATED

BERTRAND R. ADAMS

Early Settlers of Dubuque

Study for Mural in the Vestibule, Dubuque, Iowa, Post Office

6′6″ wide x 8′3″ high

KENNETH M. ADAMS

Study for Mural in the Lobby,
Goodland, Kansas, Post Office
12′ wide x 4′ high

Rural Free Delivery

CONRAD A. ALBRIZZIO

Study for Fresco in the Lobby,
De Ridder, Louisiana, Post Office
11′11″ wide x 5′3″ high

Rural Delivery

JOHN R. BALLATOR

The Building of St. Johns

Study for Mural in the Lobby, St. Johns, Oregon, Post Office

16′ wide x 8′ high

JOHN R. BALLATOR

Local Industries

Study for Mural in the Lobby, St. Johns, Oregon, Post Office

16′ wide x 8′ high

Several of the figures are actual likenesses of citizens of St. Johns who posed for the artist

California Landscape

Study for Mural in the Lobby, La Jolla, California, Post Office
11'10'' wide x 8'4'' high

STEPHEN J. BELASKI

Study for Mural in the Lobby, Rutland, Vermont, Post Offic[e]
8'6'' wide x 11' high

Benedict Arnold Commanding the First Naval Battle on Lake Champlain

STEPHEN J. BELASKI

tudy for Mural in the Lobby, Rutland, Vermont, Post Office
8'6" wide x 11' high

Freeing the First Slave in the State of Vermont

STEPHEN J. BELASKI

Ethan Allen and His
Green Mountain Boys

4′ wide x 11′ high

Top: *The Call to Unite*

6′4″ wide x 5′ high

Bottom: *The First Stroke for Vermont Independence—*
The Attack on the James Breckenridge Farm in Dorset

7′ wide x 4′6″ high

The Beech Seal

4′ wide x 11′ high

Studies for Murals in the Lobby, Rutland, Vermont, Post Office

FRANK BERGMAN

Mail Carriers of To-day

Study for Mural in the Lobby, Stockton, California, Post Office

15′ wide x 8′6″ high

GEORGE BIDDLE

Sweatshop

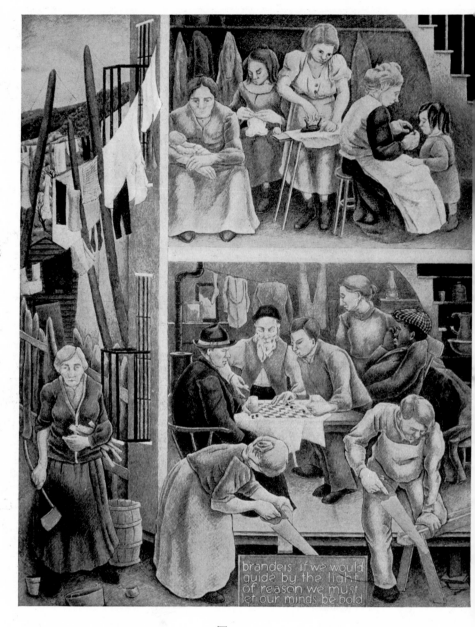

Tenement

Studies for Frescoes in the Fifth Floor Stairwell, Department of Justice Building, Washington, D. C.
Each Panel 10'7'' wide x 13'6'' high

GEORGE BIDDLE

the tenement & sweatshop of yesterday can be
the life planned with justice of tomorrow

Society Freed Through Justice

Studies for Frescoes in the Fifth Floor Stairwell, Department of Justice Building, Washington, D. C.

Each Panel 7'4'' wide x 13'6'' high

EMIL BISTTRAM

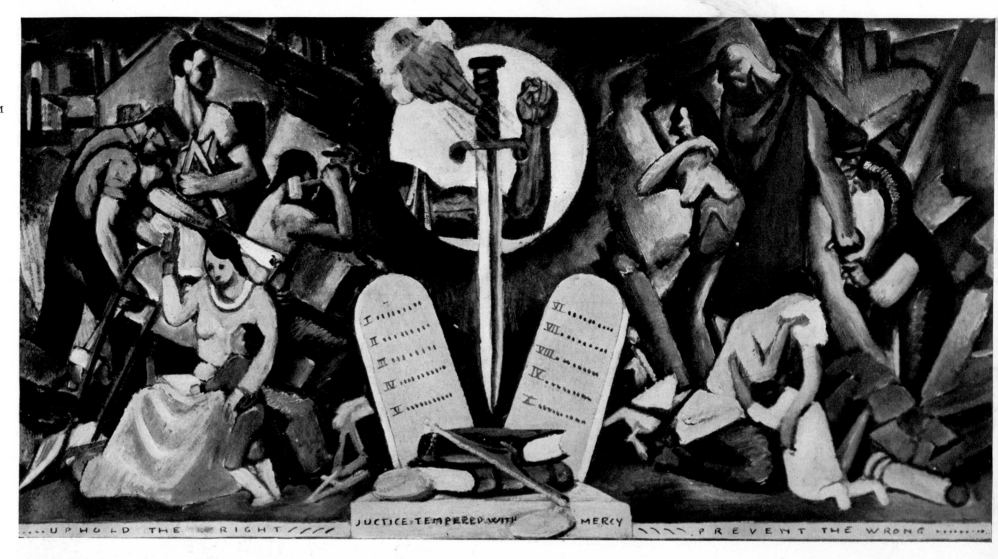

Above: Sketch of Mural in the Court
Room, Roswell, New Mexico, Court House
13'6'' wide x 7' high

Below: Studies for two Over-door Panels
3' wide x 3'6'' high

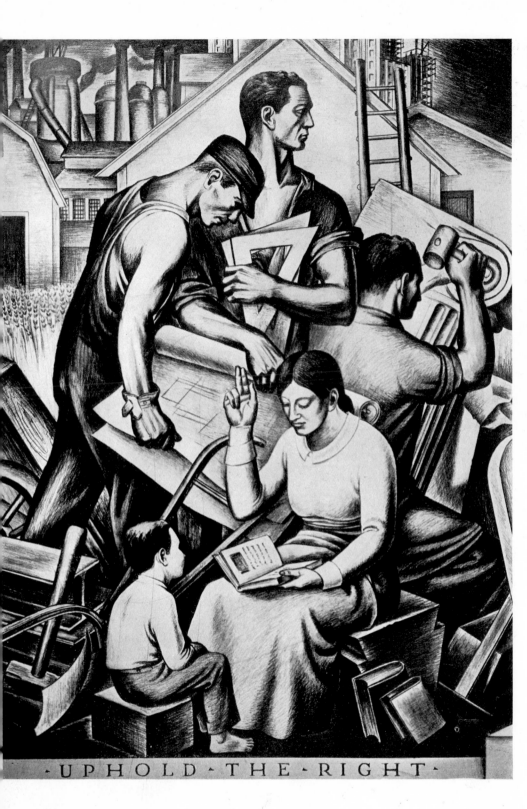

· U P H O L D · T H E · R I G H T ·

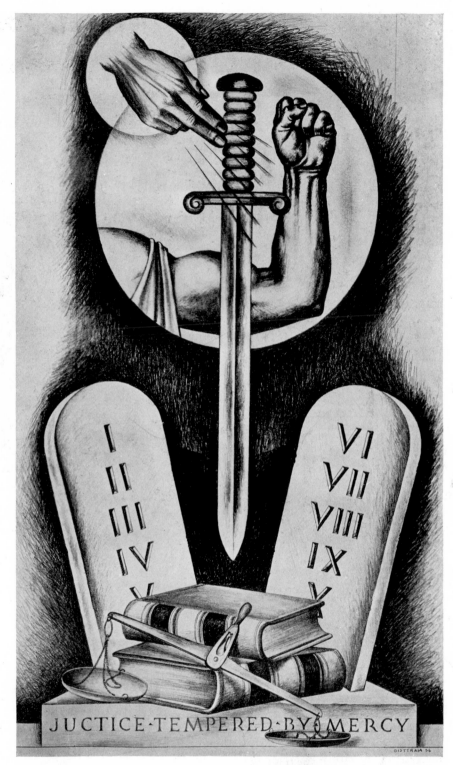

EMIL BISTTRAM

JUCTICE · TEMPERED · BY · MERCY

Details of Preceding Designs Further Developed

AARON BOHROD

Old State Capitol, Vandalia

Study for Mural in the Lobby, Vandalia, Illinois, Post Office
10′4″ wide x 4′ high

LOUIS BOUCHÉ

Violent and Peaceful Functions of the Department of Justice

Studies for Murals in the Curved Space outside the Attorney General's Office, Department of Justice Building, Washington, D. C.
Painted Surface 48′ wide x 11′ high

Arrival of the First Train

Study for Panel in the Lobby, Osceola, Iowa, Post Office

11'10″ wide x 9'11″ high

FISKE BOYD

Above: *Stage Coach Attack*   Below: *Arrival of the First Train*

Studies for Murals in the Lobby, Summit, New Jersey, Post Office
Each Panel 12′ wide x 6′6″ high

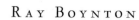
RAY BOYNTON

Gold Dredging

Study for one of a Series of Lunettes in the Lobby, Modesto, California, Post Office
7′6″ wide x 3′9″ high

RAY BOYNTON

Mining

Plowing

De-hydrating Plant

Plenty

Studies for Lunettes in the Lobby, Modesto, California, Post Office
7′6″ wide x 3′9″ high

RAY BOYNTON

Vineyards, Cattle and Orchards

Hay Cutting

Threshing

Studies for Lunettes and Panel in the Lobby, Modesto, California, Post Office

Panel 17′3″ wide x 5′ high   Each Lunette 7′6″ wide x 3′9″ high

EDGAR BRITTON

Early Settlers

Study for Fresco in the Lob
East Moline, Illinois, Post O
8′ wide x 8′6″ high

ANN BROCKMAN

View of Stamford

Study for Mural in the Main Office of the Administration Building, Stamford, Connecticut, P.W.A Housing Project. Done under the Treasury Department Art Projects, and allocated to the Stamford Housing Project

10' wide x 6' high

RICARD BROOKS

The Post Unites America

Study for Mural in the Lobby, Richland Center, Wisconsin, Post Office

12' wide x 5'6'' high

ALDIS B. BROWNE

Incidents in the History of the Coast Guard Service

Studies for All-over Murals in the Library, United States Coast Guard Academy, New London, Connecticut

Room 34′ wide x 35′ long   Painted Surface 9′ above wainscot

WILLIAM L. BUNN

Early Mississippi Steamboat

Study for Mural in the Vestibule, Dubuque, Iowa, Post Of

6'6'' wide x 8'3'' high

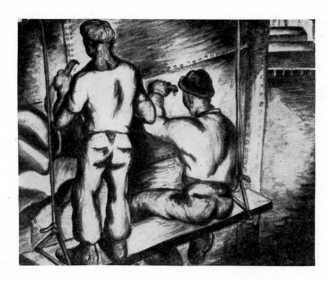

K ENNETH C ALLAHAN.

Left to Right:

Top Row: *Radio, Painting, Dock Scene, Unloading*

Middle Row: *Lifeboat Drill, Steering Wheel, Sextant, Marine Hall*

Bottom Row: *Engine Room, Ropes*

Preliminary Color Sketches for Murals in the Reception Room, Seattle, Washington, Marine Hospital

Room 26′ wide x 42′ long   Painted Surface 6′ above wainscot

KENNETH CALLAHAN

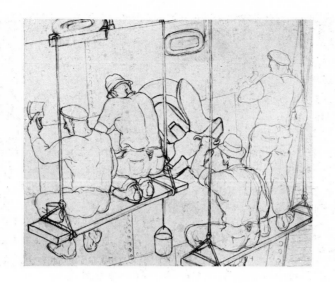

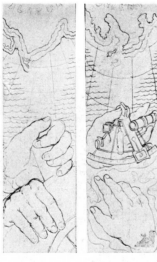

The studies on the preceding page were approved
as to color and subject matter. These revised drawings, originally made to meet problems of scale,
show further development of the subject matter

CHARLES CAMPBELL

Children Playing

Studies for Murals in the Entrance Lobby of the Auditorium Building, Cleveland, Ohio, "Whiskey Island," P.W.A.
Housing Project. Done under the Treasury Department Art Projects and allocated to the P.W.A. Housing Project

14' wide x 3'9" high

ORVILLE CARROLL

Early Settlers and Pioneer Life

Studies for Murals in the Reception Room, Louisville, Kentucky, Marine Hospital
Total length of Murals 84′, height 10′

Ohio River

Study for Mural in the Lobby, Portsmouth, Ohio, Post Office
7'2" wide x 1'7" high

Early Ravenna

Study for Mural in the Lobby, Ravenna, Ohio, Post Office
11' wide x 5' high

NORMAN S. CHAMBERLAIN

History of California

Studies for All-over Murals in the Lobby, Huntington Park, California, Post Office

Lobby 14′ wide x 85′ long   Painted Surface 5′ above wainscot

NORMAN S. CHAMBERLAIN

Further Studies for All-over Murals in the Lobby, Huntington Park, California, Post Office

GRANT CHRISTIAN

Early and Present Day Indianapolis Life
Detail: *The Blacksmith*

Studies for Murals, Second Floor Corridor, Indianapolis, Indiana, Post Office and Court House
Top Panels 2′ wide x 6′ high   Bottom Panels 2′ wide x 6′ high and 4′ wide x 6′ high

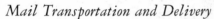

Mail Transportation and Delivery

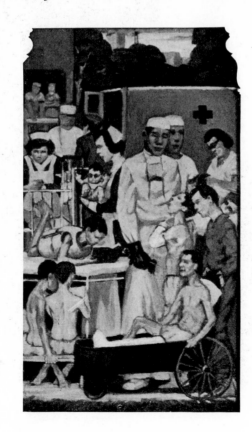

Further Studies for Murals in the Indianapolis, Indiana, Post Office and Court House

Center Panel at top 12′ wide x 6′ high, Side Panels 2′ wide x 6′ high
Bottom Panels 2′ wide x 6′ high and 4′ wide x 6′ high

HOWARD COOK

Steel Industry

Study for Fresco in Court Room No. 1, Pittsburgh, Pennsylvania, Post Office and Court House
17′5″ wide x 10′6″ high

Bridgeport Manufacturing—Brass, Casing and Sewing Machine Industries   Below: Revised Sketches

Studies for Murals in the Lobby, Bridgeport, Connecticut, Post Office

Center Panel 8'8" wide x 3'6" high   Side Panels 4'4" wide x 3'6" high

ALFRED D. CRIMI

Above: *Post Office Work Room*   Below: *Transportation of the Mail*

Studies for Frescoes in the Fourth Floor South Elevator Lobby, Post Office Department Building, Washington, D. C.

13′6″ wide x 7′ high

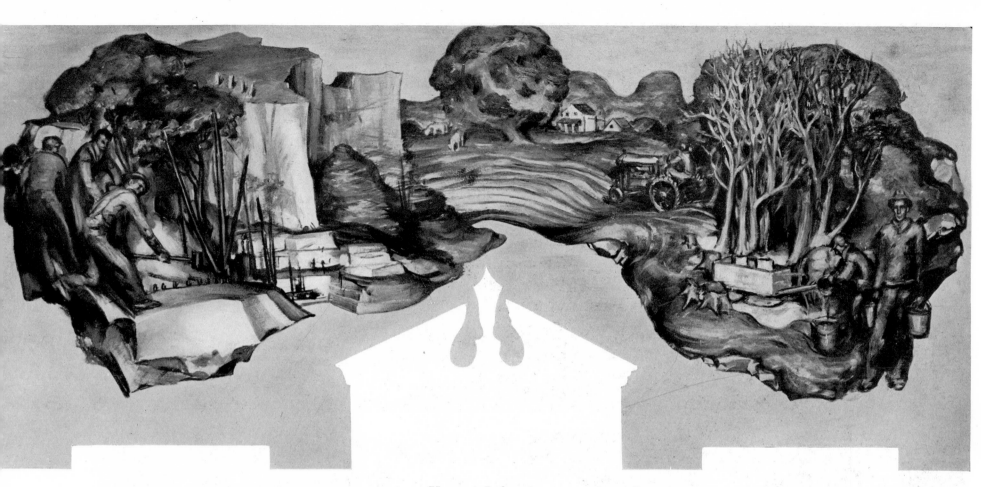

Vermont Industries

Study for Mural in the Lobby, White River Junction, Vermont, Post Office

16' wide x 6'6'' high

JOHN CSOSZ

Left to right: *Mail Coach at the Inn near Doan Corners—Sandusky—One of the First Locomotive*

Euclid Township—Nathaniel Doan—Blacksmith, Justice of the Peace, and One of the First Postmasters Giving out Mail

Studies for Continuous Mural Frieze in the Lobby

Frieze 168 runnin

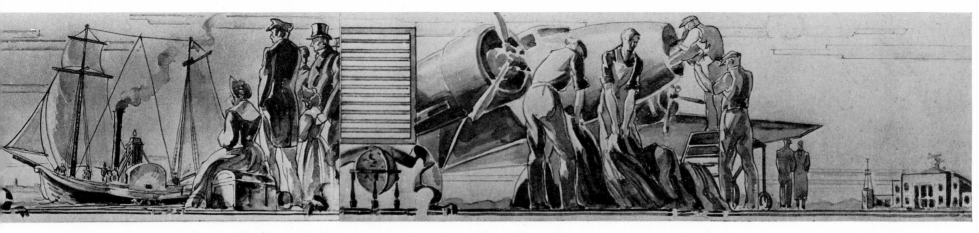

JOHN CSOSZ

'est of the Ohio River—The First Steamboat on Lake Erie—Air-Mail with Cleveland Air Port

Modern Cleveland near Doan Corners—University, Museum, Art and Scientific School, Symphony Orchestra and Hospital

University Center Station, Cleveland, Ohio, Post Office
eet, 6' high

JOHN STEUART CURRY

Top: *Movement of the Population Westward*   Bottom: *Law versus Mob Rule*

Studies for two Lunettes in the Elevator Lobby on the Fifth Floor, Department of Justice Building, Washington, D. C.
20′7″ wide x 8′3″ high

Illinois Farm

Study for Panel in the Lobby, Gillespie, Illinois, Post Office   5′ wide x 4′ high

JULIO DE DIEGO

Fruits of Nature
Detail, *Tobacco*

Studies for Murals on Side Walls of Officers' Mess Hall, Fort Sheridan, Illinois
Room 13' wide x 42' long   Painted Surface 6' above wainscot

Mail and Travel by Stage Coach

Study for Mural in the Lobby, Stockton, California, Post Office
15' wide x 8'6'' high

THOMAS DONNELLY

Indian Community Cornfield

Mount Kisco in 1850

Studies for two Lunettes in the Lobby, Mount Kisco, New York, Post Office
14'6'' wide x 7'3'' high

Washington Bridge

Study for Mural in the Lobby, Ridgefield Park, New Jersey, Post Office
12'2'' wide x 6'6'' high

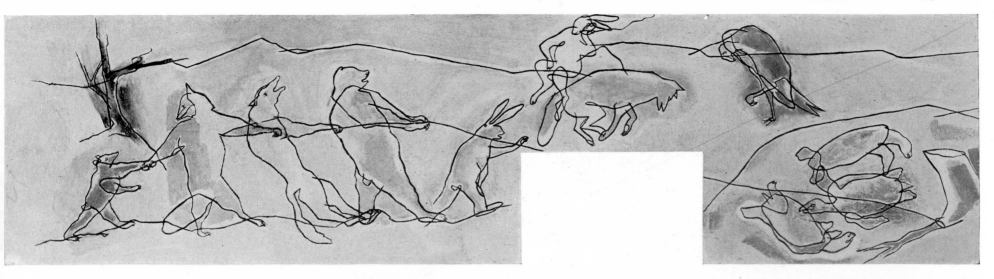

ELSIE DRIGGS

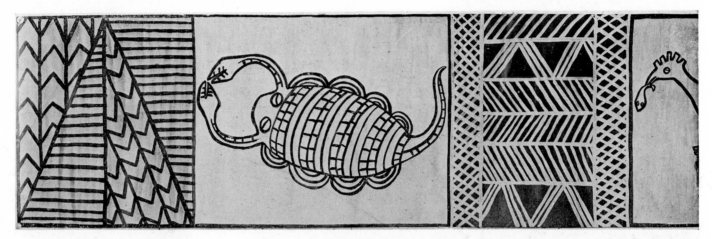

Animal Fables

Above and below: Sketches for Two Panels for a Children's Playroom—22′ wide x 6′ high
Center: Detail of a Frieze for a Children's Playroom—116 running feet x 1′4″ high
Done under the Treasury Department Art Projects and allocated to the P.W.A. Harlem Housing Project

GUY PENE DU BOIS

 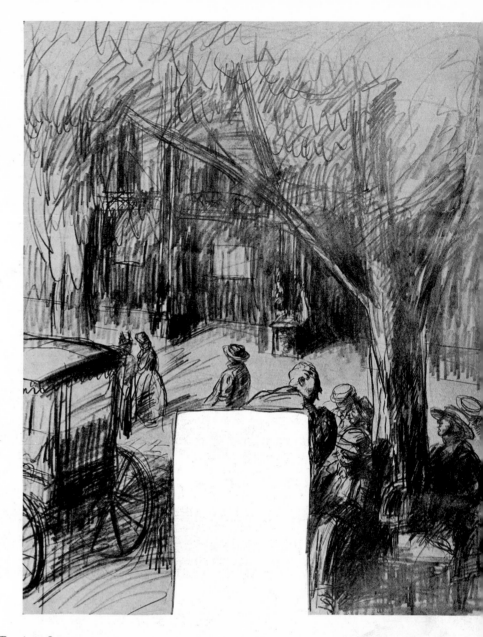

Saratoga in the Racing Season

Preliminary Drawings for Two Murals in the Lobby, Saratoga Springs, New York, Post Office
7′6″ wide x 11′ high

Saratoga in the Racing Season

Later Color Studies of Preceding Sketches

JOSEPH A. FLECK

First Mail Crossing Raton Pass

Study for Mural in the Lobby, Raton, New Mexico, Post Office
12'4'' wide x 7'6'' high

HELEN K. FORBES

Early Settlers

study for Mural in the Lobby, Merced, California, Post Office

6′ wide x 9′8″ high

Molly Pitcher

Study for Mural in the Lobby, Freehold, New Jersey, Post Office

11′8″ wide x 4′ high

Stage Coach and Train

Pencil Study for Mural in the Lobby, Cranford, New Jersey, Post Office

11′6″ wide x 4′4″ high

GERALD S. FOSTER

Pencil Studies and Details for
Murals on the Screen Wall of
the Lobby, Cranford,
New Jersey, Post Office

Lobby 11'6'' wide x 53'6'' long
Painted Surface
4'4'' above wainscot

Scenes from the Continental War

The Letter

Study for Mural in the Lobby,
East Alton, Illinois, Post Office

4' wide x 4'6'' high

French Explorers and Indians

Study for Mural in the Seventh Floor South Elevator Lobby, Post Office Department Building, Washington, D. C.

13′6″ wide x 6′6″ high

KARL R. FREE

Arrival of the Mail in New Amsterdam

Study for Mural in the Seventh Floor South Elevator Lobby, Post Office Department Building, Washington, D. C.
13′6″ wide x 6′6″ high

Wheat Farming

Chicken Hatcheries

Studies for Lunettes in the Lobby, Clinton, Missouri, Post Office
11′8″ wide x 4′4″ high

WALTER GARDNER

*The First
Locomotive*

*Washington
Irving and
Philip Hone
Visit Canal*

*The Canal
Boat*

Early Scenes on the Delaware and Ohio Canal at Honesdale

Studies for Murals in the Lobby, Honesdale, Pennsylvania, Post Office   Top and Bottom Panels 13'6'' wide x 3'6'' high   Center Panel 12' wide x 3'6'' high

Clearing the Wilderness

Details of Murals around the Entrance Door

Space 18′ wide x 10′ high

Coal and the Gravity Railroad

Studies for Murals in the Lobby, Honesdale, Pennsylvania, Post Office   15′ wide x 3′6″ high

X A V I E R   G O N Z A L E S

Strawberry Culture

Preliminary Sketches for Murals in the Lobby, Hammond, Louisiana, Post Office

Two Upper Panels 28′ wide x 4′ high   Two Lower Panels 15′6″ wide x 4′ high

XAVIER GONZALES

Strawberry Culture

Revised Sketches for Murals in the Lobby, Hammond, Louisiana, Post Office

Two Upper Panels 28′ wide x 4′ high   Two Lower Panels 15′6″ wide x 4′ high

DAVID GRANAHAN

Cultivation of Raspberries

Studies for All-over Murals in the Lobby, Hopkins, Minnesota, Post Office

Room 12′ wide x 34′ long   Painted Surface 9′6′′ above wainscot

DAVID GRANAHAN

Studies for Murals in the Lobby,
Rochester, Minnesota, Post Office

Center Panel
8′4″ wide x 12′4″ high

Side Panels
2′4″ wide x 5′4″ high

The Founding of Rochester

GORDON KENNETH GRANT

(Detail)

Agriculture an

(Detail)

Industries in Ventura

Ventura, California, Post Office

Painted Surface 7′6″ above wainscot

JACK J. GREITZER

Studies for Murals in the Entrance
Vestibule, Cleveland,
Ohio, Post Office

7'3" wide x 11'10" high

Interior of the City Post Office

Suburban Post in Winter

Preliminary Drawing and Subsequent Color Study for
Mural in the Lobby, Freeport, New York, Post Office
6'9" wide x 17'6" high

RICHARD HAINES

Iowa Farming

Study for Mural in the Lobby, Cresco, Iowa, Post Office
7′6″ wide x 5′ high

RICHARD HAINES

Kansas Farming

Above: Preliminary Study
Below: Revised Study for
Mural in the Lobby, Wich-
ita, Kansas, Post Office
10'6" wide x 4'7" high

GEORGE HARDING

Top: *Commerce of the East*   Center: *Exports, Port of Philadelphia*   Bottom: *Customs Examination*

10′2″ wide x 3′7″ high   15′7″ wide x 3′7″ high   10′2″ wide x 3′7″ high

Studies for Murals in the Philadelphia, Pennsylvania,

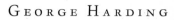

Top: *Shipbuilding*   Center: *Foreign Imports of Philadelphia*   Bottom: *Government Aids to Harbor Navigation, Buoys; Government Aids to Deep Sea Navigation*

0'2″ wide x 3'7″ high   15'7″ wide x 3'7″ high   6'5″ wide x 3'7″ high   6'5″ wide x 3'7″ high

Custom House and Appraisers' Stores

GEORGE HARDING

Studies for Murals in the Sixth
Floor South Elevator Lobby,
Post Office Department Build-
ing, Washington, D. C.

13'6'' wide x 6' high

Above: *The Carrying of Dispatches in the Revolution*   Below: *Benjamin Franklin and His Administration of the Philadelphia Post Office*

GEORGE HARRIS

Farm Life

Study for Mural in the Lobby, Woodland, California, Post Office   12' wide x 5' high

VICTOR HIGGINS

Crossing the Ford

Study for Mural in the Lobby, Rocky Ford, Colorado, Post Office   11'10'' wide x 4'2'' high

JOHN F. HOLMER

Pioneer Cincinnati

Studies for Frieze in the Elevator Lobby,
Lobby 16′ wide x 23′ long

J O H N   F.   H O L M E R

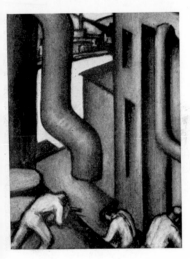

Modern Cincinnati

Cincinnati, Ohio, Post Office
Painted Surface 5′9″ above wainscot

LOWELL HOUSER

Evolution of Corn

Preliminary Study, before Changes, for Mural in the Lobby, Ames, Iowa, Post Office

Side Panels 4′ wide x 7′ high   Center Panel 4′6″ wide x 3′ high

CHARLES KASSLER, II

P.W.A. Payments Help Trade—P.W.A. Construction

Studies for Fresco Lunettes for Side Walls in the Lobby, Beverly Hills, California, Post Office
20' wide x 10'2'' high

CHARLES KASSLER, II

Above: *Post Rider*

Below: *Air Mail*

Studies for Fresco Lunettes
on the End Walls in the Lobby, Beverly Hills, California,
Post Office

14' wide x 7' high

Train Mail

Left to right: *Millwork, Shoe Factory Cutting, Air Mail, Shoe Factory Finishing, Truck and Dairy Farming*

Studies for All-over Murals in the Lobby, Johnson City, New York, Post Office

Lobby 12'8'' wide x 48' long   Painted Surface 9'6'' above wainscot

LEON KROLL

Triumph of Justice

Study for Lunette in the Attorney General's Private Office on the Fifth Floor of the Department of Justice Building, Washington, D. C.

21'8'' wide x 8'6'' high

Defeat of Justice

Study for Lunette in the Attorney General's Private Office on the Fifth Floor of the Department of Justice Building, Washington, D. C.

21′8″ wide x 8′6″ high

THOMAS LA FARGE

Across Both Pages—Top: *Morning Watch*   Center

Studies for Murals in the Lobby

Each Pane

THOMAS LA FARGE

Cutting Up, Midday   Bottom: *Furling Sail, Sunset*

New London, Connecticut, Post Office

4'3" wide x 3' high

RICHARD LAHEY

Transfer from Stage to Boat

Study for Mural in the Lobby, Brownsville, Pennsylvania, Post Office
12' wide x 4'7'' high

THOMAS LAMAN

Land   *Water*

Preliminary Sketches for Murals in the Court Room, Eureka, California, Post Office and Court House
4'4'' wide x 2'6'' high

THOMAS LAMAN

Mining (Drawing)   *Mining* (Color Sketch)   *Forestry*

Studies for Murals in the Court Room, Eureka, California, Post Office and Court House
5'6'' wide x 9'6'' high

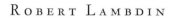

ROBERT LAMBDIN

Top: *Preliminary Study for Three Panels*   Revised Studies Below

Center: *Stage Coach and Modern Transportation*   Lower Left: *Post Rider and Modern Carriers*   Lower Right: *Continental Inn Post Office and Modern Distributors*

Studies for Murals in the Lobby, Bridgeport, Connecticut, Post Office   Center Panel 8'8" wide x 3'6" high   Side Panels 4'4" wide x 3'6" high

TOM LEA

Texas Farm

Study for Mural in the Entrance Vestibule, Benjamin Franklin Postal Station,
Post Office Department Building, Washington, D. C.

6′ wide x 11′6″ high

FREDERICO LeBRUN

Post in the Country

Post in the City (Ink Sketch)

Studies for Frescoes in the Entrance Vestibule, New York City Post Office Annex
Walls 38′ wide x 9′4″ high

DORIS LEE

Country Post

Study for Mural in the Sixth Floor North Elevator Lobby, Post Office Department Building, Washington, D. C.

13'6'' wide x 6' high

DORIS LEE

General Store and Post Office

Study for Mural in the Sixth Floor North Elevator Lobby, Post Office Department Building, Washington, D. C.

13′6″ wide x 6′ high

HILTON LEECH

Allegory of Chattanooga

Study for Mural in the Court Room, Chattanooga, Tennessee, Post Office and Court House   17'3" wide x 5' high

SCHOMER LICHTNER

Modern Life

The Lake

Indian Life

5' wide x 7'6" high   Studies for Murals in the Lobby, Sheboygan, Wisconsin, Post Office   14'6" wide x 7'6" high

The Pioneer

Study for Mural in the Lobby, Sheboygan, Wisconsin, Post Office
10′ wide x 7′6″ high

WARD LOCKWOOD

Pioneers in Kansas

Above: Preliminary Study
Below: Revised Study for Mural
in the Lobby, Wichita, Kansas,
Post Office

10'6" wide x 4'7" high

LOCKWOOD

Opening of the Southwest

Study for Mural in the Fifth Floor South Elevator Lobby, Post Office Department Building, Washington, D. C.
13′6″ wide x 6′ high

Building of the Railroads in the West

Study for Mural in the Fifth Floor South Elevator Lobby, Post Office Department Building, Washington, D. C.

13'6'' wide x 6' high

FRANK W. LONG

Top—Left: *Ohio River Traffic*   Right: *Coal Mining*

Studies for Murals in Two Side Entrances and Elevato

Each Pane

FRANK W. LONG

Center: (continuous) *Stock Farming*   Bottom: (continuous) *Agriculture*

Lobbies, Louisville, Kentucky, Post Office

38' wide x 3'3" high

FRANK W. LONG

Fox Hunting

Horse Racing

Studies for Murals in Two Side Entrances and Elevator Lobbies, Louisville, Kentucky, Post Office
10′ wide x 3′3″ high

Rural Free Delivery

FRANK W. LONG

The Star Route

Unloading a Railroad Post Office Car

City Collection

Studies for Lunettes over Elevator Doors, Louisville, Kentucky, Post Office and Court House

5′5″ wide x 3′ high

DAVID McCOSH

Lewis and Clark at Mount Kelso

Study for Mural in the Lobby, Kelso, Washington, Post Office

15'6'' wide x 6' high

KINDRED McLEARY

Modern Justice

Study for Mural in Court Room No. 2, Pittsburgh, Pennsylvania, Post Office and Court House
17′5″ wide x 10′6″ high

PEPPINO MANGRAVITE

Hempstead Settlers in 1640

Dutch and English Settlers Bargain for Land from Native Chiefs and Erect a Stockade

Study for one of the Murals in the Lobby, Hempstead, New York, Post Office, Depicting a Series of Incidents in Hempstead History Dealing with the Transportation of People, Mail and Merchandise, by Sea, Land and Air

18'6'' wide x 10' high

PEPPINO MANGRAVITE

Revolutionary War—1775

St. George's Church in the Background

Study for Mural in the Lobby, Hempstead, New York, Post Office
18'6'' wide x 10' high

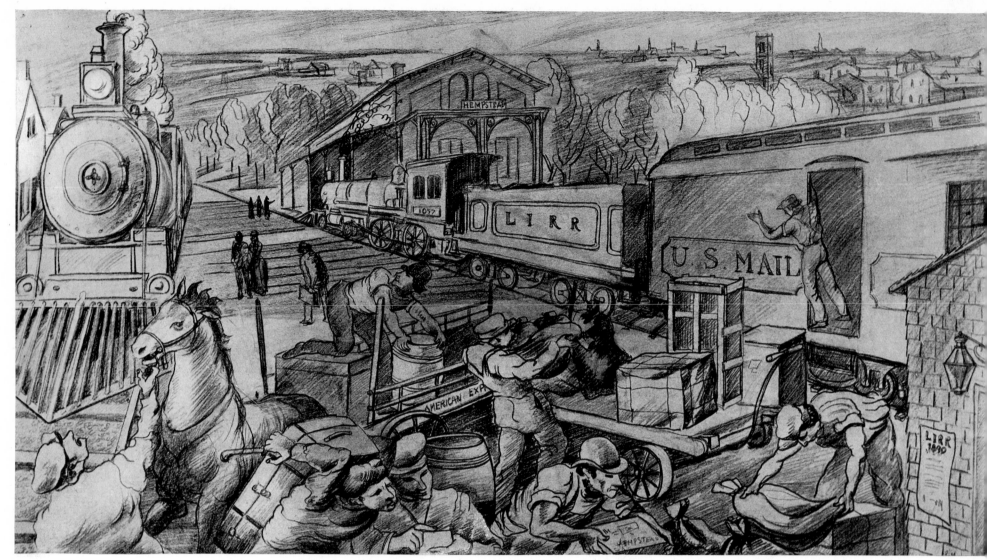

The Long Island Railroad at Hempstead—1890

The New City in the Background

Study for Mural in the Lobby, Hempstead, New York, Post Office

18′6″ wide x 10′ high

English Dirigible R34 Delivering Mail to the United States at Hempstead Field, 1919

Study for Mural in the Lobby, Hempstead, New York, Post Office

18′6″ wide x 10′ high

Sorting Mail

Preliminary Sketch for Fresco in the Fourth Floor North Elevator Lobby, Post Office Department Building, Washington, D. C.

13'6'' wide x 7' high

Transfer of Mail from Liner to Tugboat

Preliminary Sketch for Fresco in the Fourth Floor North Elevator Lobby, Post Office Department Building, Washington, D. C.

13′6″ wide x 7′ high

HENRICK MARTIN MAYER

Scenes on the Ohio River Around Louisville

Top, left to right: *The Train, Lightning* (drawing for wood carving), *Loading the Boat, Indian Sacrifice*

Center, left to right: *Pleasure Ship, Marine Hospital* (drawing for wood carving), *Ship Building*

Bottom, left to right: *Preaching to the Indians, Wind* (drawing for wood carving), *Canal Barge, Life Saving*

Studies for Murals in the Lobby, Louisville, Kentucky, Marine Hospital

Room 15' wide x 17' long
Painted Surface 7' above wainscot

P A U L   M A Y S

Studies for Murals in
the Lobby, Norris-
town, Pennsylvania,
Post Office

12′ wide x 5′6″ high

Local Industries

FRANK A. MECHAU

Dangers of the Mail

Study for Mural in the Fifth Floor North Elevator Lobby, Post Office Department Building, Washington, D.C.

13′6″ wide x 6′ high

Pony Express

Study for Mural in the Fifth Floor North Elevator Lobby, Post Office Department Building, Washington, D. C.

13'6'' wide x 6' high

FRANK A. MECHAU

Indian Fight

Study for Mural in the Lobby, Colorado Springs, Colorado, Post Office
13′6″ wide x 6′ high

The Corral

Study for Mural in the Lobby, Colorado Springs, Colorado, Post Office

13'6'' wide x 6' high

EDWARD MILLMAN

Study for Mural in the Lobby,
Moline, Illinois, Post Office

8'6" wide x 7' high

Manufacture of Plow Shares in Moline

ROSS MOFFETT

Captain Alezur Holyoke's Exploring Party on the Connecticut River

Study for Mural in the Lobby, Holyoke, Massachusetts, Post Office
16'5'' wide x 9' high

STEPHEN MOPOPE

assisted by

MONROE TSA-TO-KE
SPENCER ASAH
AND JACK AUCHIAH

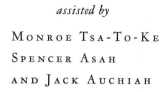

Indian Themes

Studies for Murals in the Lobby, Anadarko, Oklahoma, Post Office
Room 14′ wide x 97′ long   Painted Surface 11′ above wainscot

F. Luis Mora

Arrival of the Stage

Study for Mural in the Lobby, Catasauqua, Pennsylvania, Post Office
12′ wide x 5′6″ high

DOMENICO MORTELLITO

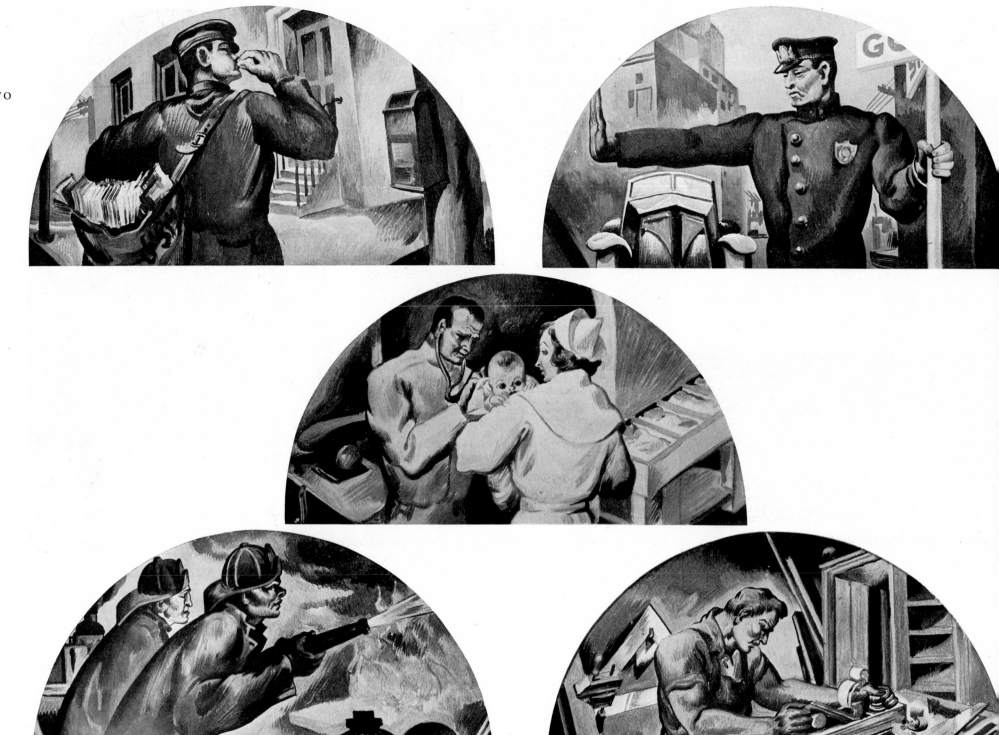

Port Chester Pursuits

Studies for Lunettes in the Lobby, Port Chester, New York, Post Office
8' wide x 4' high

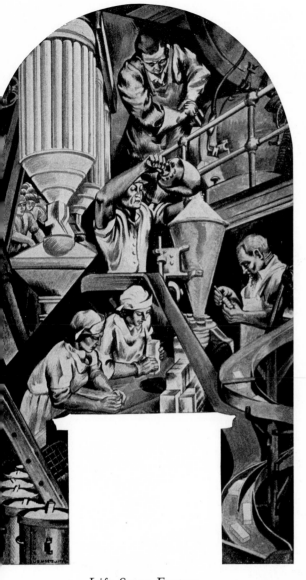  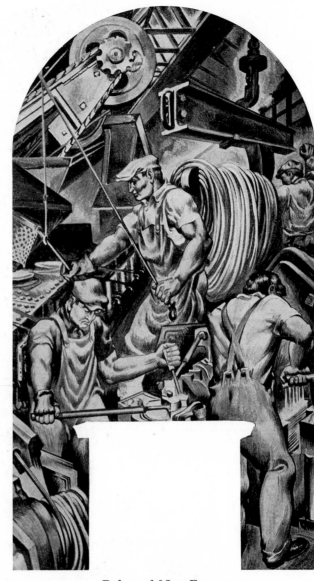

DOMENICO MORTELLITO

Life Saver Factory   *Old Port Chester*   *Bolt and Nut Factory*

Studies for Three Murals in the Lobby, Port Chester, New York, Post Office   8′ wide x 14′ high

 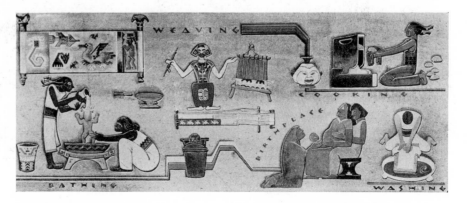

Studies for Linoleum Panels 23′ wide x 9′ high
Done under the Treasury Department Art Projects and allocated to the P.W.A. Harlem Housing Project, New York City

LOREN MOZLEY

Indian Revolt of 1680 Against the Spaniards

(Detail)

Study for Mural over the Elevator Doors, Albuquerque, New Mexico, Post Office
34' wide x 6'6" high

EARL J. NEFF

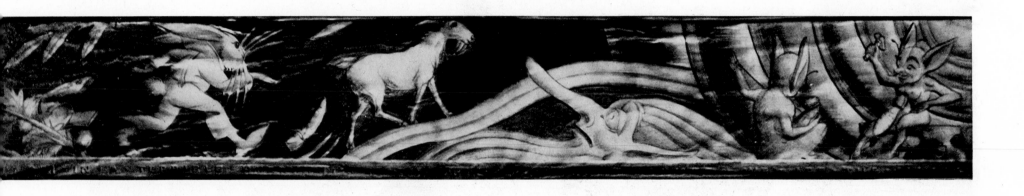

Legends and Fairy Stories

Studies for a Frieze in the Children's Playroom, Cleveland, Ohio, "Whiskey Island," P.W.A. Housing Project
Done under the Treasury Department Art Projects and allocated to the P.W.A. Housing Project

Frieze 39 running feet, 2'2" high

A R T H U R W. O A K M A N

Old Harbor in Early Times

Studies for All-over Murals in the Conference Room, Boston, Massachusetts, Old Harbor Village P.W.A. Housing Project
Done under the Treasury Department Art Projects and allocated to the P.W.A. Housing Project

Room 13′ wide by 19′ long   Painted Surface 5′9″ above wainscot

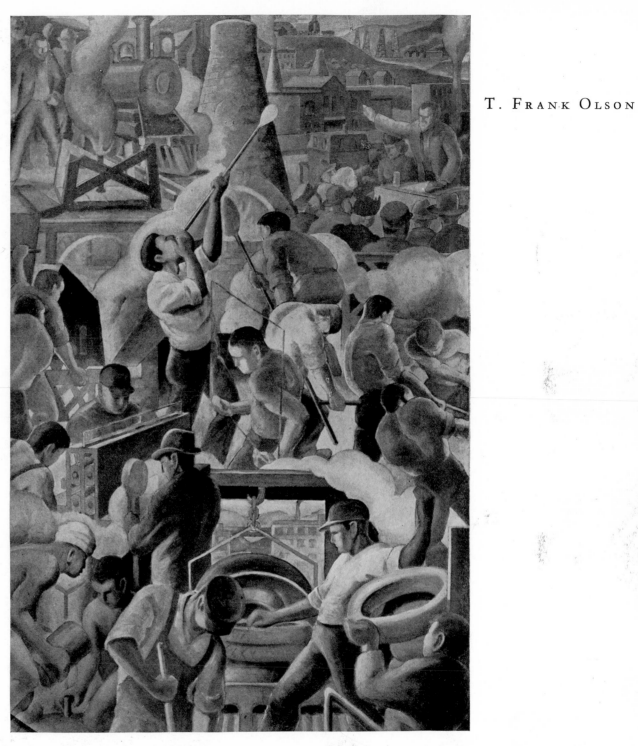

T. FRANK OLSON

History of Jeannette

Industries of Jeannette

These Studies Were Made by the Late T. Frank Olson and Are Being Carried Out by Alexander Kostellow

Studies for Murals in the Lobby, Jeannette, Pennsylvania, Post Office

Each Panel 5′9″ wide x 8′8″ high

WILLIAM C. PALMER

Covered Wagon Attacked by Indians

Study for Mural in the Seventh Floor North Elevator Lobby, Post Office Department Building, Washington, D. C.

13′6″ wide x 7′ high

Stage Coach Attacked by Bandits

Study for Mural in the Seventh Floor North Elevator Lobby, Post Office Department Building, Washington, D. C.

13'6'' wide x 7' high

ERNEST PEIXOTTO

George Washington at the Young's House, Oyster Bay, 1790

William Leverich Discusses the Treaty with the Indians, 1653

James Caldwell, First Postmaster, and First Post Office, Oyster Bay, 180

Theodore Roosevelt with His Children at Sagamore Hill

Springtime, Oyster Bay

Studies for Five Panels in the Lobby, Oyster Bay, New York, Post Office
Each Panel 6' wide x 2'6'' high

Agriculture

Street Scene

Studies for Continuous Frieze in the Lobby, Hudson Falls, New York, Post Office
Frieze 113 running feet, 4' high

G EORGE P ICKEN

Transportation and Distribution of the Mail

Family Scene

Studies for Continuous Frieze in the Lobby, Hudson Falls, New York, Post Office
Frieze 113 running feet, 4' high

GEORGE PICKEN

The Falls   12′ wide x 4′ high

Detail, *Power Plant*   Detail, *Paper Mill*

Studies for Continuous Frieze in the Lobby, Hudson Falls, New York, Post Office   Frieze 113 running feet, 4′ high

HENRY VARNUM POOR

Imprisonment   *Vocational Training*   *Release*

Side Panels 3′ wide x 13′6″ high   Studies for Frescoes in the Fifth Floor Corrido

Unloading   Examination and Customs   Surveying New Lands

of the Department of Justice Building, Washington, D. C.   Center Panels 6′6″ wide x 4′ high

HENRY VARNUM POOR

Tennessee Valley Authority

Side Panels 3′ wide x 13′6″ high

Symbols of Justice

Gold Case

Studies for Frescoes in the Fifth Floor Corridor

Anti-Trust Division   *Kidnapping*   *Bureau of Investigation*

f the Department of Justice Building, Washington, D. C.   Center Panels 6′6″ wide x 4′ high

DOROTHY PUCCINELLI

Vacheros

Study for Mural in the Lobby, Merced, California, Post Office

6' wide x 9'8'' high

Early California

Studies for All-over Murals in the Lobby, Compton, California, Post Office

Lobby 13' wide x 55' long   Painted Surface 6' above wainscot

EDNA REINDEL

Studies for All-over Murals in the Committee Room, Stamford, Connecticut, P.W.A. Housing Project
Done under the Treasury Department Art Projects and allocated to the P.W.A. Housing Project

Room 9′ wide x 10′ long   Painted Surface 8′6″ above baseboard

Developed Detail of Mural Shown on the Opposite Page

DAN RHODES

Settlers Building

Study for Mural in the Lobby, Glen Ellyn, Illinois, Post Office
12′ wide x 4′ high

WILLIAM RISEMAN

1635—Early and Modern Industries of Lynn—1935

Study for Mural in the Lobby, Lynn, Massachusetts, Post Office

16'6'' wide x 7' high

BOARDMAN ROBINSON

MENES

MOSES

HAMMURABI

Studies for Murals in the Main Stairhall
Side Panels 3'11" wide x 12'6" high

GAIUS

SOLON

JUSTINIAN

epartment of Justice Building, Washington, D. C.

enter Panels 5'7" wide x 12'6" high

BOARDMAN ROBINSON

COKE

MAGNA CHARTA

BLACKSTONE

Studies for Murals in the Main Stairhall

Side Panels, 3′11″ wide x 12′6″ high

BOARDMAN ROBINSON

MARSHALL

CONSTITUTION

KENT

Department of Justice Building, Washington, D. C.
Center Panels 10'4" wide x 12'6" high

BOARDMAN ROBINSON

HOLMES

GROTIUS

Studies for Murals in the Main Stairhal
Side Panels 3'11'' wide x 12'6'' hig

HENRY II

CHRIST

BRACTON

BOARDMAN ROBINSON

Department of Justice Building, Washington, D. C.

Center Panels 5'6'' wide x 5'3'' high

FRANK ROMANELLI

Landscape with Deer

Alcoves 9½' wide x 13' long

Studies for All-over Murals in two Alcoves off the Nurses

FRANK ROMANELLI

Landscape with Buffalo

UMBERTO ROMANO

William Pynchon Purchasing Land for Springfield from the Indians—Customs and Superstitions brought by the Colonists from England

Conflict of Religious Ideas—
Trade on the Connecticut River

Revolutionary War
—Shay's Rebellion

Each Panel 11'9'' wide x 7'6'' high

John Brown and the Fugitive Slaves—New Industries

19' wide x 6' high

Studies for Murals in the Lobby

Indians under Wequogan Sack and Burn Community—Internal Strife
11'9'' wide x 7'6'' high

World War and the Depression
13'3'' wide x 6' high

Springfield, Massachusetts, Post Office

CHARLES ROSEN

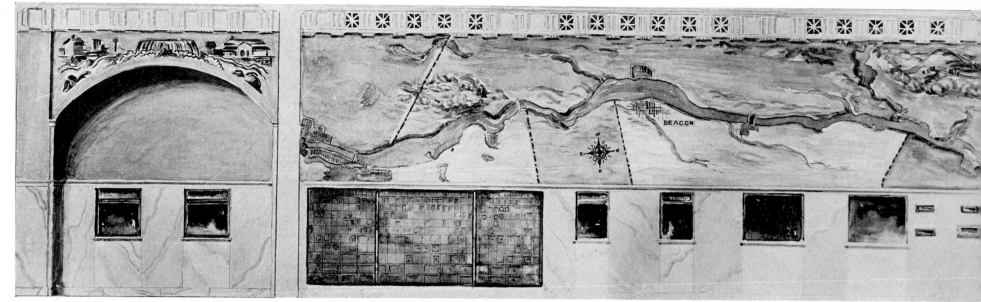

Map of the Hudson River from New York to Hudson

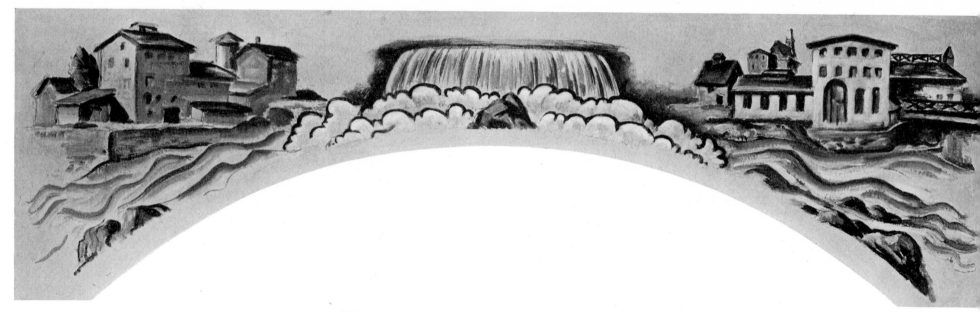

Old Power House and Water-Fall (Detail of End Wall)

Studies for All-over Murals in the Lobby, Beacon, New York, Post Office

Lobby 12'6'' wide x 40' long   Painted Surface 8' above wainscot

View of Beacon from the River

CHARLES ROSEN

Old Swedish Church, Beacon

Studies for Murals in the Lobby, Beacon, New York, Post Office

Lobby 12'6'' wide x 40' long   Painted Surface 8' above wainscot

W. Vladimir Rousseff

Fight with Indians
13′ wide x 5′9″ high

Stage Coach and Ferry Boat
12′ wide x 5′9″ high

Studies for Murals in the Lobby, Iron Mountain, Michigan, Post Office

W. VLADIMIR ROUSSEFF

Moving West
23' wide x 5'9'' high

Washing and Carrying Gold
12' wide x 10'6'' high

Watching an Early Train
23' wide x 5'9'' high

Studies for Murals in the Lobby, Iron Mountain, Michigan, Post Office

WILLIAM B. ROWE

Views of Old Buffalo

Studies for All-over Murals in the Nurses' Community Room, Buffalo, New York, Marine Hospital

Room 20′ wide x 27′6″ long   Painted Surface 8′ above the baseboard

PAUL SAMPLE

Sheep Farming and the Ocean near Redondo
36′ wide x 5′ high

Excursion Train and Picknickers in the Nineties
12′ wide x 5′ high

Fishing from Redondo Dock
12′ wide x 5′ high

Studies for All-over Murals in the Lobby, Redondo Beach, California, Post Office

MICHAEL SARISKY

Air Mail

Study for Mural in the Lobby, Barnesville, Ohio, Post Office
13′ wide x 5′6″ high

Local Life and Industries

Studies for All-over Murals in the Lobby, Scottdale, Pennsylvania, Post Office

Top Panel 36′ wide x 5′6″ high   Two Lower Panels 12′6″ wide x 5′ high

Old Post Office

Study for Mural in the Lobby, Fairfield, Illinois, Post Office
4' wide x 3' high

ROLAND SCHWEINSBURG

Study for Lunette in the Lobby,
East Liverpool, Ohio,
Post Office

15'3" wide x 5' high

The Old Bennet Pottery Plant

ELISE SEEDS

Air Mail

Study for Mural in the Lobby,
Oceanside, California,
Post Office

11'2" wide x 5'7" high

GLENN SHAW

Pouring Steel Ingots

The Soaking Pit

Studies for a Series of Murals Depicting the Steel Industry, in the Lobby, Canton, Ohio, Post Office   6′9″ wide x 11′ high

Tapping the Blast Furnace

Teeming the Electric Furnace

Studies for Murals in the Lobby, Canton, Ohio, Post Office   6'9'' wide x 11' high

GLENN SHAW

The Breakdown Mill   *Seamless Tube Mill*

Studies for Murals in the Lobby, Canton, Ohio, Post Office   6'9" wide x 11' high

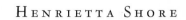

Limestone Quarries   6' wide x 3' high

Artichoke Culture   *Cabbage Culture*

8' wide x 4' high

Fishing   6' wide x 3' high

Studies for Lunettes in the Lobby, Santa Cruz, California, Post Office

DAVID SILVETTE

The Founding of New Bern by Graffenried

The Bayard-Singleton Case

The First Provincial Convention in North Carolina

Studies for Murals in the Court Room, New Bern, North Carolina, Court House

Center Panel 13′6″ wide x 6′8″ high   Side Panels 8′6″ wide x 6′8″ high

JACOB GETLAR SMITH

Indian Wars—Meeting of John André and Benedict Arnold—Underground Tunnel

23' wide x 6'8'' high

Indians Watching Hendrick Hudson—Dutch Settlers

Section of Panel 15' wide x 6'8'' high

Nyack in the Early Nineteenth Century

Section of Panel 13' wide x 6'8'' high

Studies for Murals in the Lobby, Nyack, New York, Post Office

HARRY STERNBERG

Carrying the Mail

Study for Mural in the Lobby, Sellersville, Pennsylvania, Post Office

12′ wide x 5′8″ high

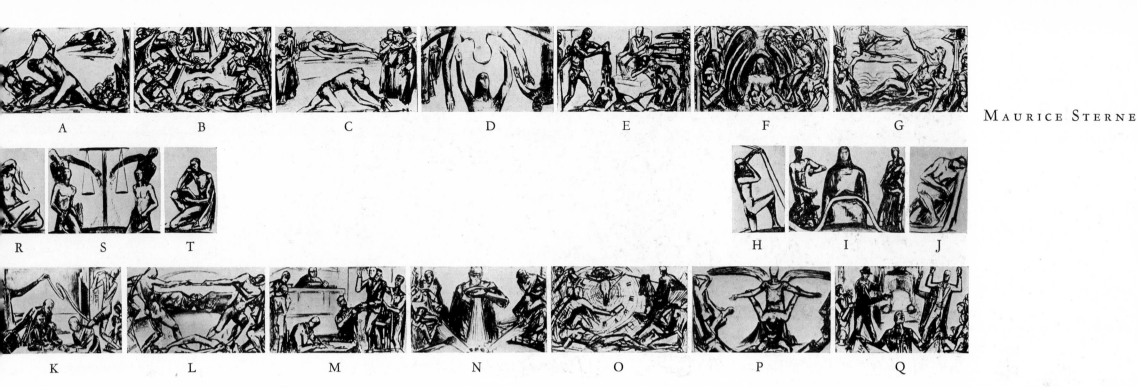

MAURICE STERNE

A —Brute Force

Two figures struggling; flock of sheep in foreground suggesting fight over property. Background, mountain lion attacking a deer.

B —Greed

A group fighting over and casting dice for the garments of Christ at the foot of the Cross, oblivious of the drama which is taking place above.

C —Cruelty

Trial by fire; man carrying two red-hot irons, collapsing at the altar where he is supposed to place them after having walked three paces.

D —Justice Tempered by Mercy

"He who is without sin should cast the first stone." The panel shows a pool and figure with uplifted arms.

E —Intolerance

Old Roman scene. Figure, collapsed over book, besmirched with tar. Man setting fire to the group. Background, a dictator surrounded by Roman soldiers.

F —Tradition

A figure nursing two babes, inside of skeleton. To the left, Hammurabi, Moses and Justinian. To the right, a Roman, Medieval and Modern soldier.

G —Superstition

The Delphic Sybil in a trance, surrounded by attendants. Background, a sacrifice.

Continuity of the Law

H —The Future   **I—The Law**   **J—The Past**

The Law seated over the earth, with scroll—figure to the immediate left with pair of wolves on a leash. To the right, a woman with baby and small child.

K —Magic

A magician making a piper figure of ticker tape, being followed by people entranced by playing. Gamblers in foreground.

L —Competition

Men at each end of tug-of-war. Background, two steers fighting.

M—False Witness

Man delivering an oath on the Bible; he has two faces, one a sweet, honest mask, the other hiding behind it; figure of Bribery behind the man.

N —Justice and Science

Central figure holding lens, which throws light on finger-print card; rays deflected on left to kidnapping; on right to criminal in barber shop being manicured.

O —Red Tape

Huge spiderweb around animal's skull. Clock suggests passage of time. People caught in this net being released by Don Quixote.

P —Ambition

Jacob wrestling with the angel, surrounded by people climbing up a rock, representing earthly ambition.

Q —Environment

Children witnessing a hold-up. Sob sister handing flowers to criminal. A barker with "Daily Yellow Gazette" in his hands.

Attributes of Justice

R —Intuition   **S—Scale of Justice**   **T—Reason**

The Scale of Justice coming from the earth, flanked by reapers with sowers behind, suggests the inevitability between "Cause" and "Effect."

Key for Murals in the Library, Department of Justice Building, Washington, D. C.

MAURICE STERNE

Intuition
3' wide x 6' high

Justice and the Law of Compensation
8' wide x 6' high

Reason
3' wide x 6' high

Brute Force
10' wide x 6' high

MAURICE STERNE

Greed

Cruelty

Justice Tempered by Mercy

Intolerance

Each Panel 10′ wide x 6′ high

MAURICE STERNE

Intuition

Superstition

Magic

Competition

Each Panel 10′ wide x 6′ high

False Witness

MAURICE STERNE

Justice and Science

Red Tape

Ambition

Each Panel 10′ wide x 6′ high

MAURICE STERNE

Environment
10′ wide x 6′ high

The Future
3′ wide x 6′ high

The Continuity of the Law
8′ wide x 6′ high

The Past
3′ wide x 6′ high

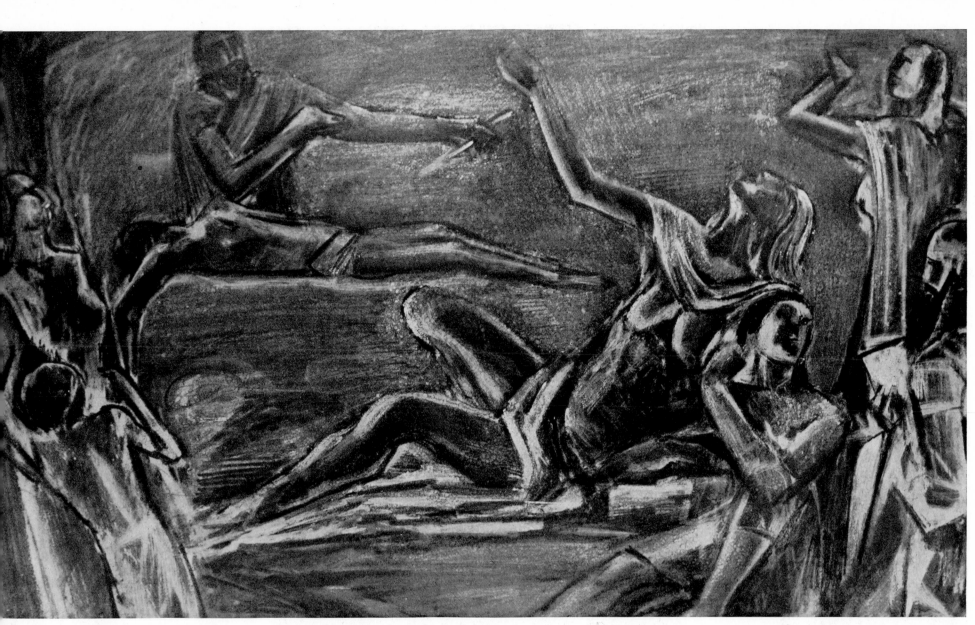

MAURICE STERNE

Superstition

Color Sketch

WILLIAM LESTER STEVENS

Early Rural School

Early Rural Mail Delivery

Studies for Murals in the Lobby, Dedham, Massachusetts, Post Office
13'6'' wide x 7' high

Postman in Storm

Study for Panel in the Lobby, Independence, Iowa, Post Office
5′7″ wide x 3′6″ high

LORIN THOMPSON

*The Growth of the Town: Early Domestic Scenes; Education;
Clearing the Wilderness; Producing the Modern Town*

18′ wide x 8′6″ high

*Early Methods of Transportation
and Making of the Railroad*

18′ wide x 12′ high

Studies for Murals in the Lobby, Altoona, Pennsylvania, Post Of

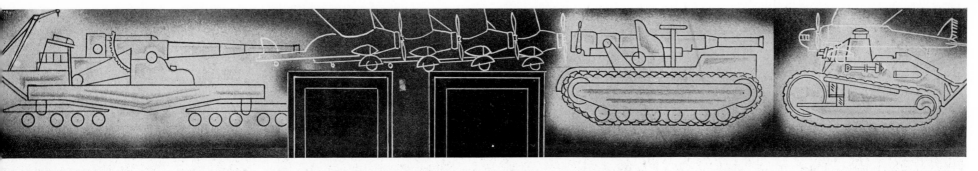

CHARLES TURZAK

Symbols and Instruments Relating to the Army

Studies for Mural Designs in the Corridor Outside the Office of the General in Charge, Army Sixth Corps Area, Chicago, Illinois, Post Office

Corridor 10′ wide x 64′ long   Painted Surface 5′6″ above wainscot

CHARLES TURZAK

Further Studies for Murals Outside the General's Office, Chicago, Illinois, Post Office

Study for One of Four Walls Showing Decorative Maps of the Region in the Office of the General in Charge of the Sixth Corps

Room 24′ wide x 27′ long   Painted Surface 9′ above baseboard

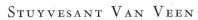

STUYVESANT VAN VEEN

View of Pittsburgh

Study for Mural in Court Room No. 3, Pittsburgh, Pennsylvania, Post Office and Court House

17'5'' wide x 10'6'' high

CHARLES W. WARD

The Second Battle of Trenton

Rural Delivery

Studies for Murals in the Lobby, Trenton, New Jersey, Post Office
17' wide x 5'6'' high

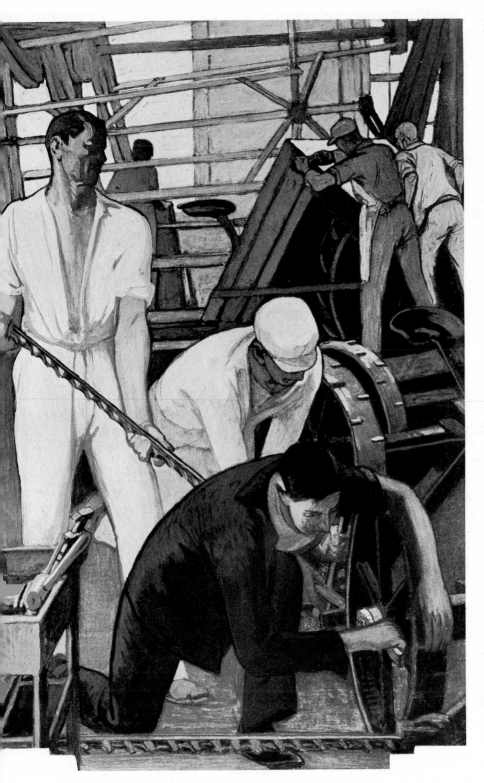

HERMAN H. WESSEL

Printing in Springfield

Studies for Murals in the Lobby, Springfield, Ohio, Post Office

4′ wide x 6′ high

Fuel Depot and Loading Platform. With Predella Showing Various Procurement Division Activities

Surveying

Pouring Concrete

Steel Foundations

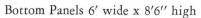

Top Panel 20'5" wide x 10' high

Bottom Panels 6' wide x 8'6" high

Studies for Murals in the Lobby, Treasury Department,

HAROLD WESTON

Recent Buildings Built by the Treasury and Older Buildings Built by the Government. With Predella Showing Various Procurement Division Activities

Steel Superstructures

Procurement Division, Washington, D. C.

Brickwork

Top Panel 20′5″ wide x 10′ high

Roofing

Bottom Panels 6′ wide x 8′6″ high

Community Service

FRANCIS ROBERT WHITE

assisted by

DON GLASELL
EVERETT JEFFREY
HOWARD JOHNSON
AND HARRY JONES

Conquest, Expansion and Development of the West

American Archaeological Research

Lynch Law versus Settled Tribunal—Superstition and Science

(Detail)

Studies for All-over Murals in the Court Room, Cedar Rapids, Iowa
Court House

Room 48' wide x 60' long
Painted Surface 5'6'' above wainscot

WILLIAM D. WHITE

Spring
8′ wide x 9′ high

Summer
8′ wide x 9′ high

Harvest

13′ wide x 9′ high

...udies for Murals in the Lobby, Dover,
Delaware, Post Office

RICHARD ZOELLNER

Fort Hamilton

Agriculture

Machine Tools

Paper Mill

Iron and Coke Industry

Studies for Murals in the Lobby, Hamilton, Ohio, Post Office

Top Lunette 14′ wide x 3′5″ high   Lower Lunettes 6′5″ wide x 3′5″ high

Ohio River Ferry Boat

Study for Mural in the Lobby, Portsmouth, Ohio, Post Office

4′7″ wide x 3′1″ high

RICHARD ZOELLNER

Ohio River Coal Barge

Study for Mural in the Lobby, Portsmouth, Ohio, Post Office
4'7'' wide x 3'1'' high

ARCHITECTURAL DRAWINGS

THE FOLLOWING architectural drawings are arranged alphabetically according to the place names. They consist of floor plans and wall elevations showing the relation of the murals to the rooms in which they are located. The scale used in the murals is indicated by a partial or complete outline drawing.

S.A.O. refers to the Supervising Architect's Office. The three Supervising Architects under whom these buildings were erected are given below with the dates of their tenure of office.

James Knox Taylor, Supervising Architect—October, 1897 – July, 1912
James A. Wetmore, Acting Supervising Architect—June, 1915 – October, 1933
Louis A. Simon, Supervising Architect—October, 1933 –

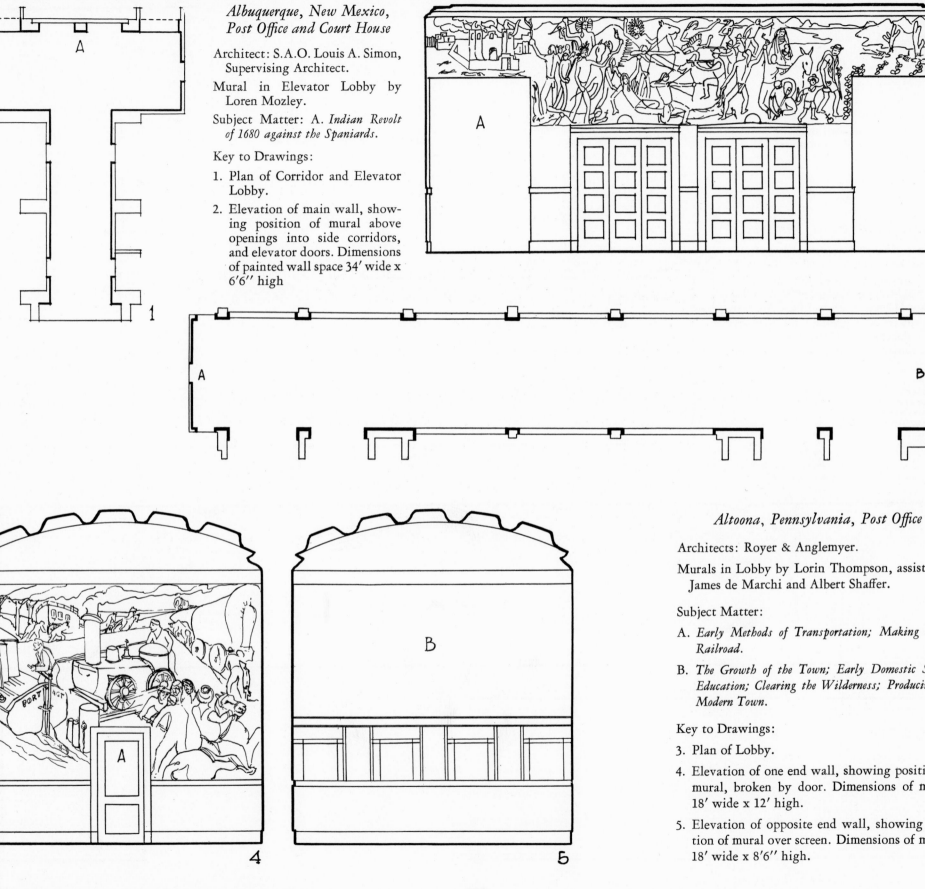

Albuquerque, New Mexico, Post Office and Court House

Architect: S.A.O. Louis A. Simon, Supervising Architect.

Mural in Elevator Lobby by Loren Mozley.

Subject Matter: A. *Indian Revolt of 1680 against the Spaniards.*

Key to Drawings:

1. Plan of Corridor and Elevator Lobby.

2. Elevation of main wall, showing position of mural above openings into side corridors, and elevator doors. Dimensions of painted wall space 34′ wide x 6′6″ high

Altoona, Pennsylvania, Post Office

Architects: Royer & Anglemyer.

Murals in Lobby by Lorin Thompson, assisted by James de Marchi and Albert Shaffer.

Subject Matter:

A. *Early Methods of Transportation; Making of the Railroad.*

B. *The Growth of the Town; Early Domestic Scenes; Education; Clearing the Wilderness; Producing the Modern Town.*

Key to Drawings:

3. Plan of Lobby.

4. Elevation of one end wall, showing position of mural, broken by door. Dimensions of mural, 18′ wide x 12′ high.

5. Elevation of opposite end wall, showing position of mural over screen. Dimensions of mural, 18′ wide x 8′6″ high.

217

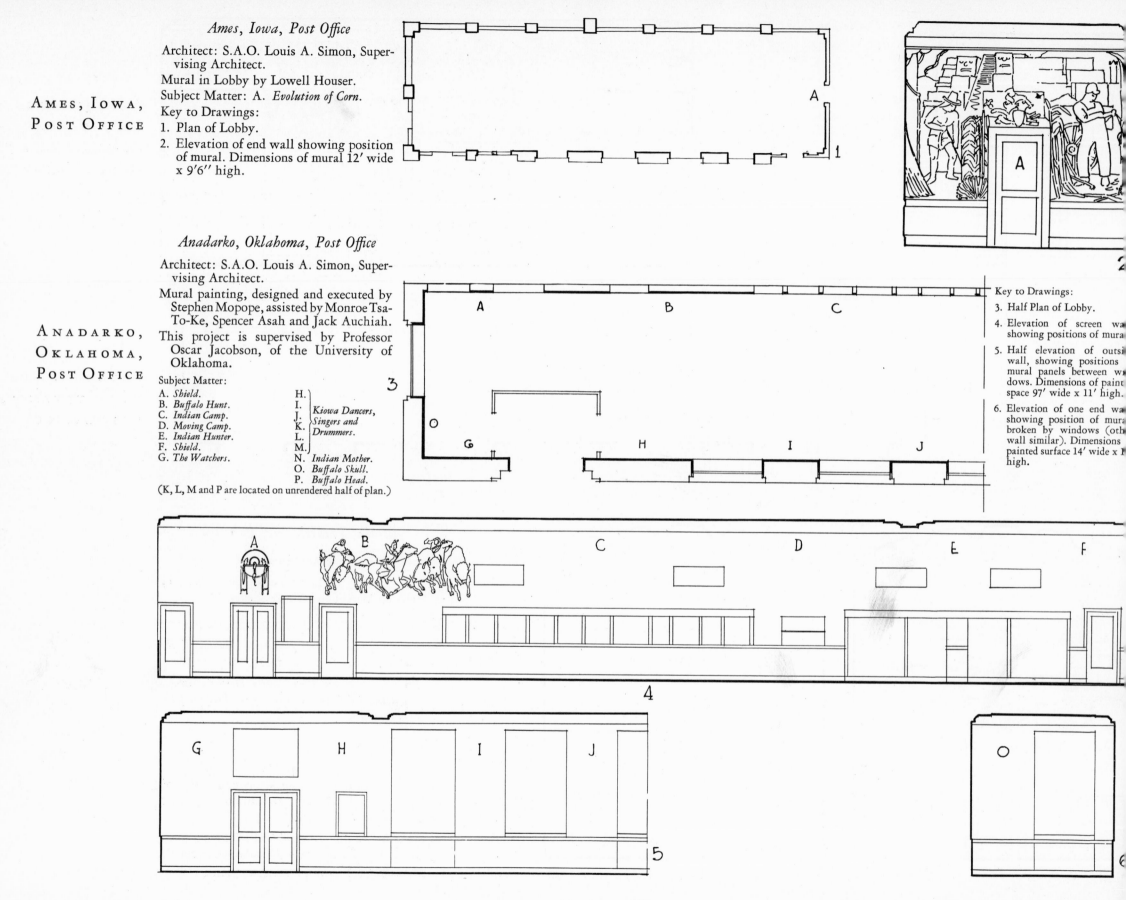

AMES, IOWA, POST OFFICE

Ames, Iowa, Post Office

Architect: S.A.O. Louis A. Simon, Supervising Architect.

Mural in Lobby by Lowell Houser.

Subject Matter: A. *Evolution of Corn.*

Key to Drawings:

1. Plan of Lobby.
2. Elevation of end wall showing position of mural. Dimensions of mural 12′ wide x 9′6″ high.

A

1

2

ANADARKO, OKLAHOMA, POST OFFICE

Anadarko, Oklahoma, Post Office

Architect: S.A.O. Louis A. Simon, Supervising Architect.

Mural painting, designed and executed by Stephen Mopope, assisted by Monroe Tsa-To-Ke, Spencer Asah and Jack Auchiah.

This project is supervised by Professor Oscar Jacobson, of the University of Oklahoma.

Subject Matter:

A. *Shield.*	H.
B. *Buffalo Hunt.*	I.
C. *Indian Camp.*	J. *Kiowa Dancers,*
D. *Moving Camp.*	K. *Singers and*
E. *Indian Hunter.*	L. *Drummers.*
F. *Shield.*	M.
G. *The Watchers.*	N. *Indian Mother.*
	O. *Buffalo Skull.*
	P. *Buffalo Head.*

(K, L, M and P are located on unrendered half of plan.)

Key to Drawings:

3. Half Plan of Lobby.
4. Elevation of screen wa showing positions of mura
5. Half elevation of outsi wall, showing positions mural panels between wi dows. Dimensions of paint space 97′ wide x 11′ high.
6. Elevation of one end wa showing position of mura broken by windows (oth wall similar). Dimensions painted surface 14′ wide x high.

A B C

3

O

G H I J

A B C D E F

4

G H I J

5

O

6

218

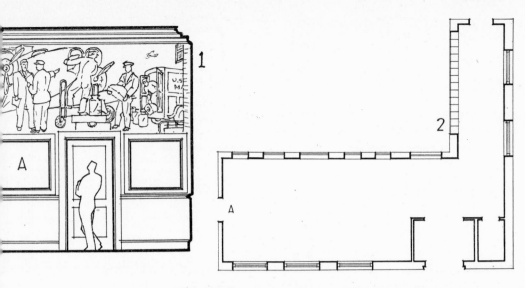

1

2

BARNESVILLE, OHIO, POST OFFICE

Beacon, New York, Post Office (below)

Architects: S.A.O. Gilbert Stanley Underwood and Benjamin C.
  Flournoy, Consulting Architects.
Murals in Lobby by Charles Rosen, assisted by Clarence Bolton.
Subject Matter: A. *Map of Hudson River from New York to Hudson.*
  B. *Old Swedish Church, Beacon.*   D. *Old Power House and Water Fall.*
  C. *Map of Hudson River near Beacon.*   E. *View of Beacon.*

Key to Drawings:
3. Plan of Lobby.
4. Elevation of screen wall, showing position of mural. Dimensions
  of mural 40′ wide x 8′ high.
5. Elevation of end wall, showing position of mural over opening
  into alcove and landscape panel on end wall of alcove. Dimensions
  of alcove wall 12′6′′ wide x 6′6′′ high.
6. Elevation of outside wall, showing position of mural, broken by a
  doorway and windows. Dimensions of mural 40′ wide x 8′ high.
7. Elevation of end wall, showing position of mural over opening
  into stair hallway and landscape panel, broken by windows in stair
  hallway. Dimensions of landscape mural 12′6′′ wide x 6′6′′ high.

BARNESVILLE, OHIO, POST OFFICE

Barnesville, Ohio, Post Office (above)

chitect: S.A.O. Louis A. Simon, Supervising Architect.
ural in Lobby by Michael Sarisky.
bject Matter: A. *Air Mail.*
y to Drawings:
 Elevation of end wall, showing position of mural. Dimensions of mural 13′ wide x 5′6′′ high.
 Plan of Lobby.

BEACON, NEW YORK, POST OFFICE

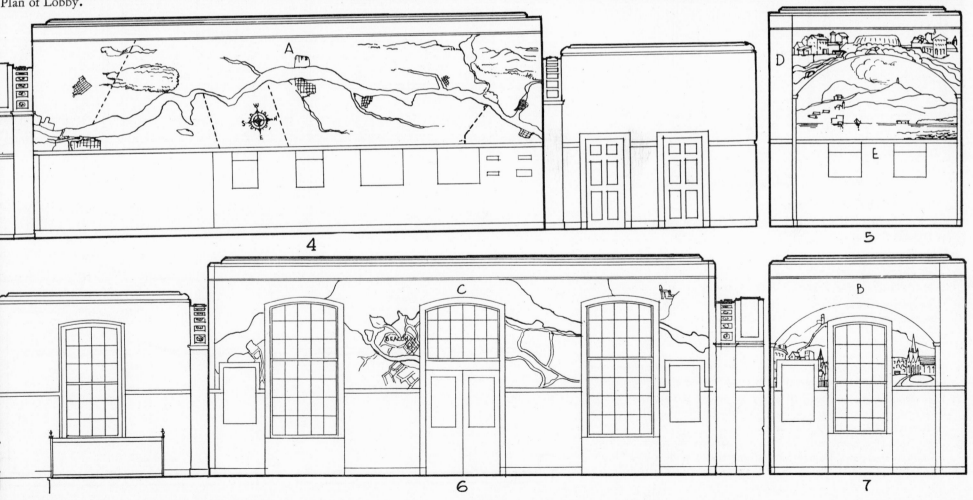

3

4

5

6

7

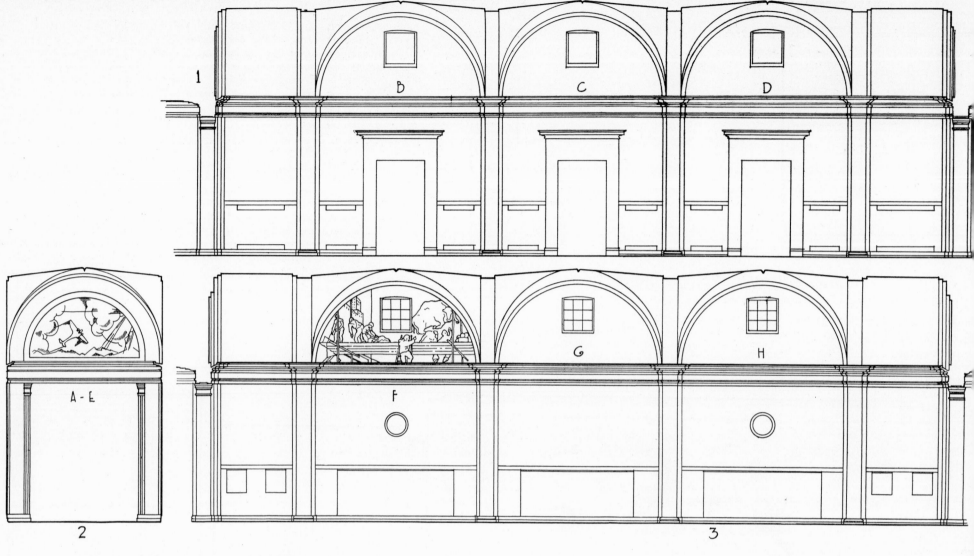

Beverly Hills, California, Post Office

Architect: Ralph C. Flewelling.

Series of eight fresco lunettes in Lobby by Charles Kassler II, assisted by Arnold Rubio.

Subject Matter:

A. *Post Rider.*   E. *Air Mail.*

P.W.A. Payments Affect Trade: *P.W.A. Construction:*

B. *Unemployed Obtain Work.*   F. *Building—Painting.*

C. *Are Paid and Buy Meat.*   G. *Building.*

D. *Groceries.*   H. *Building—Sculpture.*

Key to Drawings:

1. Elevation of outside wall, showing positions of three lunettes over entrance doors. Dimensions of lunettes 20′ wide x 10′2″ high.

2. Elevation of one end wall of lobby, showing position of lunette over opening into lower side lobby. Other end similar. Dimensions of lunette 14′3″ wide x 7′6″ high.

3. Elevation of screen wall, showing positions of three lunettes, broken by windows. Dimensions of lunettes 20′ wide x 10′2″ high.

4. Plan of Lobby.

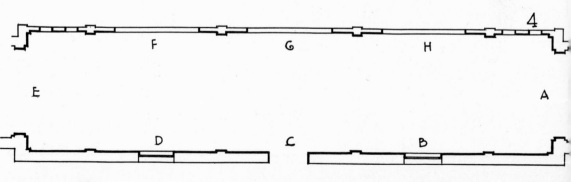

220

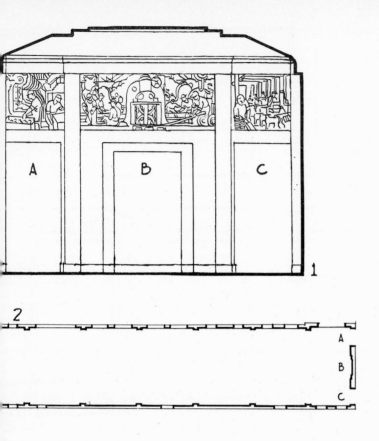

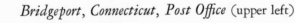

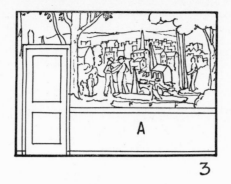

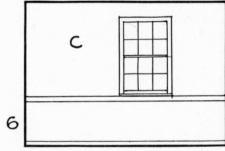

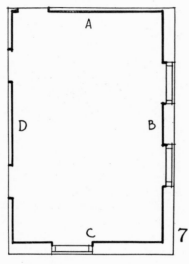

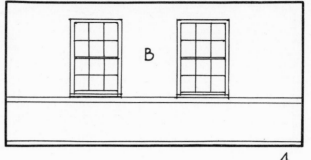

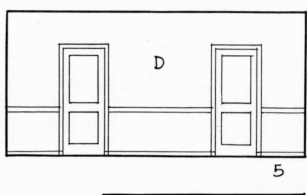

BOSTON,
MASSACHUSETTS,
P.W.A. HOUSING
PROJECT

BRIDGEPORT,
CONNECTICUT,
POST OFFICE

BROWNSVILLE,
PENNSYLVANIA,
POST OFFICE

Bridgeport, Connecticut, Post Office (upper left)

Architect: Charles W. Walker.

Murals at one end of Lobby by Arthur Covey.

Murals at opposite end of Lobby by Robert Lambdin.

Subject Matter:

Manufactures of Bridgeport:

A. *Casing Industry.*   C. *Sewing Machine Industry.*
B. *Brass Industry.*

History of the Mail:

A. *Transportation.*   C. *Sorting Mail.*
B. *Mail Coach.*

Key to Drawings:

1. Elevation of one end wall, showing positions of murals. Other wall similar. Dimensions of center panels 8'8" wide x 3'6" high. Dimensions of flanking panels 4'4" wide x 3'6" high, each.
2. Half Plan of Lobby.

Brownsville, Pennsylvania, Post Office (left)

Architect: S.A.O. Louis A Simon, Supervising Architect.

Mural in Lobby by Richard Lahey.

Subject Matter: A. *Transfer from Stage to Boat.*

Key to Drawings:

8. Elevation of end wall of Lobby, showing position of mural. Dimensions of mural 12' wide x 4'7" high.
9. Plan of Lobby.

Boston, Massachusetts, "Old Harbor Village" P.W.A. Housing Project (above)

Architect: Joseph Leland, Chief Architect.

All-over Murals in Conference Room by Arthur Oakman.

Subject Matter: A, B, C, D. *Old Harbor in Early Times.*

Key to Drawings:

3. Elevations of four walls of Conference
4. Room, showing positions of murals,
5. broken by doors and windows. Dimen-
6. sions of painted surface on short walls 13' wide x 5'9" high; on long walls 19' wide x 5'9" high.
7. Plan of Conference Room.

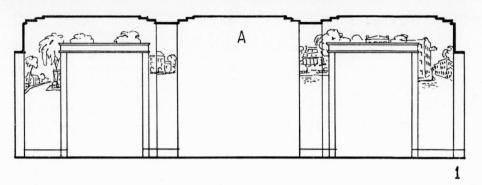

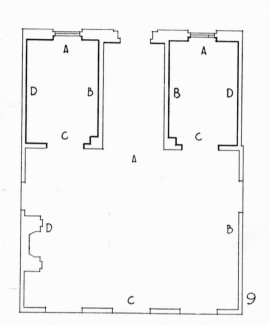

Buffalo, New York, Marine Hospital

Architects: S.A.O. Louis A. Simon, Supervising Architect.
Murals in Nurses' Community Room by William B. Rowe.
Subject Matter: *Views of Old Buffalo.*

Key to Drawings:

1.
2.
3. Elevations of four sides of Community Room, showing positions of murals,
4. broken by doors and windows. Dimensions of painted surface on long walls
    27'6'' wide x 8' high, on short walls 20' wide x 8' high.

Murals in two identical alcoves, off Nurses' Community Room, by Frank Romanelli.

Subject Matter:

Alcove No. 1— *Deer.*
Alcove No. 2— *Buffalo.*

Key to Drawings:

5.
6. Elevation of four sides of one alcove, showing positions of murals, broken by
7. openings (other alcove similar). Dimensions of painted surface on two long
8. walls 13' wide x 8' high, on two short walls 9'6'' wide x 8' high.

9. Plan of Nurses' Community Room and of two alcoves.

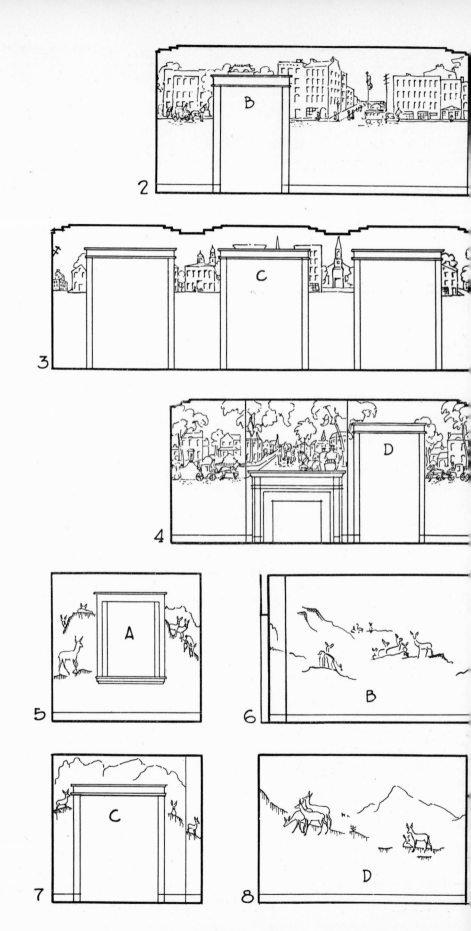

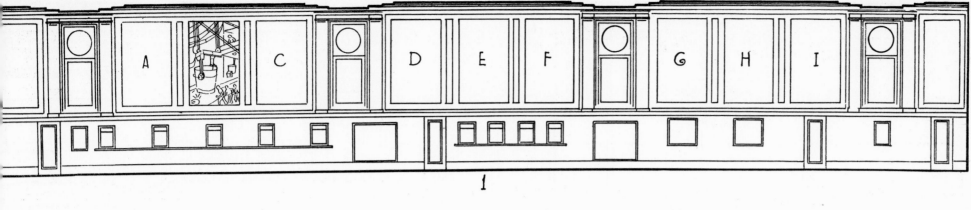

1

CANTON, OHIO,
POST OFFICE

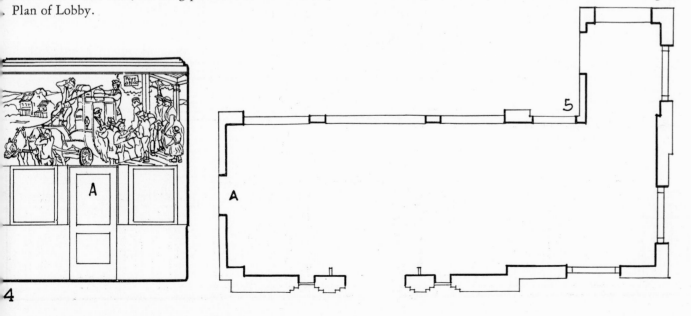

2

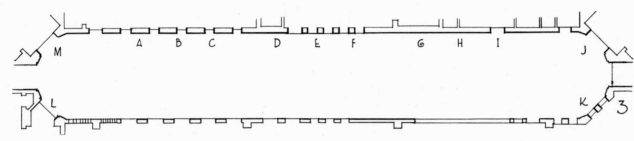

M A B C D E F G H I J

L K 3

CATASAUQUA,
PENNSYLVANIA,
POST OFFICE

Canton, Ohio, Post Office (above)

Architects: Charles Firestone and L. Christman.
Murals in Lobby by Glenn Shaw, assisted by Daniel Boza.

Subject Matter:

A. *Tapping Blast Furnace.*   C. *Pouring Steel Ingots.*   E. *Breakdown Mill.*   G. *Rolling Mill.*   I. *Electric Welding.*
B. *Teeming Electric Furnace.*   D. *Soaking Pit.*   F. *Seamless Tube Mill.* H. *Drop Forging.*   J, K, L and M, subject matter as yet undeveloped.

Key to Drawings:

1. Elevation of screen wall, showing positions of nine murals. Dimensions of each mural 6'9" wide x 11' high.
2. Elevation of end wall, showing positions of two murals (other end similar). Dimensions of murals 3' wide x 7'6" high, each.
3. Plan of Lobby.

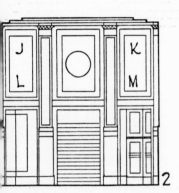

4

5

A

*Catasauqua, Pennsylvania,
Post Office* (left)

Architect: S.A.O. Louis A. Simon, Supervising Architect.

Mural in Lobby by F. Luis Mora.

Subject Matter: A. *Arrival of the Stage.*

Key to Drawings:

4. Elevation of end wall, showing position
of mural. Dimensions of mural 12' wide
x 5'6" high.
5. Plan of Lobby.

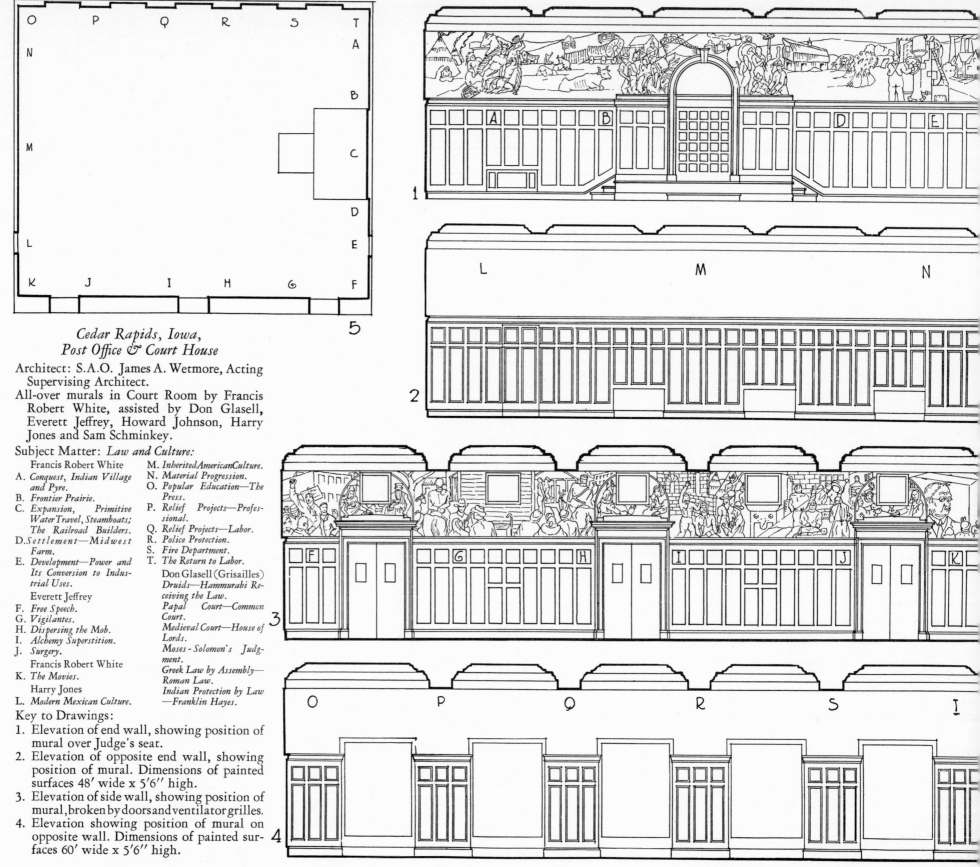

CEDAR RAPIDS, IOWA,
POST OFFICE AND
COURT HOUSE

Cedar Rapids, Iowa,
Post Office & Court House

Architect: S.A.O. James A. Wetmore, Acting
  Supervising Architect.
All-over murals in Court Room by Francis
  Robert White, assisted by Don Glasell,
  Everett Jeffrey, Howard Johnson, Harry
  Jones and Sam Schminkey.
Subject Matter: *Law and Culture:*

Francis Robert White

A. *Conquest, Indian Village and Pyre.*
B. *Frontier Prairie.*
C. *Expansion, Primitive Water Travel, Steamboats; The Railroad Builders.*
D. *Settlement—Midwest Farm.*
E. *Development—Power and Its Conversion to Industrial Uses.*

Everett Jeffrey

F. *Free Speech.*
G. *Vigilantes.*
H. *Dispersing the Mob.*
I. *Alchemy Superstition.*
J. *Surgery.*

Francis Robert White

K. *The Movies.*

Harry Jones

L. *Modern Mexican Culture.*

M. *Inherited American Culture.*
N. *Material Progression.*
O. *Popular Education—The Press.*
P. *Relief Projects—Professional.*
Q. *Relief Projects—Labor.*
R. *Police Protection.*
S. *Fire Department.*
T. *The Return to Labor.*

Don Glasell (Grisailles)
Druids—Hammurabi Receiving the Law.
Papal Court—Common Court.
Medieval Court—House of Lords.
Moses - Solomon's Judgment.
Greek Law by Assembly—Roman Law.
Indian Protection by Law —Franklin Hayes.

Key to Drawings:

1. Elevation of end wall, showing position of mural over Judge's seat.
2. Elevation of opposite end wall, showing position of mural. Dimensions of painted surfaces 48′ wide x 5′6″ high.
3. Elevation of side wall, showing position of mural, broken by doors and ventilator grilles.
4. Elevation showing position of mural on opposite wall. Dimensions of painted surfaces 60′ wide x 5′6″ high.

224

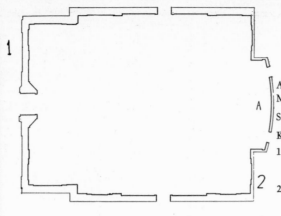

Chattanooga, Tennessee, Post Office and Court House (left)

Architect: R. H. Hunt.
Mural in Court Room by Hilton Leech.

Subject Matter: A. *Allegory of Chattanooga.*

Key to Drawings:

1. Elevation of end wall of Court Room, showing position of mural above Judge's seat. Dimensions of mural 17′3″ wide x 5′ high.

2. Plan of Court Room.

Chicago, Illinois, Post Office (below)

Architects: Graham, Anderson, Probst & White.

Murals in Main Office of General in Charge of the Army Sixth Corps Area, on the fourth floor, and in the corridor outside, by Charles Turzak, assisted by Desiderio Lavin.

Subject Matter: Office— A, B, C, D. *Decorative Maps of the Sixth Corps Area.*
Corridor—A, B, C, D. *Abstract Treatment of Symbols and Instruments Relating to the Army.*

Key to Drawings:

OFFICE

3. 4. 5. 6. Elevation of side walls of office, showing positions of murals, broken by doors and windows. Dimensions of murals 51 running feet. Painted surface 9′ high above baseboard.

7. Plan of Office.

CORRIDOR

8 and 9. Elevations of two side walls of corridor, showing positions of murals broken by doors.

10. Elevation of end wall, showing position of mural. Dimensions of corridor 64′ long x 7′, 10′ and 14′ wide. Painted surface 5′6″ above wainscot.

11. Plan of Corridor.

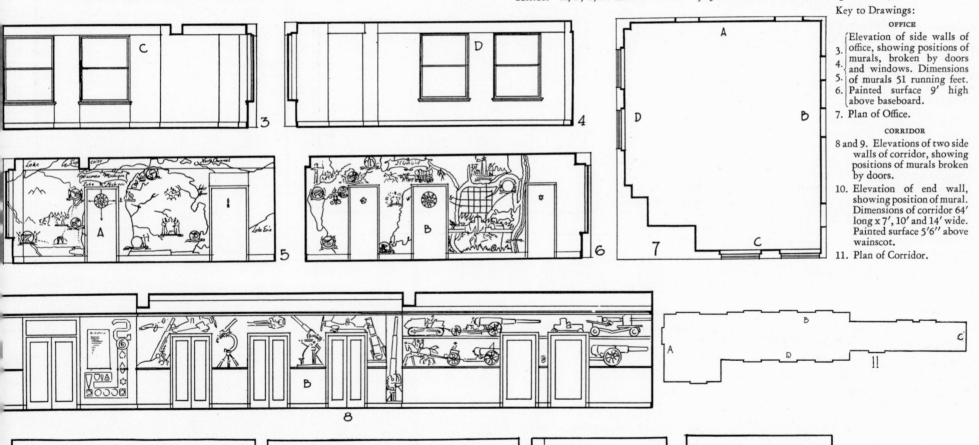

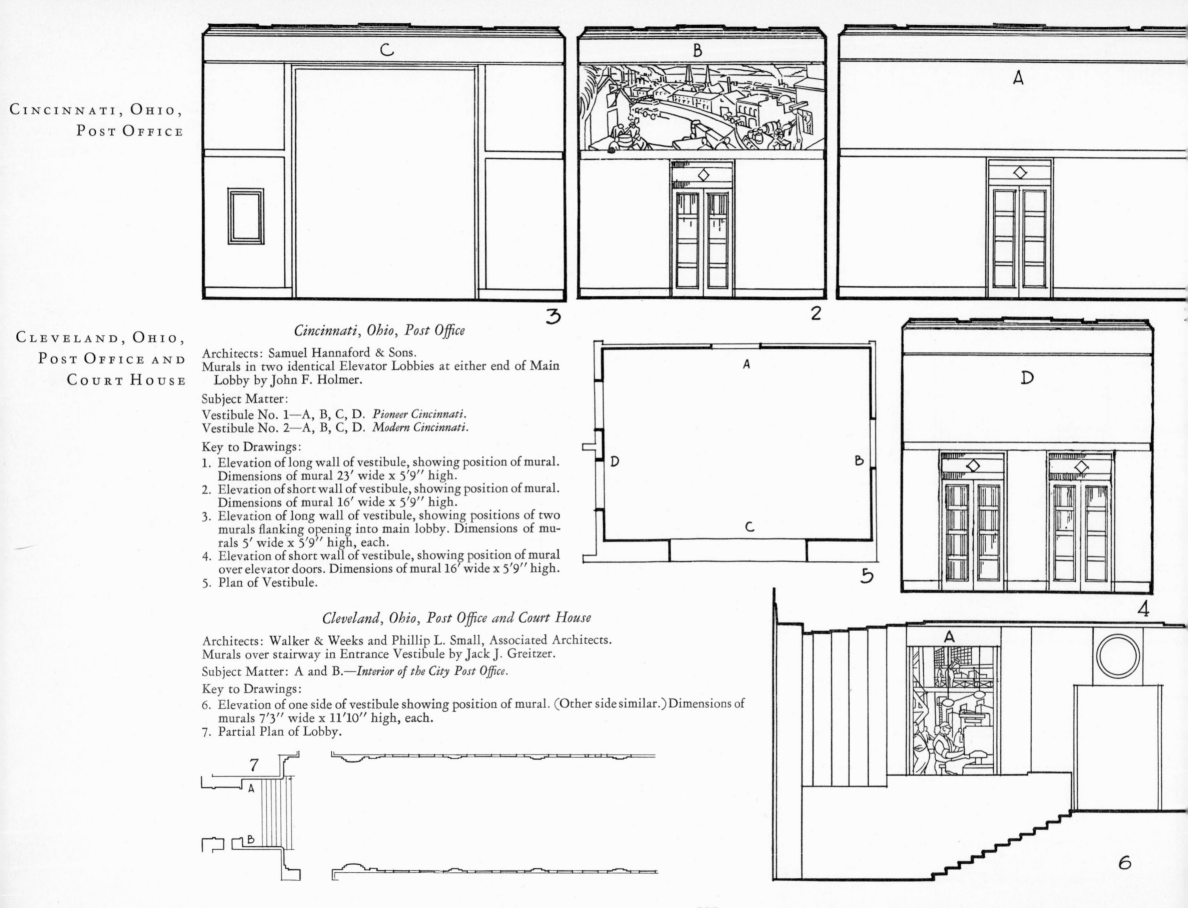

CINCINNATI, OHIO,
POST OFFICE

CLEVELAND, OHIO,
POST OFFICE AND
COURT HOUSE

Cincinnati, Ohio, Post Office

Architects: Samuel Hannaford & Sons.
Murals in two identical Elevator Lobbies at either end of Main
  Lobby by John F. Holmer.

Subject Matter:
Vestibule No. 1—A, B, C, D. *Pioneer Cincinnati.*
Vestibule No. 2—A, B, C, D. *Modern Cincinnati.*

Key to Drawings:
1. Elevation of long wall of vestibule, showing position of mural.
   Dimensions of mural 23′ wide x 5′9″ high.
2. Elevation of short wall of vestibule, showing position of mural.
   Dimensions of mural 16′ wide x 5′9″ high.
3. Elevation of long wall of vestibule, showing positions of two
   murals flanking opening into main lobby. Dimensions of murals 5′ wide x 5′9″ high, each.
4. Elevation of short wall of vestibule, showing position of mural
   over elevator doors. Dimensions of mural 16′ wide x 5′9″ high.
5. Plan of Vestibule.

Cleveland, Ohio, Post Office and Court House

Architects: Walker & Weeks and Phillip L. Small, Associated Architects.
Murals over stairway in Entrance Vestibule by Jack J. Greitzer.

Subject Matter: A and B.—*Interior of the City Post Office.*

Key to Drawings:
6. Elevation of one side of vestibule showing position of mural. (Other side similar.) Dimensions of
   murals 7′3″ wide x 11′10″ high, each.
7. Partial Plan of Lobby.

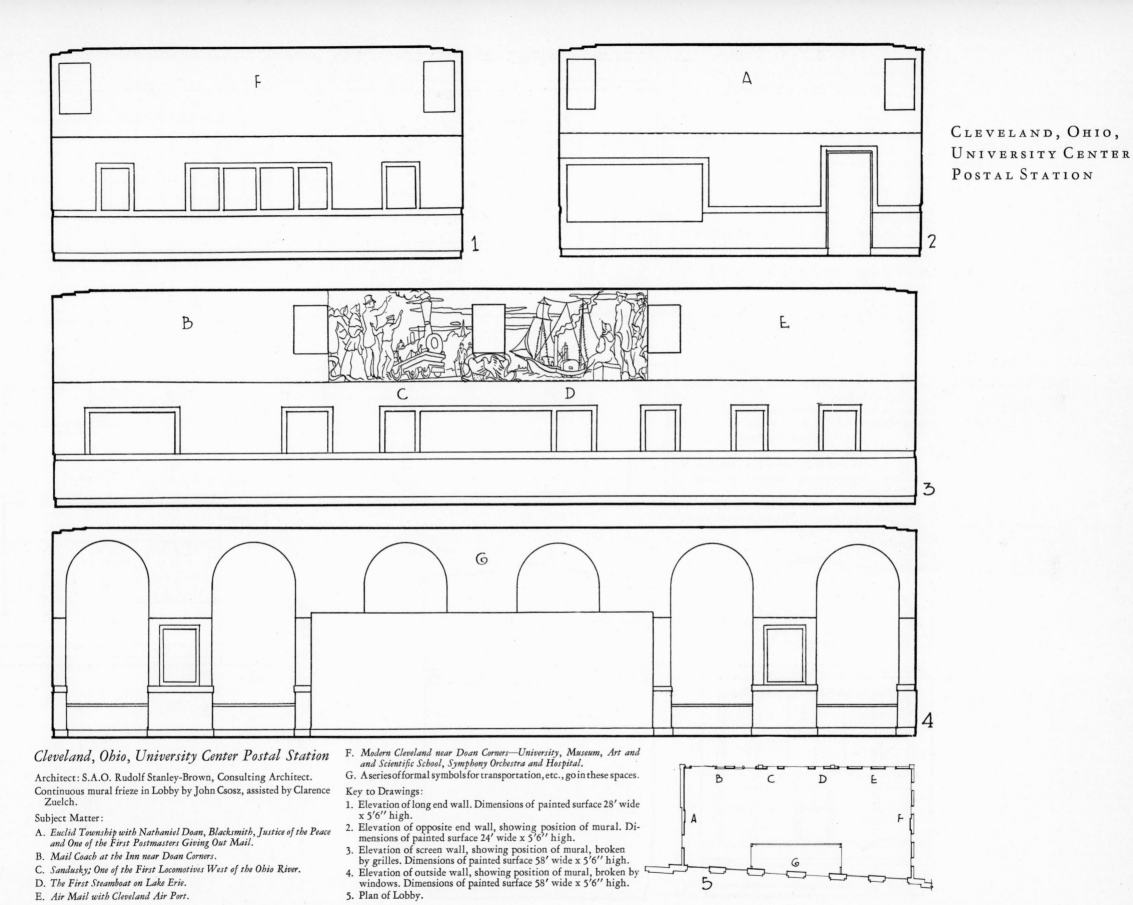

1

2

B

E

C

D

3

G

4

Cleveland, Ohio, University Center Postal Station

Architect: S.A.O. Rudolf Stanley-Brown, Consulting Architect.

Continuous mural frieze in Lobby by John Csosz, assisted by Clarence Zuelch.

Subject Matter:

A. *Euclid Township with Nathaniel Doan, Blacksmith, Justice of the Peace and One of the First Postmasters Giving Out Mail.*

B. *Mail Coach at the Inn near Doan Corners.*

C. *Sandusky; One of the First Locomotives West of the Ohio River.*

D. *The First Steamboat on Lake Erie.*

E. *Air Mail with Cleveland Air Port.*

F. *Modern Cleveland near Doan Corners—University, Museum, Art and and Scientific School, Symphony Orchestra and Hospital.*

G. A series of formal symbols for transportation, etc., go in these spaces.

Key to Drawings:

1. Elevation of long end wall. Dimensions of painted surface 28′ wide x 5′6″ high.

2. Elevation of opposite end wall, showing position of mural. Dimensions of painted surface 24′ wide x 5′6″ high.

3. Elevation of screen wall, showing position of mural, broken by grilles. Dimensions of painted surface 58′ wide x 5′6″ high.

4. Elevation of outside wall, showing position of mural, broken by windows. Dimensions of painted surface 58′ wide x 5′6″ high.

5. Plan of Lobby.

B   C   D   E

A   F

G

5

CLEVELAND, OHIO,
P.W.A. HOUSING PROJECT

CLINTON, MISSOURI,
POST OFFICE

*Cleveland, Ohio, "Whiskey Island"
P.W.A. Housing Project*

Architects: Conrad, Weinberg and Teare.
Murals in Childrens' Playroom by Earl J. Neff.
Subject Matter: A. *Legends and Fairy Stories.*
Key to Drawings:
1. Elevation of one side of playroom, showing position of mural. Dimensions of center panel 8'6" wide x 5'6" high. Dimensions of continuous frieze 39 running feet x 2'2" high.
2. Plan of Children's Playroom.
Murals in Entrance Vestibule to Auditorium in Main Community Building, by Charles Campbell.
Subject Matter: A and B—*Children at Play.*
Key to Drawings:
3. Plan of Vestibule.
4. Elevation of one side of vestibule, showing position of mural. (Other side similar.) Dimensions of murals 14' wide x 3'9" high, each.

Clinton, Missouri, Post Office

Architect: S.A.O. James Knox Taylor, Supervising Architect.
Murals in Lobby by Harry Louis Freund.
Subject Matter: A. *Wheat Farming.*
           B. *Chicken Hatcheries.*
Key to Drawings:
5. Elevation of end wall, showing position of lunette. Dimensions of lunette 11'8" wide x 4'4" high.
6. Elevation of opening into side lobby, showing position of lunette. Dimensions of lunette 11'8" wide x 4'4" high.
7. Plan of Lobby.

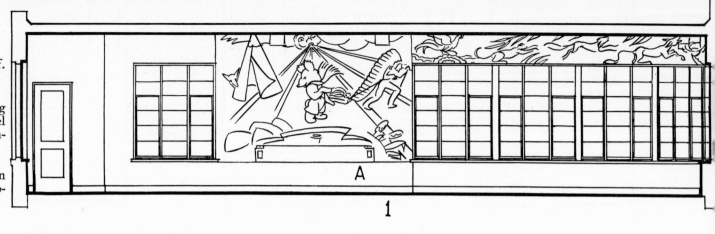

1

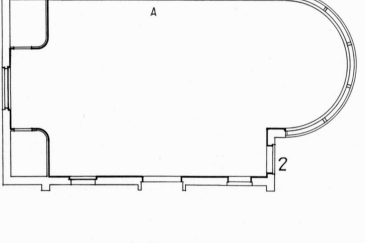

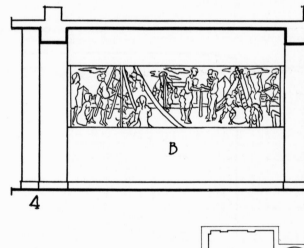

3

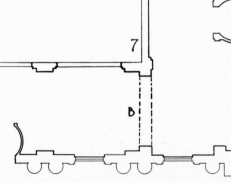

4

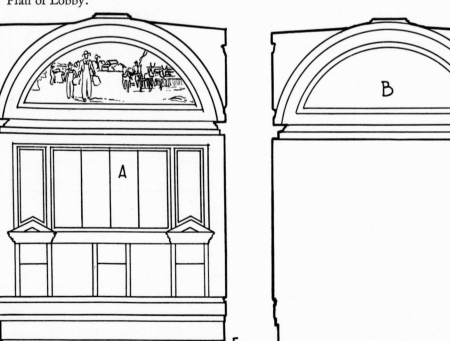

5

6

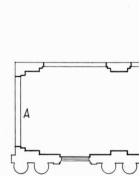

7

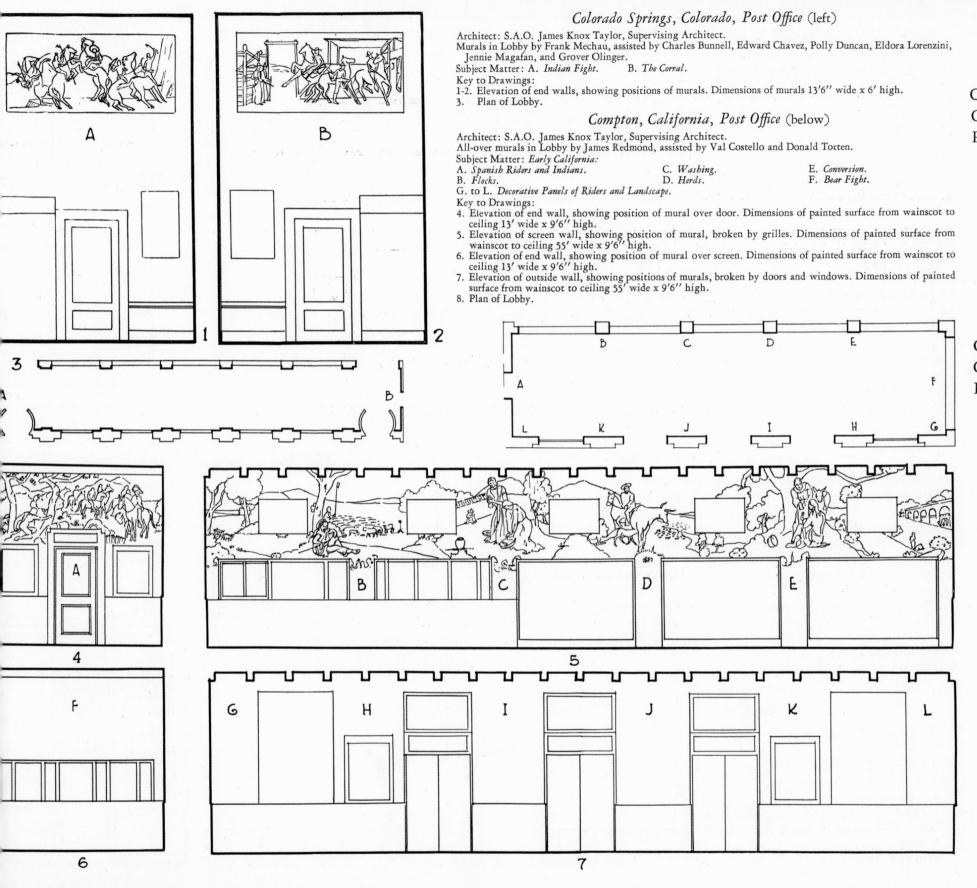

Colorado Springs, Colorado, Post Office (left)

Architect: S.A.O. James Knox Taylor, Supervising Architect.
Murals in Lobby by Frank Mechau, assisted by Charles Bunnell, Edward Chavez, Polly Duncan, Eldora Lorenzini, Jennie Magafan, and Grover Olinger.
Subject Matter: A. *Indian Fight.*   B. *The Corral.*
Key to Drawings:
1-2. Elevation of end walls, showing positions of murals. Dimensions of murals 13'6" wide x 6' high.
3. Plan of Lobby.

Compton, California, Post Office (below)

Architect: S.A.O. James Knox Taylor, Supervising Architect.
All-over murals in Lobby by James Redmond, assisted by Val Costello and Donald Totten.
Subject Matter: *Early California:*

A. *Spanish Riders and Indians.*   C. *Washing.*   E. *Conversion.*
B. *Flocks.*   D. *Herds.*   F. *Bear Fight.*
G. to L. *Decorative Panels of Riders and Landscape.*

Key to Drawings:
4. Elevation of end wall, showing position of mural over door. Dimensions of painted surface from wainscot to ceiling 13' wide x 9'6" high.
5. Elevation of screen wall, showing position of mural, broken by grilles. Dimensions of painted surface from wainscot to ceiling 55' wide x 9'6" high.
6. Elevation of end wall, showing position of mural over screen. Dimensions of painted surface from wainscot to ceiling 13' wide x 9'6" high.
7. Elevation of outside wall, showing positions of murals, broken by doors and windows. Dimensions of painted surface from wainscot to ceiling 55' wide x 9'6" high.
8. Plan of Lobby.

229

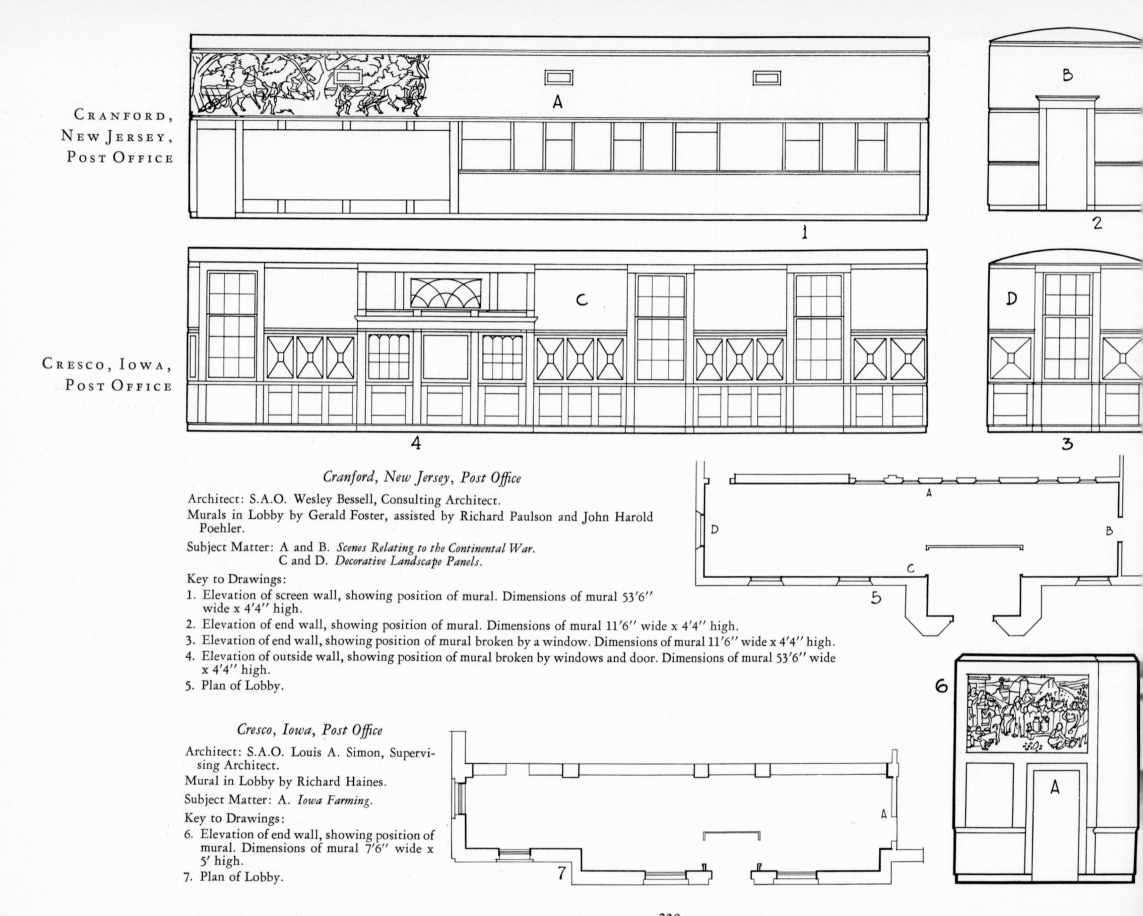

CRANFORD,
NEW JERSEY,
POST OFFICE

A

1

2

CRESCO, IOWA,
POST OFFICE

C

4

D

3

Cranford, New Jersey, Post Office

Architect: S.A.O. Wesley Bessell, Consulting Architect.

Murals in Lobby by Gerald Foster, assisted by Richard Paulson and John Harold Poehler.

Subject Matter: A and B. *Scenes Relating to the Continental War.*
C and D. *Decorative Landscape Panels.*

Key to Drawings:

1. Elevation of screen wall, showing position of mural. Dimensions of mural 53'6" wide x 4'4" high.
2. Elevation of end wall, showing position of mural. Dimensions of mural 11'6" wide x 4'4" high.
3. Elevation of end wall, showing position of mural broken by a window. Dimensions of mural 11'6" wide x 4'4" high.
4. Elevation of outside wall, showing position of mural broken by windows and door. Dimensions of mural 53'6" wide x 4'4" high.
5. Plan of Lobby.

5

Cresco, Iowa, Post Office

Architect: S.A.O. Louis A. Simon, Supervising Architect.

Mural in Lobby by Richard Haines.

Subject Matter: A. *Iowa Farming.*

Key to Drawings:

6. Elevation of end wall, showing position of mural. Dimensions of mural 7'6" wide x 5' high.
7. Plan of Lobby.

6

7

A

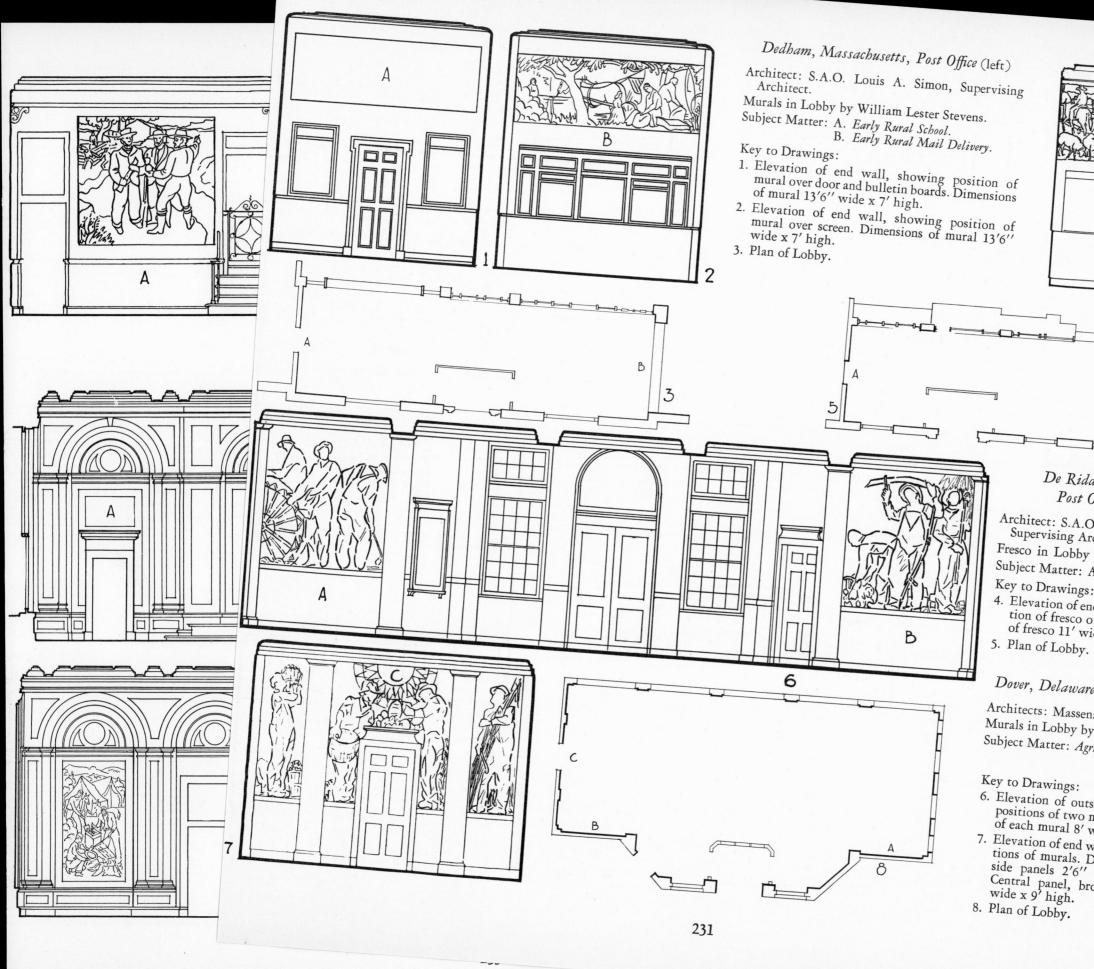

Dedham, Massachusetts, Post Office (left)

Architect: S.A.O. Louis A. Simon, Supervising Architect.
Murals in Lobby by William Lester Stevens.
Subject Matter: A. *Early Rural School.*
B. *Early Rural Mail Delivery.*

Key to Drawings:
1. Elevation of end wall, showing position of mural over door and bulletin boards. Dimensions of mural 13'6'' wide x 7' high.
2. Elevation of end wall, showing position of mural over screen. Dimensions of mural 13'6'' wide x 7' high.
3. Plan of Lobby.

DEDHAM,
MASSACHUSETTS,
POST OFFICE

De Ridder, Louisiana, Post Office (above)

Architect: S.A.O. Louis A. Simon, Supervising Architect.
Fresco in Lobby by Conrad Albrizzio.
Subject Matter: A. *Rural Delivery.*

Key to Drawings:
4. Elevation of end wall, showing position of fresco over door. Dimensions of fresco 11' wide x 5' high.
5. Plan of Lobby.

DE RIDDER,
LOUISIANA,
POST OFFICE

Dover, Delaware, Post Office (left)

Architects: Massena and Dupont.
Murals in Lobby by William D. White.
Subject Matter: *Agriculture:* A. *Spring.*
B. *Summer.*
C. *Harvest.*

Key to Drawings:
6. Elevation of outside wall, showing positions of two murals. Dimensions of each mural 8' wide x 9' high.
7. Elevation of end wall, showing positions of murals. Dimensions of two side panels 2'6'' wide x 9' high. Central panel, broken by door, 8' wide x 9' high.
8. Plan of Lobby.

DOVER, DELAWARE,
POST OFFICE

231

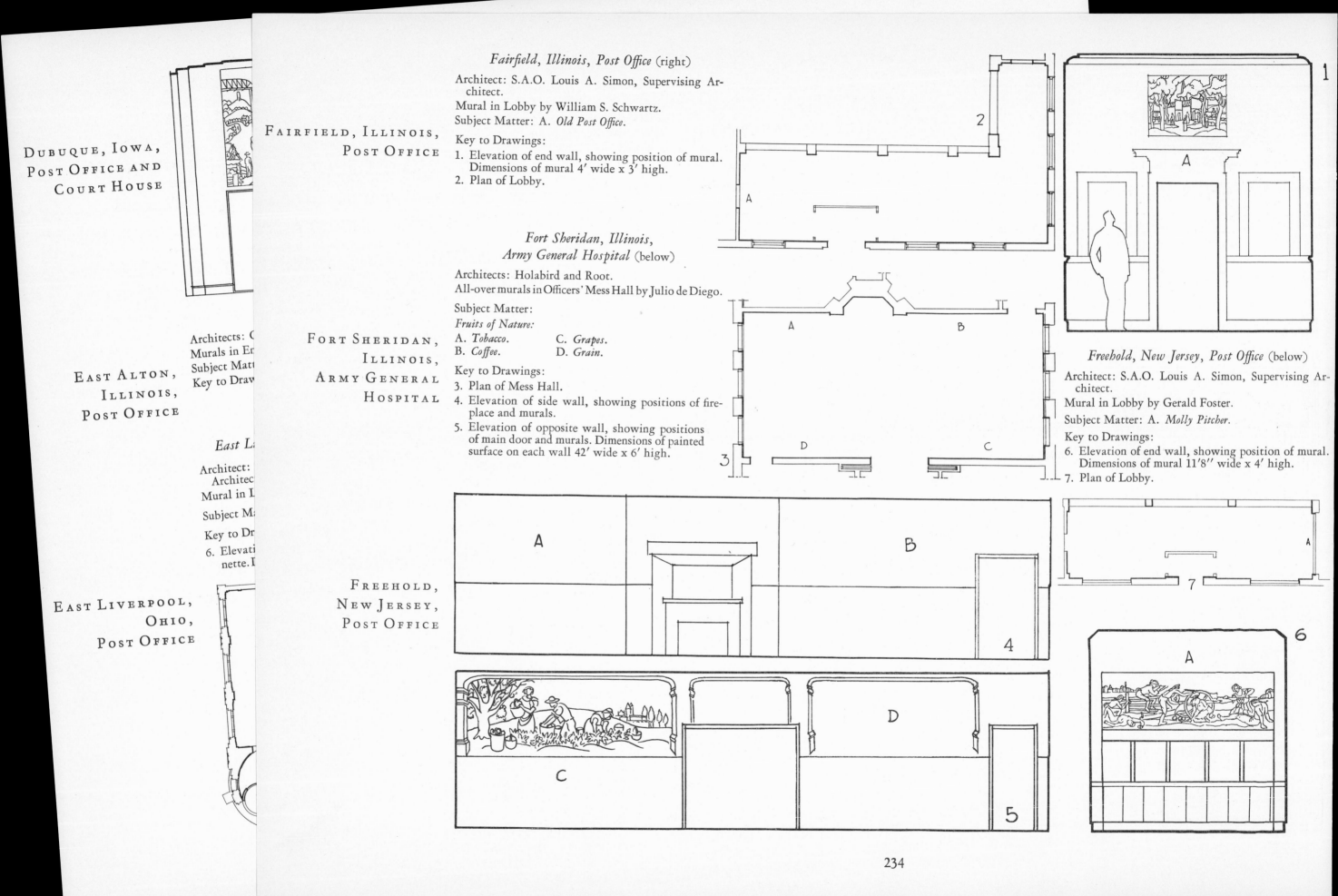

DUBUQUE, IOWA,
POST OFFICE AND
COURT HOUSE

Fairfield, Illinois, Post Office (right)

Architect: S.A.O. Louis A. Simon, Supervising Architect.

Mural in Lobby by William S. Schwartz.

Subject Matter: A. *Old Post Office.*

Key to Drawings:

1. Elevation of end wall, showing position of mural. Dimensions of mural 4' wide x 3' high.
2. Plan of Lobby.

FAIRFIELD, ILLINOIS,
POST OFFICE

EAST ALTON,
ILLINOIS,
POST OFFICE

Architects: (

Murals in En

Subject Matt

Key to Draw

East L.

Architect:

Architec

Mural in L

Subject Ma

Key to Dra

6. Elevati

nette. I

*Fort Sheridan, Illinois,
Army General Hospital* (below)

Architects: Holabird and Root.

All-over murals in Officers' Mess Hall by Julio de Diego.

Subject Matter:
Fruits of Nature:
A. *Tobacco.*   C. *Grapes.*
B. *Coffee.*   D. *Grain.*

Key to Drawings:

3. Plan of Mess Hall.
4. Elevation of side wall, showing positions of fireplace and murals.
5. Elevation of opposite wall, showing positions of main door and murals. Dimensions of painted surface on each wall 42' wide x 6' high.

Freehold, New Jersey, Post Office (below)

Architect: S.A.O. Louis A. Simon, Supervising Architect.

Mural in Lobby by Gerald Foster.

Subject Matter: A. *Molly Pitcher.*

Key to Drawings:

6. Elevation of end wall, showing position of mural. Dimensions of mural 11'8" wide x 4' high.
7. Plan of Lobby.

FORT SHERIDAN,
ILLINOIS,
ARMY GENERAL
HOSPITAL

EAST LIVERPOOL,
OHIO,
POST OFFICE

FREEHOLD,
NEW JERSEY,
POST OFFICE

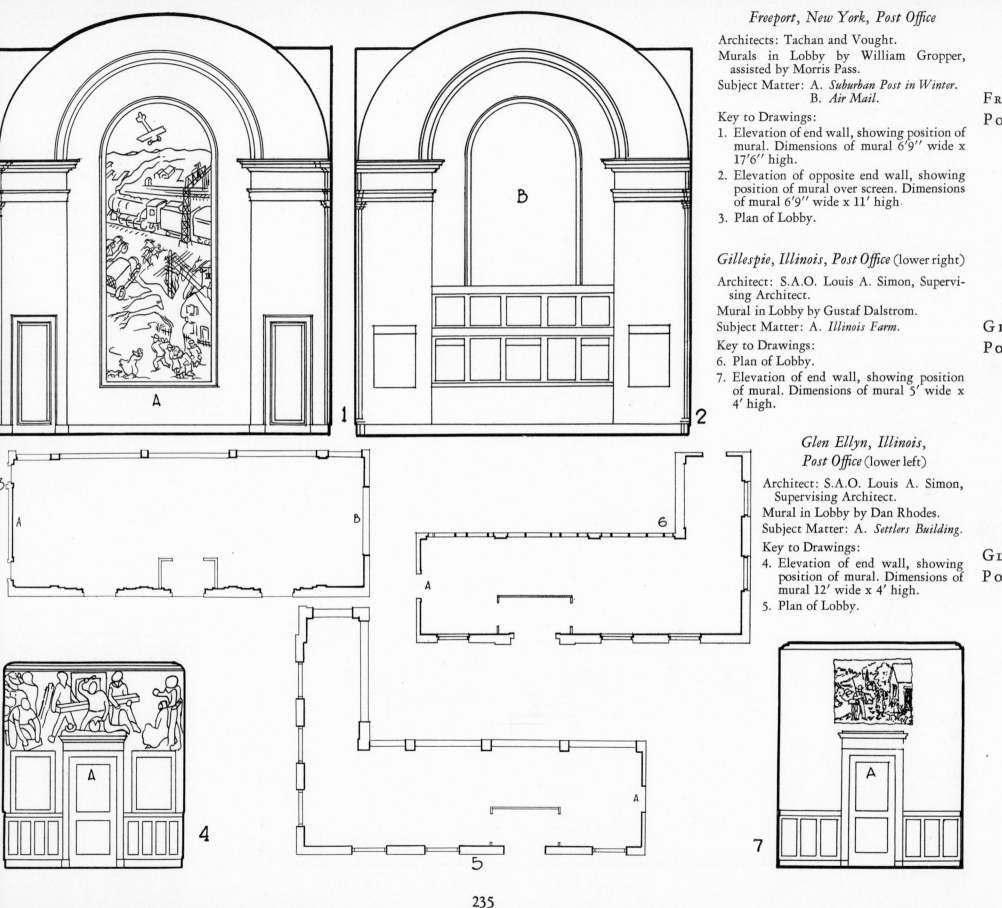

Freeport, New York, Post Office

Architects: Tachan and Vought.

Murals in Lobby by William Gropper, assisted by Morris Pass.

Subject Matter: A. *Suburban Post in Winter.*
B. *Air Mail.*

Key to Drawings:

1. Elevation of end wall, showing position of mural. Dimensions of mural 6'9" wide x 17'6" high.

2. Elevation of opposite end wall, showing position of mural over screen. Dimensions of mural 6'9" wide x 11' high.

3. Plan of Lobby.

Gillespie, Illinois, Post Office (lower right)

Architect: S.A.O. Louis A. Simon, Supervising Architect.

Mural in Lobby by Gustaf Dalstrom.

Subject Matter: A. *Illinois Farm.*

Key to Drawings:

6. Plan of Lobby.

7. Elevation of end wall, showing position of mural. Dimensions of mural 5' wide x 4' high.

Glen Ellyn, Illinois, Post Office (lower left)

Architect: S.A.O. Louis A. Simon, Supervising Architect.

Mural in Lobby by Dan Rhodes.

Subject Matter: A. *Settlers Building.*

Key to Drawings:

4. Elevation of end wall, showing position of mural. Dimensions of mural 12' wide x 4' high.

5. Plan of Lobby.

FREEPORT, NEW YORK, POST OFFICE

GILLESPIE, ILLINOIS, POST OFFICE

GLEN ELLYN, ILLINOIS, POST OFFICE

GOODLAND, KANSAS, POST OFFICE

Goodland, Kansas, Post Office

Architect: S.A.O. Louis A. Simon, Supervising Architect.

Mural in Lobby by Kenneth Adams.

Subject Matter: A. *Rural Delivery.*

Key to Drawings:

1. Elevation of end wall, showing position of mural. Dimensions of mural 12′ wide x 4′ high.
2. Plan of Lobby.

HAMILTON, OHIO, POST OFFICE

Hamilton, Ohio, Post Office

Architect: S.A.O. James A. Wetmore, Acting Supervising Architect.

Murals in Lobby by Richard Zoellner, assisted by Paul Chidlaw.

Subject Matter:

A. *Agriculture.*   D. *Paper Mill.*
B. *Stove Industry.*   E. *Iron and Coke Industry.*
C. *Machine Tools.*   F. *Fort Hamilton.*

Key to Drawings:

3. Elevation of end wall, showing position of single lunette. Dimensions of lunette 14′ wide x 3′5″ high.
4. Elevation of outside wall, showing positions of five lunettes. Dimensions of each lunette 6′5″ wide x 3′5″ high.
5. Plan of Lobby.

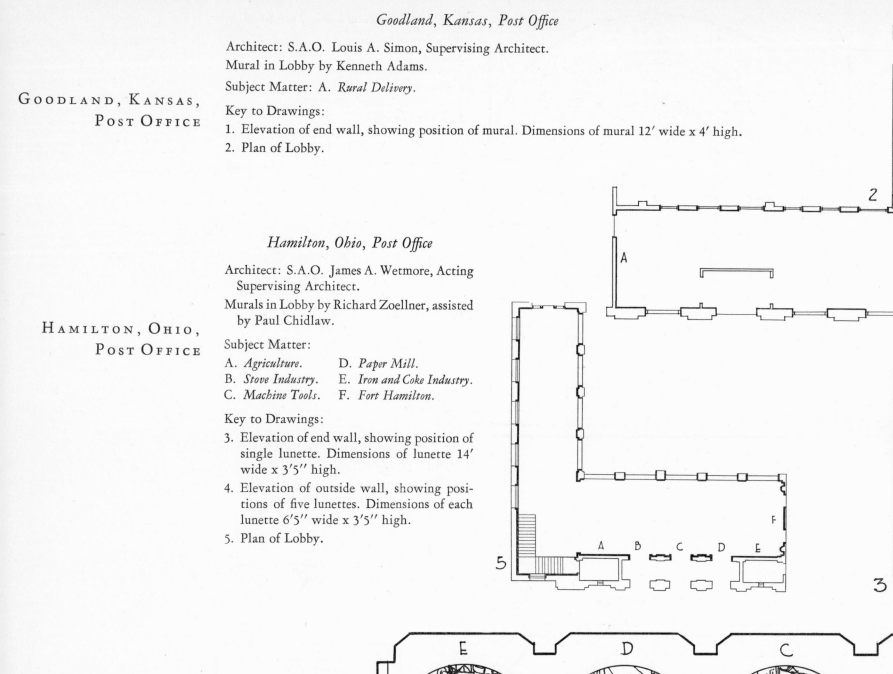

236

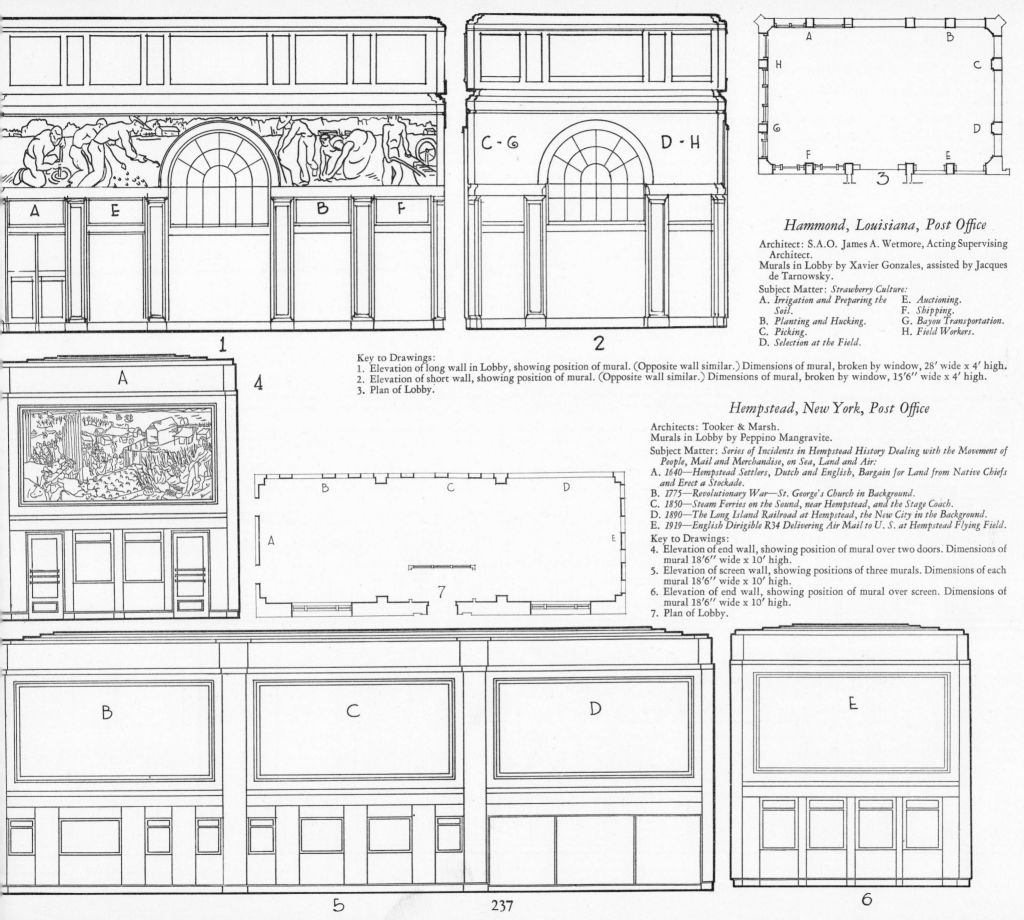

Hammond, Louisiana, Post Office

Architect: S.A.O. James A. Wetmore, Acting Supervising
Architect.

Murals in Lobby by Xavier Gonzales, assisted by Jacques
de Tarnowsky.

Subject Matter: *Strawberry Culture:*

A. *Irrigation and Preparing the*   E. *Auctioning.*
   Soil.   F. *Shipping.*
B. *Planting and Hucking.*   G. *Bayou Transportation.*
C. *Picking.*   H. *Field Workers.*
D. *Selection at the Field.*

Key to Drawings:
1. Elevation of long wall in Lobby, showing position of mural. (Opposite wall similar.) Dimensions of mural, broken by window, 28' wide x 4' high.
2. Elevation of short wall, showing position of mural. (Opposite wall similar.) Dimensions of mural, broken by window, 15'6'' wide x 4' high.
3. Plan of Lobby.

Hempstead, New York, Post Office

Architects: Tooker & Marsh.

Murals in Lobby by Peppino Mangravite.

Subject Matter: *Series of Incidents in Hempstead History Dealing with the Movement of*
People, Mail and Merchandise, on Sea, Land and Air:

A. *1640—Hempstead Settlers, Dutch and English, Bargain for Land from Native Chiefs*
   and Erect a Stockade.
B. *1775—Revolutionary War—St. George's Church in Background.*
C. *1850—Steam Ferries on the Sound, near Hempstead, and the Stage Coach.*
D. *1890—The Long Island Railroad at Hempstead, the New City in the Background.*
E. *1919—English Dirigible R34 Delivering Air Mail to U. S. at Hempstead Flying Field.*

Key to Drawings:
4. Elevation of end wall, showing position of mural over two doors. Dimensions of mural 18'6'' wide x 10' high.
5. Elevation of screen wall, showing positions of three murals. Dimensions of each mural 18'6'' wide x 10' high.
6. Elevation of end wall, showing position of mural over screen. Dimensions of mural 18'6'' wide x 10' high.
7. Plan of Lobby.

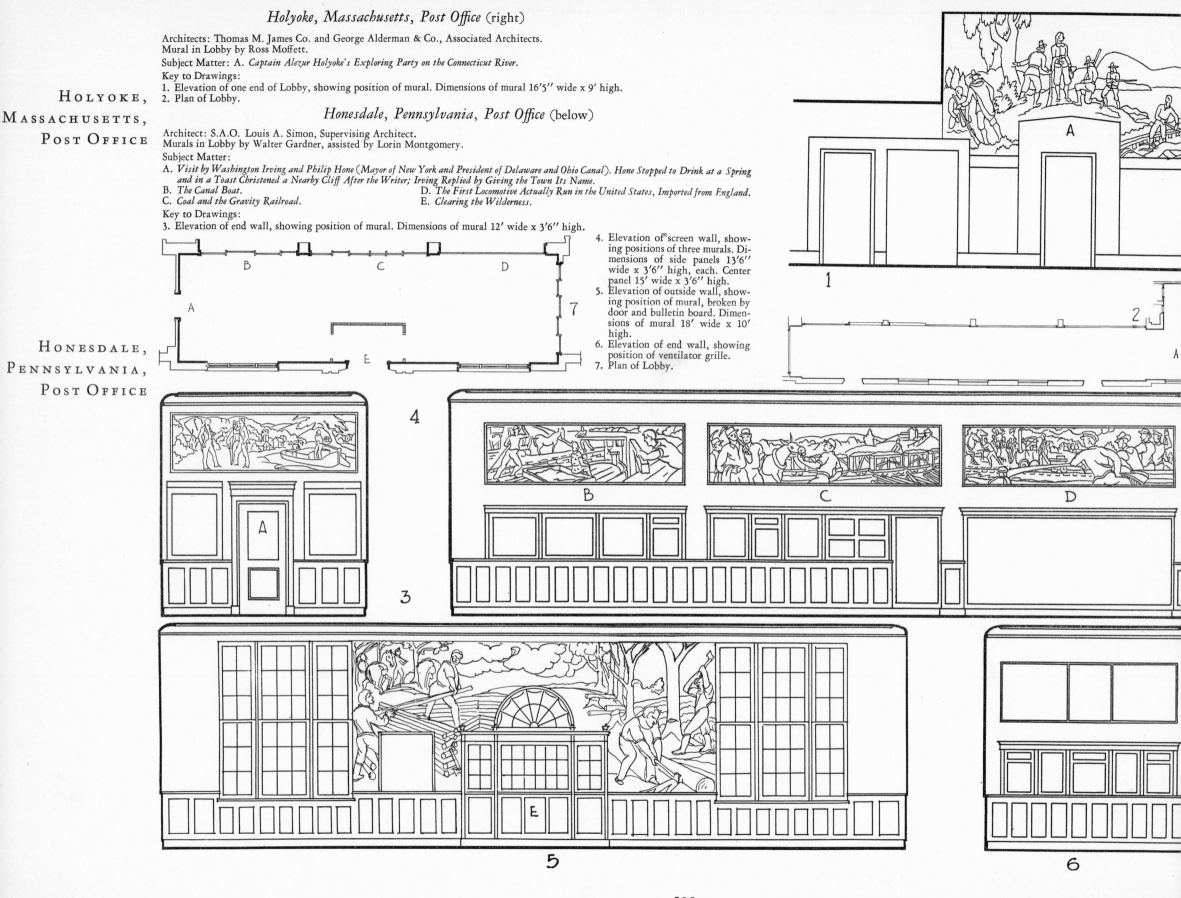

HOLYOKE, MASSACHUSETTS, POST OFFICE

Holyoke, Massachusetts, Post Office (right)

Architects: Thomas M. James Co. and George Alderman & Co., Associated Architects.
Mural in Lobby by Ross Moffett.
Subject Matter: A. *Captain Alezur Holyoke's Exploring Party on the Connecticut River.*
Key to Drawings:
1. Elevation of one end of Lobby, showing position of mural. Dimensions of mural 16'5" wide x 9' high.
2. Plan of Lobby.

Honesdale, Pennsylvania, Post Office (below)

Architect: S.A.O. Louis A. Simon, Supervising Architect.
Murals in Lobby by Walter Gardner, assisted by Lorin Montgomery.
Subject Matter:
A. *Visit by Washington Irving and Philip Hone (Mayor of New York and President of Delaware and Ohio Canal). Hone Stopped to Drink at a Spring and in a Toast Christened a Nearby Cliff After the Writer; Irving Replied by Giving the Town Its Name.*
B. *The Canal Boat.* D. *The First Locomotive Actually Run in the United States, Imported from England.*
C. *Coal and the Gravity Railroad.* E. *Clearing the Wilderness.*
Key to Drawings:
3. Elevation of end wall, showing position of mural. Dimensions of mural 12' wide x 3'6" high.

4. Elevation of screen wall, showing positions of three murals. Dimensions of side panels 13'6" wide x 3'6" high, each. Center panel 15' wide x 3'6" high.
5. Elevation of outside wall, showing position of mural, broken by door and bulletin board. Dimensions of mural 18' wide x 10' high.
6. Elevation of end wall, showing position of ventilator grille.
7. Plan of Lobby.

HONESDALE, PENNSYLVANIA, POST OFFICE

238

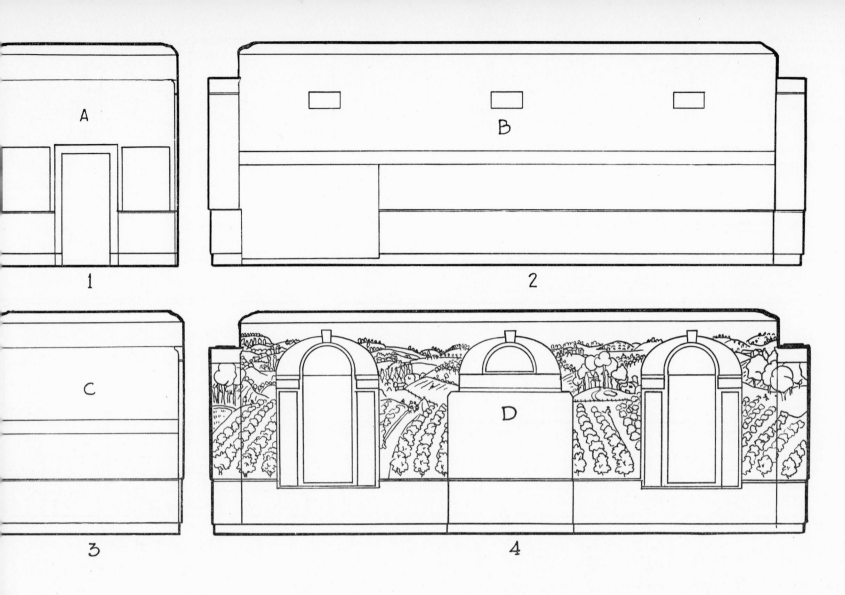

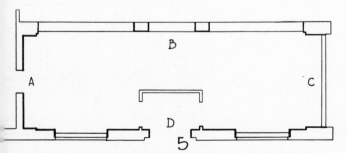

Hopkins, Minnesota, Post Office

Architect: S.A.O. Louis A. Simon, Supervising Architect.

All-over murals in Lobby by David Granahan, assisted by Henry Holmstrom, John Rolph and Jefferson T. Warren.

Subject Matter: A, B, C, D. *Cultivation of Raspberries.*

Key to Drawings:

1. Elevation of end wall, showing position of mural over door and bulletin boards. Dimensions of mural 12' wide x 9'6'' high.

2. Elevation of screen wall, showing position of mural broken by grilles. Dimensions of mural 34' wide x 6' high.

3. Elevation of end wall, showing position of mural above screen. Dimensions of mural 12' wide x 6' high.

4. Elevation of outside wall, showing position of mural broken by windows and vestibule door. Dimensions of mural 34' wide x 9'6'' high.

5. Plan of Lobby.

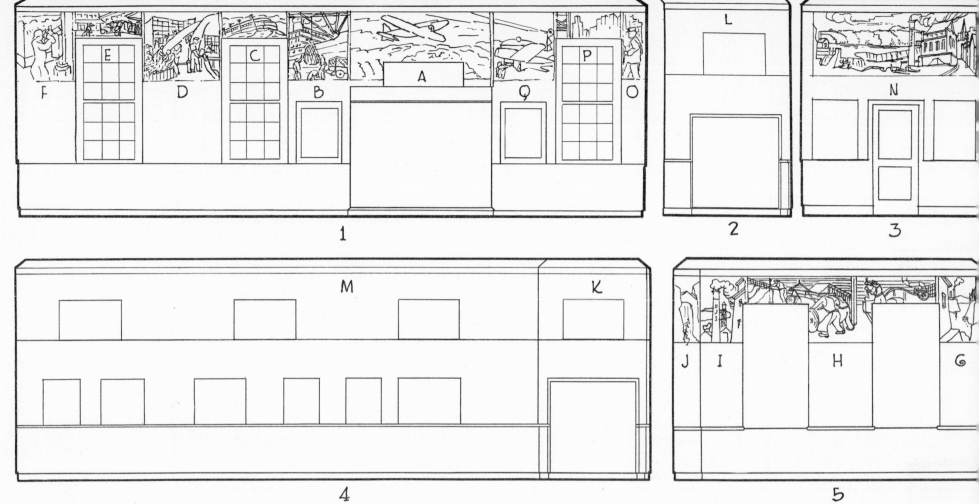

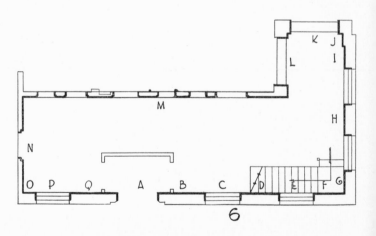

Hudson Falls, New York, Post Office

Architect: S.A.O. Louis A. Simon, Supervising Architect.
Frieze in Lobby by George Picken, assisted by Joseph Kaplan, Ludwig Mactarian and Ralph W. Walkley.

Subject Matter:

A. *Air Mail.*
B. *Unloading Mail from Ship.*
C. *Streamlined Mail Train.*
D. *Post Office Work Room.*
E. *Village Post Office.*
F. *Posting a Letter.*

G. *Upper New York Landscape and Power Plant.*
H. *Paper Mill.*
I. *Upper New York Landscape and Power Plant.*
J. *Waterfall.*
K. *Family Scene.*
L. *Village Scene.*

M. *Agriculture.*
N. *Local Power Plant.*
O. *Postman.*
P. *City Scene.*
Q. *Flying Field.*

Key to Drawings:

1. Elevation of outside wall, showing position of frieze broken by windows. Dimensions of painted wall space 41′ wide x 4′ high.
2. Elevation of inside wall, showing position of frieze "L." Dimensions of painted wall space broken by grille 9′ wide x 4′ high.
3. Elevation of end wall, showing position of frieze over door. Dimensions of painted wall space 12′ wide x 4′ high.
4. Elevation of screen wall, showing position of frieze broken by grilles. Dimensions of painted wall space 41′ wide x 4′ high.
5. Elevation of outside wall, showing position of frieze broken by windows. Dimensions of painted wall space 20′ wide x 4′ high.
6. Plan of Lobby.

240

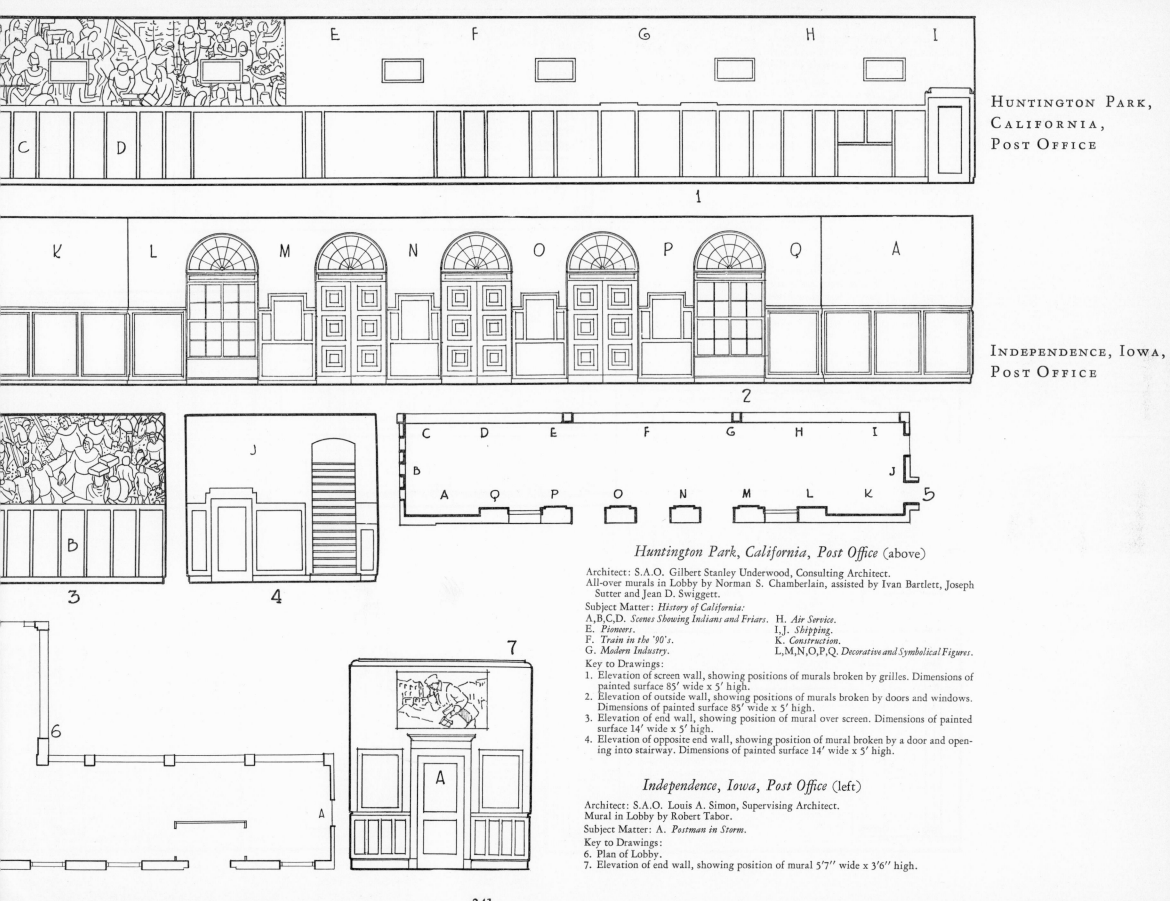

HUNTINGTON PARK,
CALIFORNIA,
POST OFFICE

INDEPENDENCE, IOWA,
POST OFFICE

Huntington Park, California, Post Office (above)

Architect: S.A.O. Gilbert Stanley Underwood, Consulting Architect.
All-over murals in Lobby by Norman S. Chamberlain, assisted by Ivan Bartlett, Joseph
 Sutter and Jean D. Swiggett.

Subject Matter: *History of California:*

A,B,C,D. *Scenes Showing Indians and Friars.*   H. *Air Service.*
E. *Pioneers.*   I,J. *Shipping.*
F. *Train in the '90's.*   K. *Construction.*
G. *Modern Industry.*   L,M,N,O,P,Q. *Decorative and Symbolical Figures.*

Key to Drawings:

1. Elevation of screen wall, showing positions of murals broken by grilles. Dimensions of
   painted surface 85' wide x 5' high.
2. Elevation of outside wall, showing positions of murals broken by doors and windows.
   Dimensions of painted surface 85' wide x 5' high.
3. Elevation of end wall, showing position of mural over screen. Dimensions of painted
   surface 14' wide x 5' high.
4. Elevation of opposite end wall, showing position of mural broken by a door and opening into stairway. Dimensions of painted surface 14' wide x 5' high.

Independence, Iowa, Post Office (left)

Architect: S.A.O. Louis A. Simon, Supervising Architect.
Mural in Lobby by Robert Tabor.

Subject Matter: A. *Postman in Storm.*

Key to Drawings:
6. Plan of Lobby.
7. Elevation of end wall, showing position of mural 5'7'' wide x 3'6'' high.

Indianapolis, Indiana, Post Office & Court House

Architects: McGuire and Shook.

Murals in one corner of Main Corridor on second floor by Grant Christian, assisted by Reynolds Selfridge.

Subject Matter: *Early and Present Day Indianapolis Life:*

A. *Pioneering; the Log Cabin.*
B. *Sowing.*
C. *Blacksmith.*
D. *Freeing the Slaves.*
E. *Covered Wagon.*
F. *Modern Soldiers.*
G. *County Fair.*
H. *Children's Play.*
I. *Children's Hospital.*
J. *Children's School.*
K. *Early Train.*
L. *Modern Mail Service.*
M. *Business and Transportation.*

Key to Drawings:

1. Elevation of one long wall, showing opening into corridor and four flanking panels.
2. Elevation of opposite wall, showing office door and four flanking panels. Dimensions of four wide panels 4′ wide x 6′ high, each. Dimensions of four narrower panels 2′ wide x 6′ high, each.
3. Elevation of one narrow wall, showing positions of two mural panels flanking opening into corridor. Dimensions of panels 2′ wide x 6′ high, each.
4. Elevation of opposite wall, showing position of opening into stairwell and positions of murals. Dimensions of two narrow panels 2′ wide x 6′ high, each. Dimensions of center panel, broken by door, 12′ wide x 6′ high.
5. Plan of corner of second-floor Corridor.

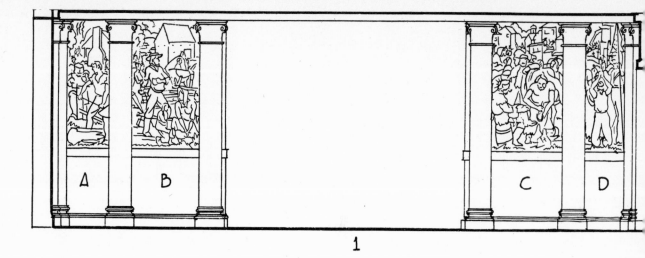

1

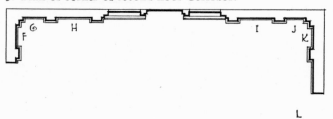

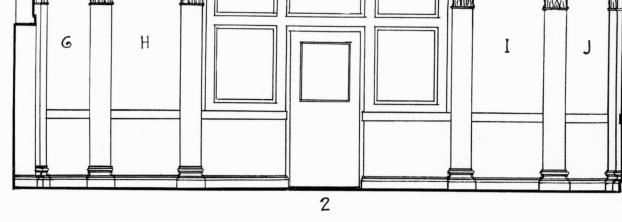

2

5

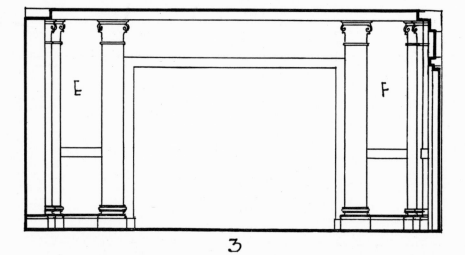

3

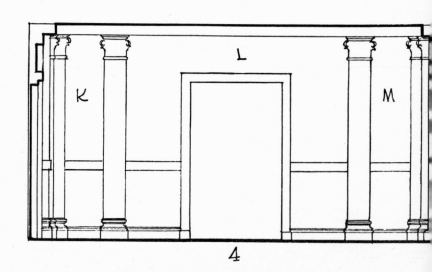

4

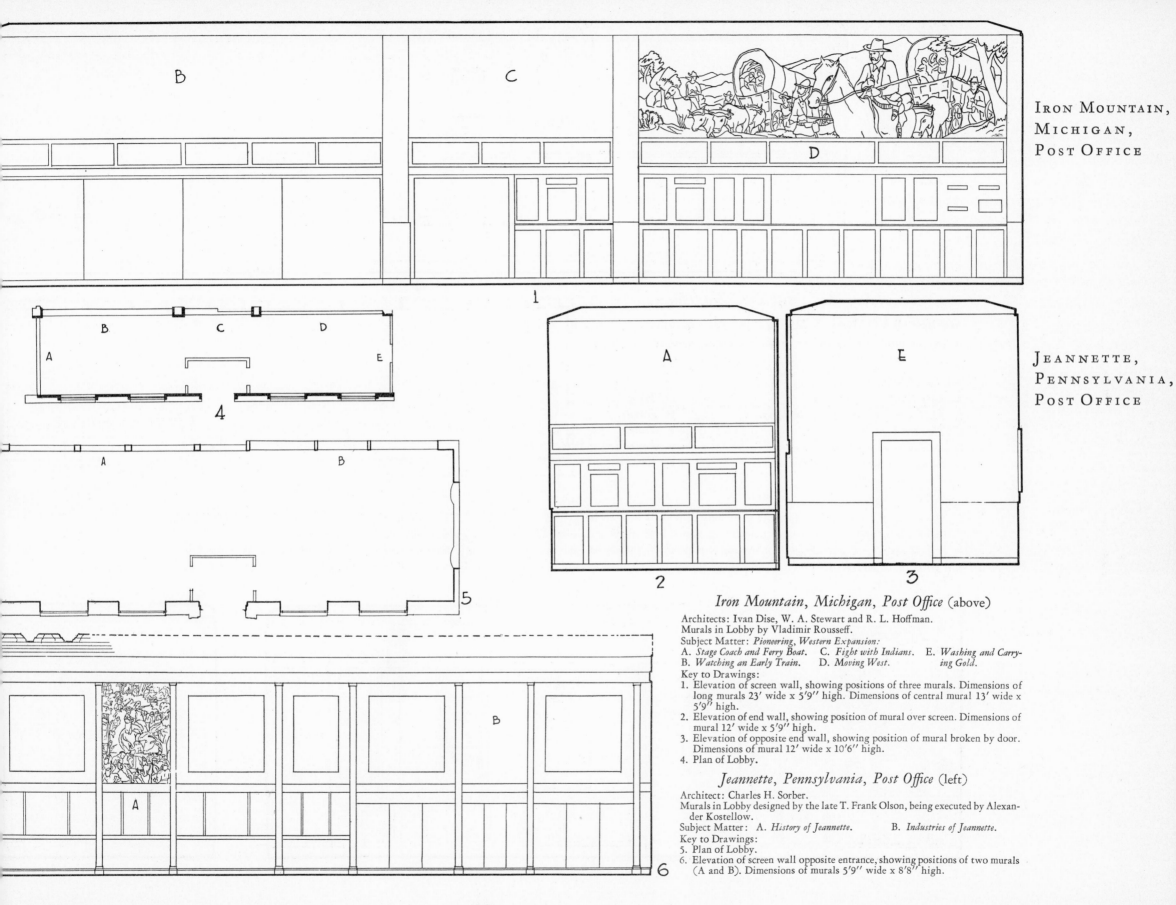

IRON MOUNTAIN,
MICHIGAN,
POST OFFICE

JEANNETTE,
PENNSYLVANIA,
POST OFFICE

Iron Mountain, Michigan, Post Office (above)

Architects: Ivan Dise, W. A. Stewart and R. L. Hoffman.
Murals in Lobby by Vladimir Rousseff.
Subject Matter: *Pioneering, Western Expansion:*
A. *Stage Coach and Ferry Boat.* C. *Fight with Indians.* E. *Washing and Carry-*
B. *Watching an Early Train.* D. *Moving West.* *ing Gold.*
Key to Drawings:
1. Elevation of screen wall, showing positions of three murals. Dimensions of
   long murals 23′ wide x 5′9″ high. Dimensions of central mural 13′ wide x
   5′9″ high.
2. Elevation of end wall, showing position of mural over screen. Dimensions of
   mural 12′ wide x 5′9″ high.
3. Elevation of opposite end wall, showing position of mural broken by door.
   Dimensions of mural 12′ wide x 10′6″ high.
4. Plan of Lobby.

Jeannette, Pennsylvania, Post Office (left)

Architect: Charles H. Sorber.
Murals in Lobby designed by the late T. Frank Olson, being executed by Alexan-
   der Kostellow.
Subject Matter: A. *History of Jeannette.* B. *Industries of Jeannette.*
Key to Drawings:
5. Plan of Lobby.
6. Elevation of screen wall opposite entrance, showing positions of two murals
   (A and B). Dimensions of murals 5′9″ wide x 8′8″ high.

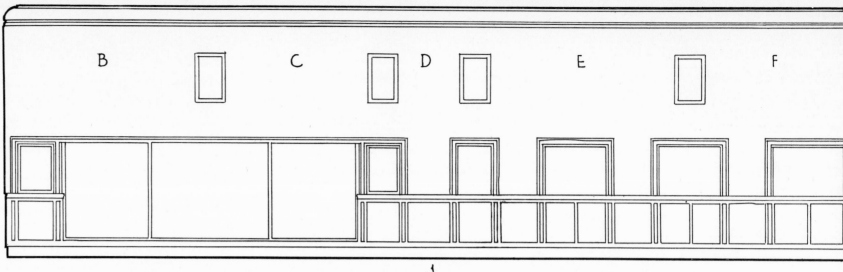

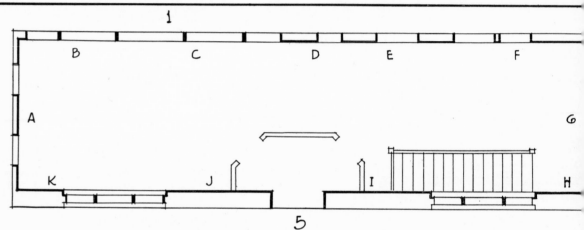

1

Johnson City, New York, Post Office

Architect: S.A.O. Louis A. Simon, Supervising Architect.

All-over murals in Lobby by Frederic Knight, assisted by Oliver
Baker, Bernard Finestone and James Mitchell.

Subject Matter:

A. *Ship Mail.*
B. *Mill Work and the Camera Industry.*
C. *Shoe Industry; Tanning.*
D. *Unloading of Air Mail.*
E. *Shoe Industry; Sewing on Tops, etc.*
F. *Truck and Dairy Farming.*

G. *Train Mail.*
H. *Schools.*
I. *Track.*
J. *Football.*
K. *Hospitals.*

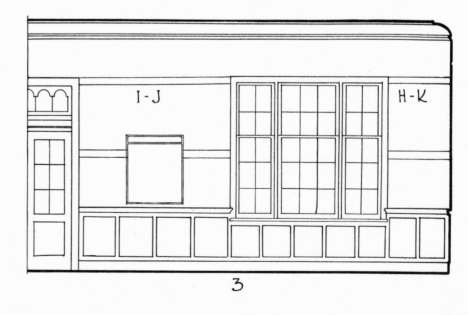

5

Key to Drawings:

1. Elevation of screen wall, showing positions of murals broken by grilles and windows. Dimensions of painted surface 48′ wide x 9′6″ high.
2. Elevation of end wall, showing position of mural broken by windows. Dimensions of painted surface 12′8″ wide x 9′6″ high.
3. Half elevation of outside wall, showing positions of murals broken by windows and doors. Dimensions of painted surface 48′ wide x 9′6″ high.
4. Elevation of end wall, showing position of mural broken by door and bulletin boards. Dimensions of painted surface 12′8″ wide x 9′6″ high.
5. Plan of Lobby.

2

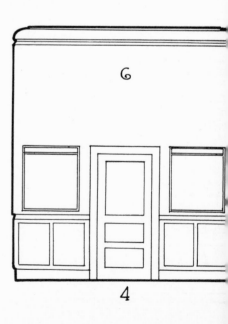

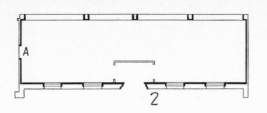

1

2

Kelso, Washington, Post Office

Architect: S.A.O. Louis A. Simon, Supervising Architect.
Mural in Lobby by David McCosh.

Subject Matter:
A. *Lewis and Clark at Mount Kelso.*

Key to Drawings:
1. Elevation of end wall, showing position of mural. Dimensions of mural 15'6" wide x 6' high.
2. Plan of Lobby.

La Jolla, California, Post Office

Architect: S.A.O. Louis A. Simon, Supervising
Architect.
Mural in Lobby by Belle Baranceanu.

Subject Matter:
A. *California Landscape.*

Key to Drawings:
3. Elevation of end wall, showing position of
mural. Dimensions of mural 11'10" wide x
8'4" high.
4. Plan of Lobby.

3

4

Lafayette, Indiana, Post Office

Architect: Walter Scholer.
Murals in Lobby by Henrick Martin Mayer.

Subject Matter:
A. *Sad News.*   B. *Rural Free Delivery.*

Key to Drawings:
5. Elevation of central bay of screen wall, showing positions of murals. Dimensions of each
mural 3' wide x 7'6" high.
6. Partial Plan of Lobby.

5

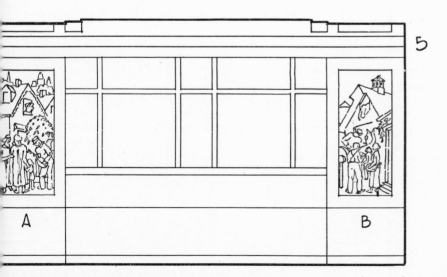

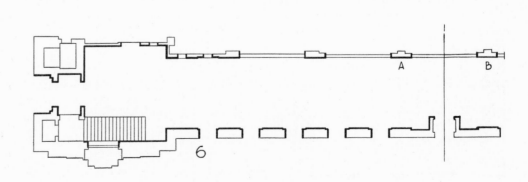

6

Louisville, Kentucky, Marine Hospital

LOUISVILLE,
KENTUCKY,
MARINE HOSPITAL

Architects: D. X. Murphy & Brothers.

All-over murals in Reception Room by Orville Carroll, assisted by Paul Childers.

Subject Matter: A to H. *Early Settlers and Pioneer Life.*

Key to Drawings:

1.
2. Elevations of walls, showing positions of murals broken by doors and windows. Room 11′ x 38′; murals 84 running feet, 10′ high from wainscot to
3. ceiling.
4.

5. Plan of Reception Room.

All-over murals in Lobby by Henrick Martin Mayer.

Subject Matter: *Scenes of the Ohio River Around Louisville, Kentucky:*

A. *Indian Sacrifice.*   D. *The Train.*   G. *Canal Barge.*
B. *Life Saving.*   E. *Ship Building.*   H. *Preaching to the*
C. *Loading the Boat.*   F. *Pleasure Ship.*   *Indians.*

Key to Drawings:

6. Elevation of entrance wall, showing positions of two murals flanking entrance door. Dimensions of each mural 3′10″ wide x 7′ high.

7. Elevation of side wall, showing positions of murals flanking information window, with carved wooden cartouche over window. Dimensions of murals 5′6″ wide x 7′ high. Dimensions of cartouche 5′ wide x 3″ high.

8. Elevation of wall, opposite the entrance, showing position of murals flanking opening into corridor and carved wooden cartouche over opening. Dimensions of murals 5′6″ wide x 7′ high. Dimensions of cartouche 4′ wide x 3′1″ high.

9. Elevation of wall, showing position of opening into reception room, flanked by murals with carved wooden cartouche over opening. Dimensions of murals 7′ wide x 7′ high. Dimensions of cartouche 3′6″ wide x 2′8″ high.

10. Plan of Lobby.

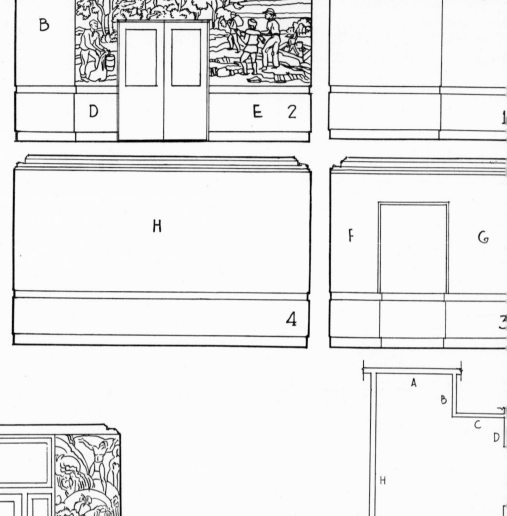

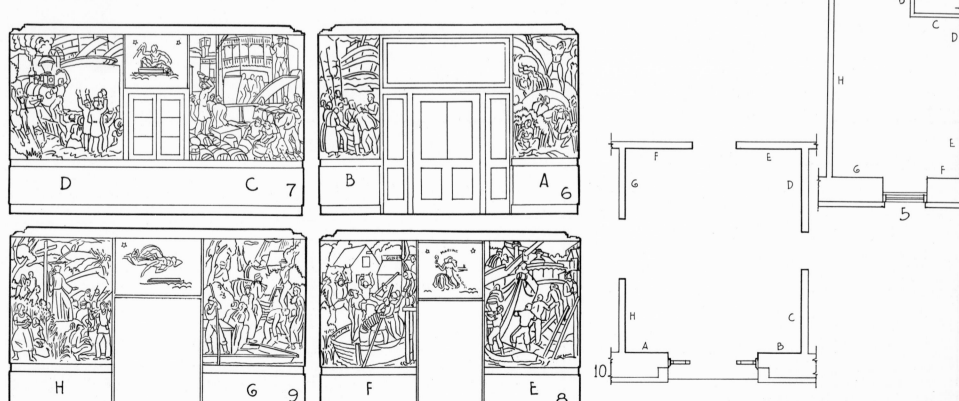

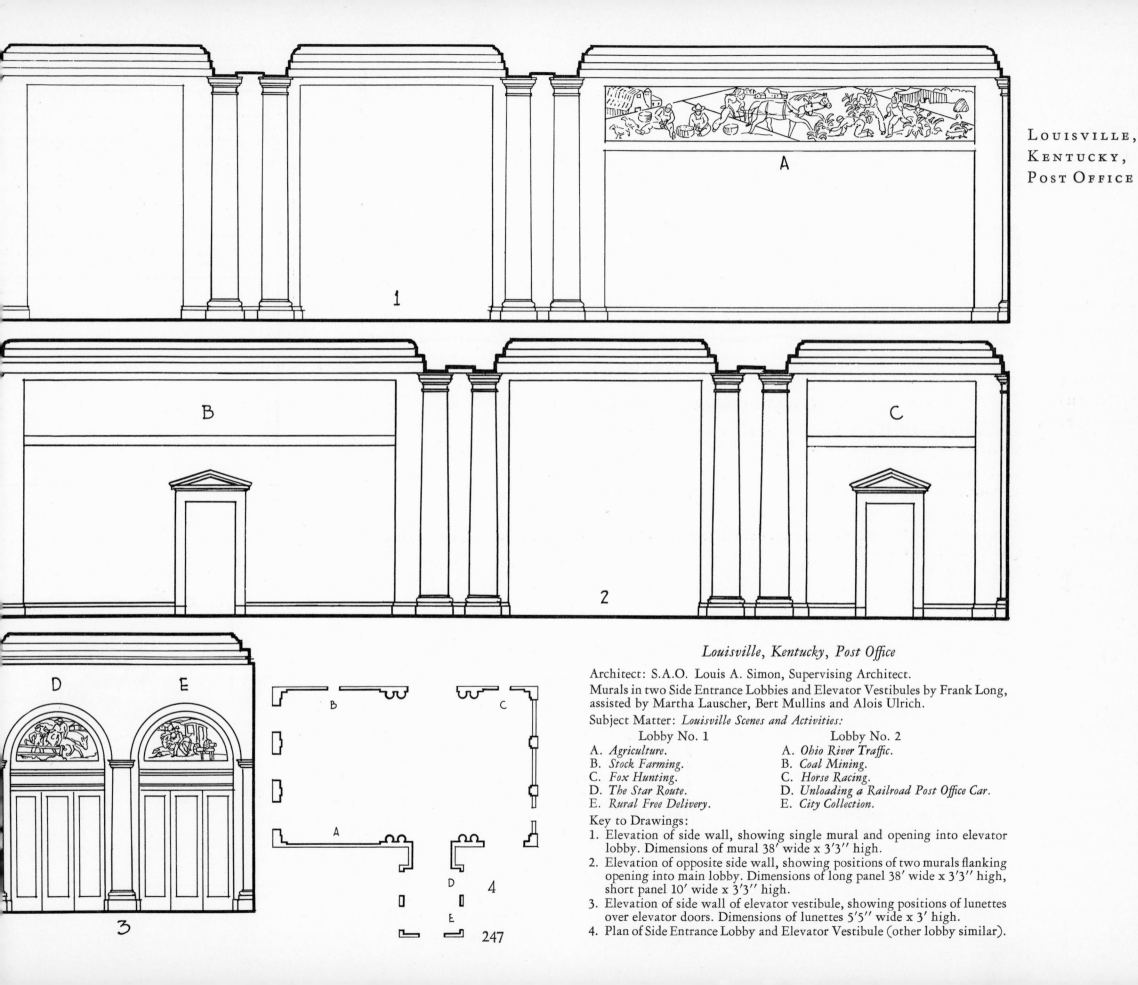

LOUISVILLE,
KENTUCKY,
POST OFFICE

Louisville, Kentucky, Post Office

Architect: S.A.O. Louis A. Simon, Supervising Architect.
Murals in two Side Entrance Lobbies and Elevator Vestibules by Frank Long, assisted by Martha Lauscher, Bert Mullins and Alois Ulrich.
Subject Matter: *Louisville Scenes and Activities:*

Lobby No. 1	Lobby No. 2
A. *Agriculture.*	A. *Ohio River Traffic.*
B. *Stock Farming.*	B. *Coal Mining.*
C. *Fox Hunting.*	C. *Horse Racing.*
D. *The Star Route.*	D. *Unloading a Railroad Post Office Car.*
E. *Rural Free Delivery.*	E. *City Collection.*

Key to Drawings:
1. Elevation of side wall, showing single mural and opening into elevator lobby. Dimensions of mural 38′ wide x 3′3″ high.
2. Elevation of opposite side wall, showing positions of two murals flanking opening into main lobby. Dimensions of long panel 38′ wide x 3′3″ high, short panel 10′ wide x 3′3″ high.
3. Elevation of side wall of elevator vestibule, showing positions of lunettes over elevator doors. Dimensions of lunettes 5′5″ wide x 3′ high.
4. Plan of Side Entrance Lobby and Elevator Vestibule (other lobby similar).

247

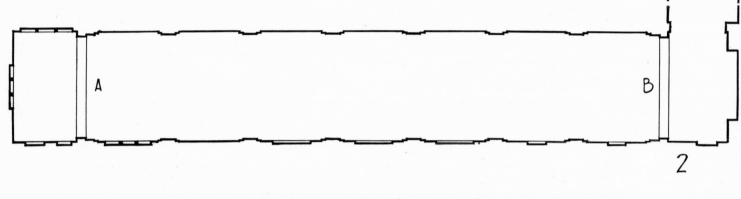

2

Lynn, Massachusetts, Post Office (above)

Architects: Edward H. Hoyt & Associates, and Ripley & Le Boutillier.

Murals in Lobby by William Riseman.

Subject Matter:

A. *Early and Modern Industries of Lynn.*   B. *Colonial and Contemporary Civic Culture.*

Key to Drawings:

1. Elevation of opening from main lobby to lower side lobby, showing position of mural. (Two ends similar.) Dimensions of each panel 16′6″ wide x 7′ high.

2. Plan of Lobby.

Merced, California, Post Office

Architects: Allison & Allison.

Mural at one end of Lobby by Helen Forbes (A).

Mural at other end of Lobby by Dorothy Puccinelli (B).

Subject Matter:

A. *Early Settlers.*   B. *Vacheros.*

Key to Drawings:

3. Elevation of one end wall, showing position of mural. (Opposite wall similar.) Dimensions of each mural 6′ wide x 9′8″ high.

4. Plan of Lobby.

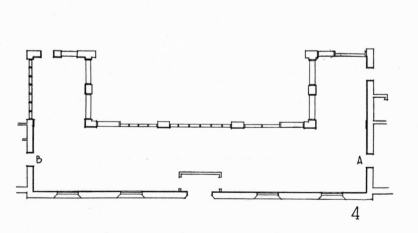

4

3

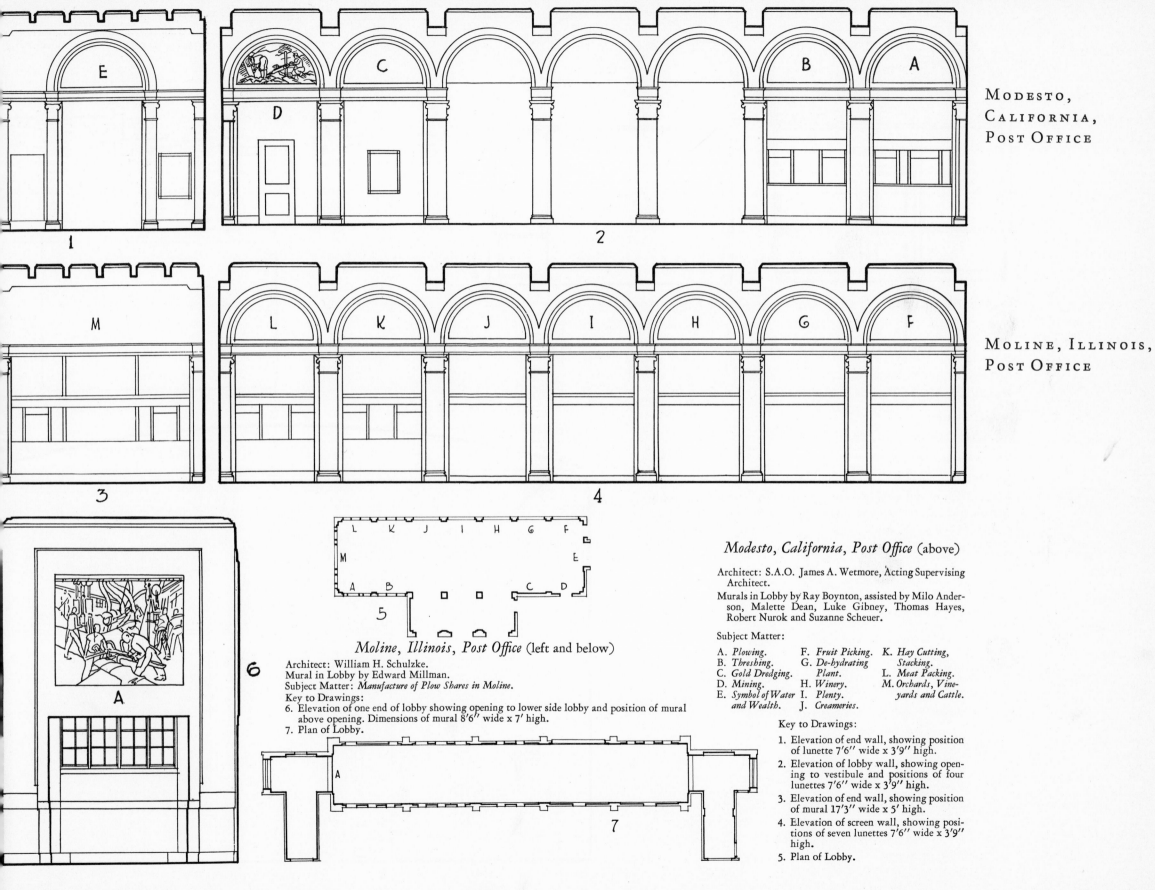

MODESTO,
CALIFORNIA,
POST OFFICE

MOLINE, ILLINOIS,
POST OFFICE

Modesto, California, Post Office (above)

Architect: S.A.O. James A. Wetmore, Acting Supervising
Architect.

Murals in Lobby by Ray Boynton, assisted by Milo Anderson, Malette Dean, Luke Gibney, Thomas Hayes,
Robert Nurok and Suzanne Scheuer.

Subject Matter:

A. *Plowing.*	F. *Fruit Picking.*	K. *Hay Cutting,*
B. *Threshing.*	G. *De-hydrating*	*Stacking.*
C. *Gold Dredging.*	*Plant.*	L. *Meat Packing.*
D. *Mining.*	H. *Winery.*	M. *Orchards, Vine-*
E. *Symbol of Water*	I. *Plenty.*	*yards and Cattle.*
and Wealth.	J. *Creameries.*	

Key to Drawings:

1. Elevation of end wall, showing position
of lunette 7'6" wide x 3'9" high.

2. Elevation of lobby wall, showing opening to vestibule and positions of four
lunettes 7'6" wide x 3'9" high.

3. Elevation of end wall, showing position
of mural 17'3" wide x 5' high.

4. Elevation of screen wall, showing positions of seven lunettes 7'6" wide x 3'9"
high.

5. Plan of Lobby.

Moline, Illinois, Post Office (left and below)

Architect: William H. Schulzke.
Mural in Lobby by Edward Millman.
Subject Matter: *Manufacture of Plow Shares in Moline.*
Key to Drawings:
6. Elevation of one end of lobby showing opening to lower side lobby and position of mural
above opening. Dimensions of mural 8'6" wide x 7' high.
7. Plan of Lobby.

MOUNT KISCO,
NEW YORK,
POST OFFICE

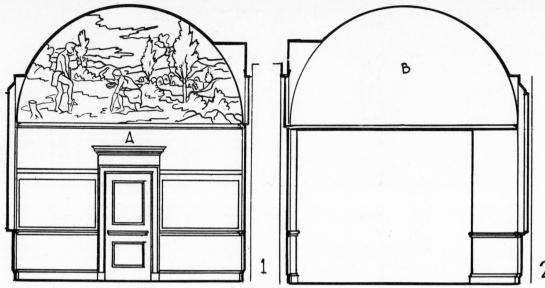

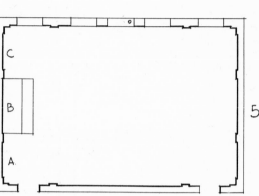

NEW BERN,
NORTH CAROLINA,
COURT HOUSE

Mount Kisco, New York, Post Office

Architect: Mott B. Schmidt.

Murals in Lobby by Thomas Donnelly.

Subject Matter:

A. *Indian Community Cornfield.*   B. *Mount Kisco in 1850.*

Key to Drawings:

1. Elevation of end wall, showing position of lunette over door.
2. Elevation of end wall, showing position of lunette over opening from main lobby to lower side lobby. Dimensions of each lunette 14'6" wide x 7'3" high.
3. Plan of Lobby.

New Bern, North Carolina, Court House

Architect: Robert F. Smallwood.

Murals in Court Room by David Silvette.

Subject Matter: *Colonial Episodes of New Bern History:*

A. *The Bayard-Singleton Case.*
B. *The Founding of New Bern by Graffenried.*
C. *The First Provincial Convention in North Carolina.*

Key to Drawings:

4. Elevation of wall, showing Judge's seat and positions of three murals. Dimensions of center panel 13'6" wide x 6'8" high. Dimensions of two side panels 8'6" wide x 6'8" high.
5. Plan of Court Room.

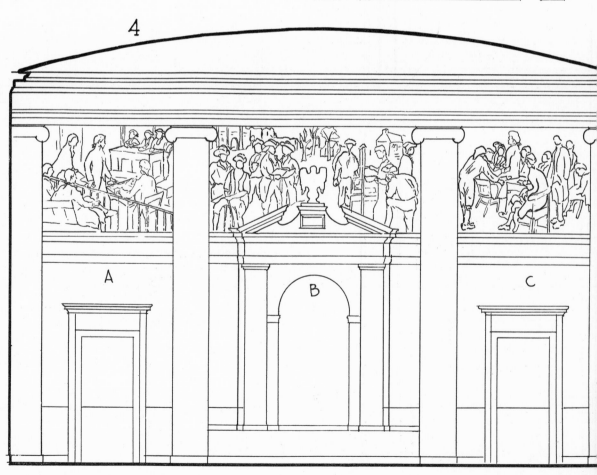

250

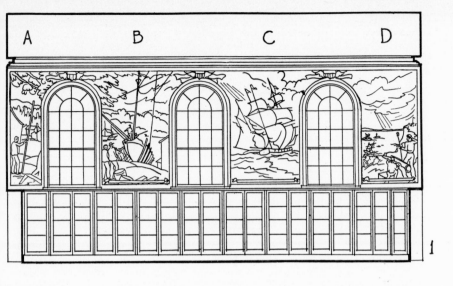

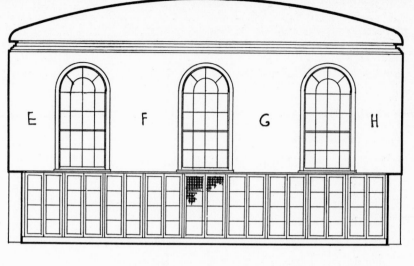

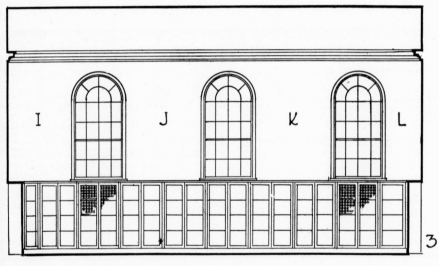

1

2

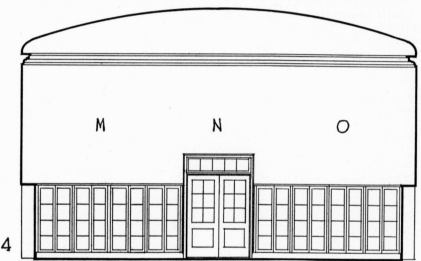

3

4

New London, Connecticut, Coast Guard Academy

Architect: S.A.O. Louis A. Simon, Supervising Architect.

All-over mural in Library by Aldis B. Browne, assisted by Mariano Corda and Robert Galvin.

Subject Matter: *Incidents in the History of the Coast Guard Service:*

A and B. *First Revenue Cutter, "Massachusetts," at Newburyport.*
C. *Cutter "Pickering" Capturing a French Pirate.*
D. *Defending Cutter "Eagle" from British (War of 1812).*
E. *Attacking a Pirates' Den in Florida.*
F. *Landing Party During Seminole Indian War.*
G. *"Harriet Lane" Firing First Shot in Civil War.*
H. *"McCulloch" Entering Manilla Bay.*
I. *"Bear" Rescues 112 Whalers, Pt. Barrow, Alaska.*

J. *"Tampa" on Convoy Duty.*
K. *Overhauling Suspected Rum-runner "Chase."*
L. *Escorting Refugees from Danger Zone, in San Sebastian, to Coast Guard Cutter "Cayuga," Summer of 1936.*
M. *International Ice Patrol.*
N. *Coast Guard Amphibian.*
O. *Bringing Passengers Ashore by Breeches Buoy.*

Key to Drawings:

1. Elevation of side wall, showing position of mural, broken by windows. Dimensions of mural 35′ wide x 9′ high.

2. Elevation of wall opposite main entrance, showing position of mural, broken by windows. Dimensions of mural 34′ wide x 9′ high.

3. Elevation of side wall, showing position of mural, broken by windows. Dimensions of mural 35′ wide x 9′ high.

4. Elevation of entrance wall, showing position of mural. Dimension of mural 34′ wide x 9′ high.

5. Plan of Lobby.

251

New London, Connecticut, Post Office

Architects: Payne & Keefe.

Murals in Lobby by Thomas La Farge.

Subject Matter: *Whaling Scenes:*

A. *Morning Watch.* C. *Cutting Up (Midday).*

B. *Furling Sail (Sunset).*

Key to Drawings:

1. Elevation of end wall, showing positions of two murals over doors.

2. Elevation of end wall, showing positions of two murals over screen.

3. Elevation of side wall, showing positions of two murals over door and screen windows. Dimensions of each mural 14′3″ wide x 3′ high.

4. Plan of Lobby.

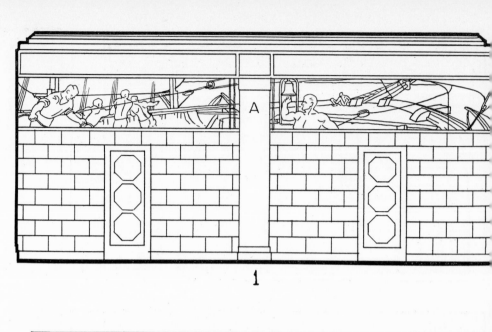

1

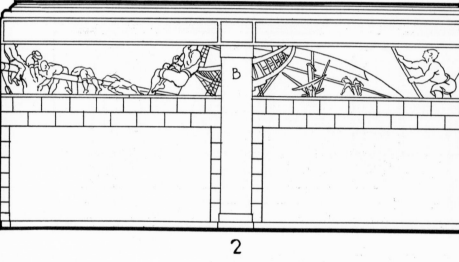

2

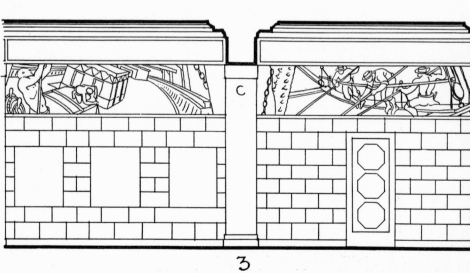

3

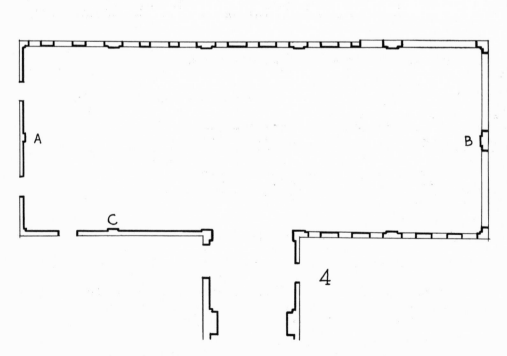

4

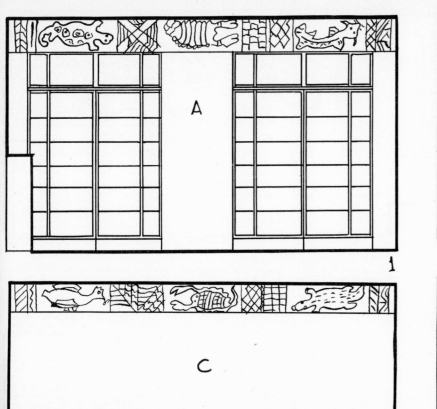

1

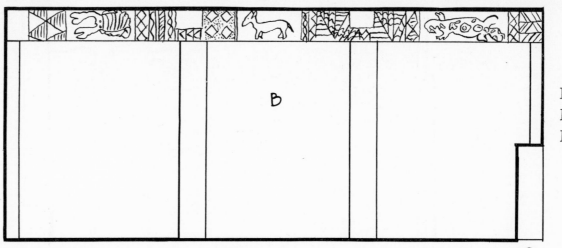

2

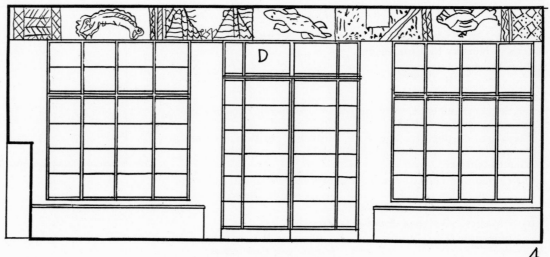

3

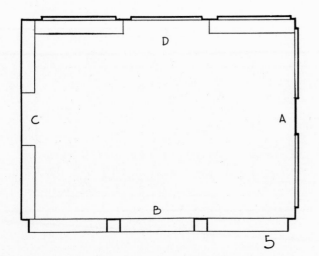

4

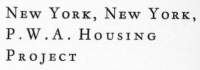

New York, New York,
P.W.A. Housing
Project

5

New York, New York, "Harlem," P.W.A.
Housing Project

Architect: Archibald Manning Brown, Chief Architect.
Murals in Nursery by Elsie Driggs.

Subject Matter:

A, B, C, D. *Decorative Animals and Abstract Design.*

Key to Drawings:

1.
2. Elevations of four walls, showing continuous frieze.
3. Dimensions of frieze 116 running feet, by 1'4" high.
4.
5. Plan of Nursery.

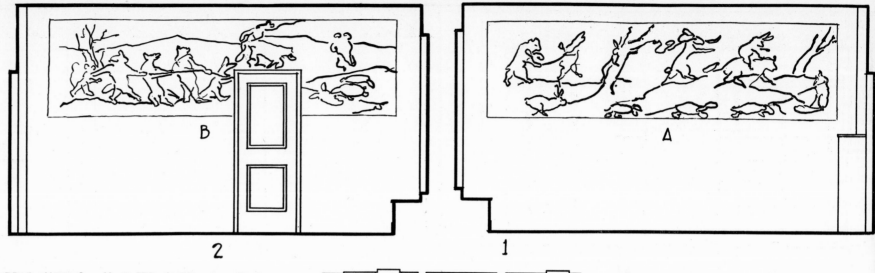

New York, New York, "Harlem," P.W.A. Housing Project

Architect: Archibald Manning Brown, Chief Architect.

Murals in Nursery by Elsie Driggs.

Subject Matter: A. } *Animal Fables.*
              B. }

Key to Drawings:

1. Elevation of end wall, showing position of mural. Dimensions of mural 22′ wide x 6′ high.

2. Elevation of opposite end wall, showing position of mural, broken by door. Dimensions of mural 22′ wide x 6′ high.

3. Plan of Nursery.

Eight carved and colored linoleum panels in two openings to the street from either end of the main court yard by Domenico Mortellito, assisted by Theodore Van Cina.

Subject Matter: *Aboriginal American Culture:*

Opening I.	Opening II.
A. *Domestic.*	A. *Building and Construction.*
B. *Hunting and Fishing.*	B. *The Crafts.*
C. *Dance and Festival.*	C. *The Arts.*
D. *Harvest.*	D. *Sports.*

Key to Drawings:

4. Plan of one opening divided in two passage ways. (Other opening similar.)

5. Elevation of one side wall of opening, showing position of linoleum panel. (Other walls similar.) Dimensions of panel 23′ wide x 9′ high.

6. Front elevation of one opening, showing two passageways on either side of central pier.

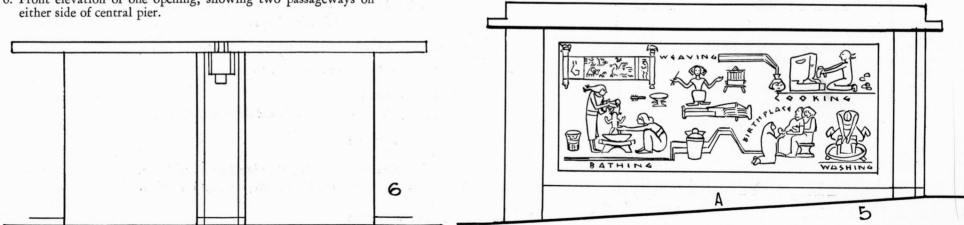

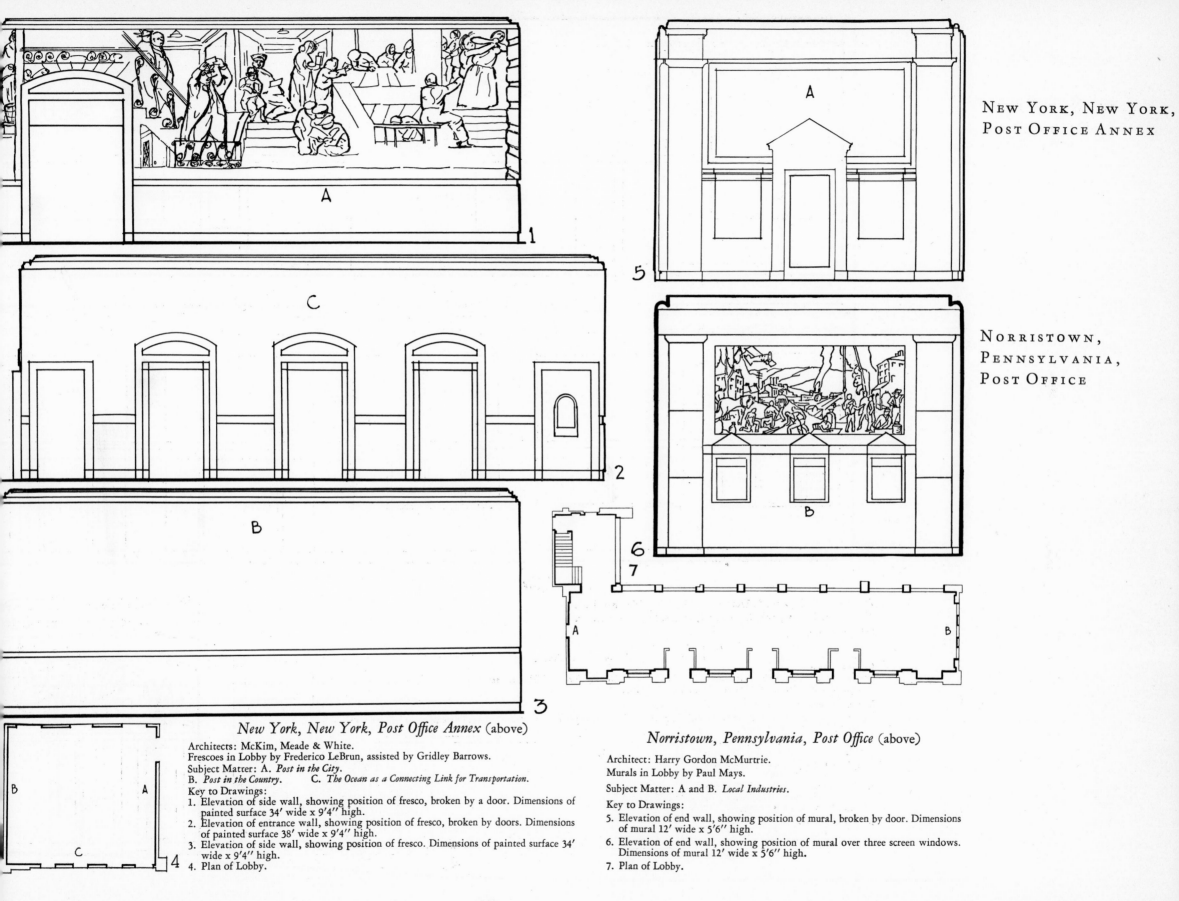

NEW YORK, NEW YORK,
POST OFFICE ANNEX

NORRISTOWN,
PENNSYLVANIA,
POST OFFICE

New York, New York, Post Office Annex (above)

Architects: McKim, Meade & White.
Frescoes in Lobby by Frederico LeBrun, assisted by Gridley Barrows.
Subject Matter: A. *Post in the City.*
B. *Post in the Country.*   C. *The Ocean as a Connecting Link for Transportation.*
Key to Drawings:
1. Elevation of side wall, showing position of fresco, broken by a door. Dimensions of painted surface 34′ wide x 9′4″ high.
2. Elevation of entrance wall, showing position of fresco, broken by doors. Dimensions of painted surface 38′ wide x 9′4″ high.
3. Elevation of side wall, showing position of fresco. Dimensions of painted surface 34′ wide x 9′4″ high.
4. Plan of Lobby.

Norristown, Pennsylvania, Post Office (above)

Architect: Harry Gordon McMurtrie.
Murals in Lobby by Paul Mays.

Subject Matter: A and B. *Local Industries.*

Key to Drawings:
5. Elevation of end wall, showing position of mural, broken by door. Dimensions of mural 12′ wide x 5′6″ high.
6. Elevation of end wall, showing position of mural over three screen windows. Dimensions of mural 12′ wide x 5′6″ high.
7. Plan of Lobby.

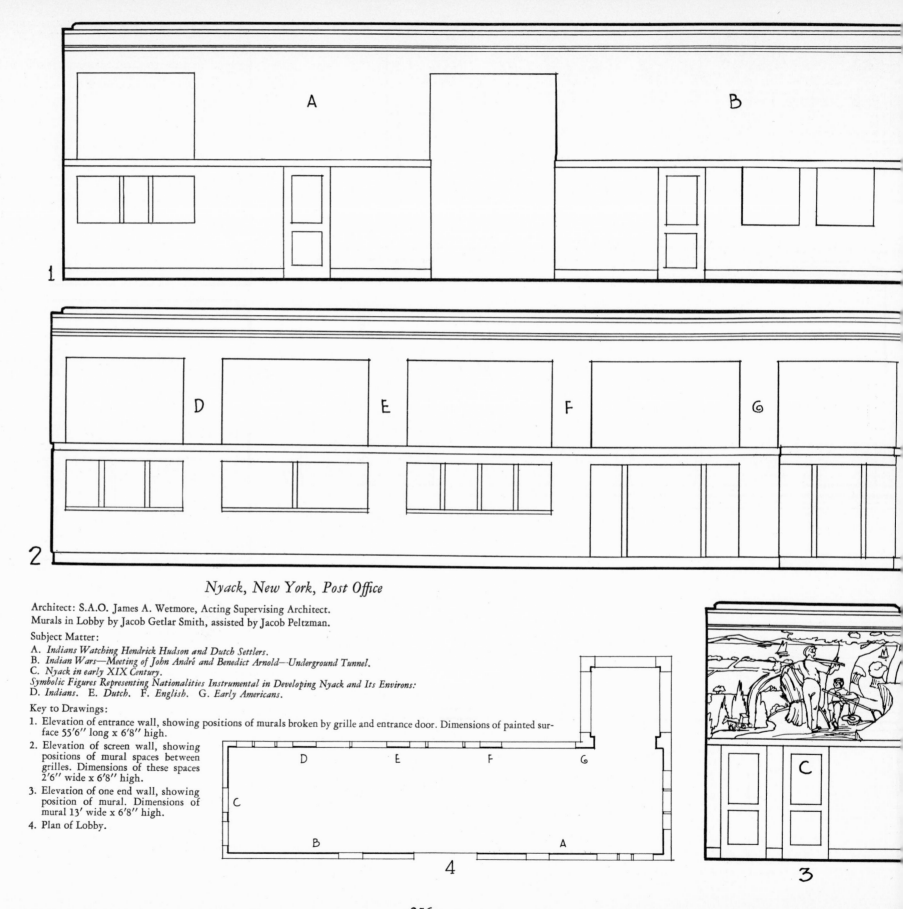

NYACK, NEW YORK,
POST OFFICE

Nyack, New York, Post Office

Architect: S.A.O. James A. Wetmore, Acting Supervising Architect.
Murals in Lobby by Jacob Getlar Smith, assisted by Jacob Peltzman.

Subject Matter:

A. *Indians Watching Hendrick Hudson and Dutch Settlers.*
B. *Indian Wars—Meeting of John André and Benedict Arnold—Underground Tunnel.*
C. *Nyack in early XIX Century.*
Symbolic Figures Representing Nationalities Instrumental in Developing Nyack and Its Environs:
D. *Indians.* E. *Dutch.* F. *English.* G. *Early Americans.*

Key to Drawings:

1. Elevation of entrance wall, showing positions of murals broken by grille and entrance door. Dimensions of painted surface 55'6" long x 6'8" high.

2. Elevation of screen wall, showing positions of mural spaces between grilles. Dimensions of these spaces 2'6" wide x 6'8" high.

3. Elevation of one end wall, showing position of mural. Dimensions of mural 13' wide x 6'8" high.

4. Plan of Lobby.

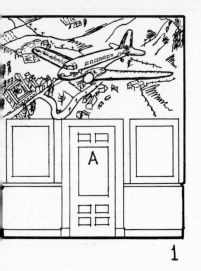

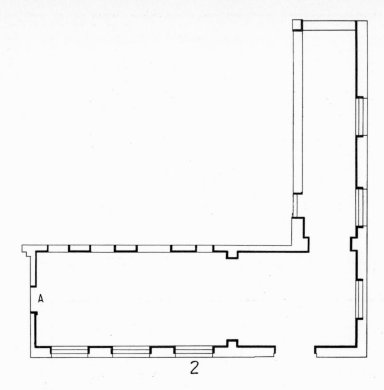

1

2

Oceanside, California, Post Office

Architect: S.A.O. Louis A. Simon, Supervising Architect. Mural in Lobby by Elise Seeds.

Subject Matter: A. *Air Mail*.

Key to Drawings:

1. Elevation of end wall, showing position of mural. Dimensions of mural 11′2″ wide x 5′7″ high.
2. Plan of Lobby.

Osceola, Iowa, Post Office

Architect: S.A.O. Louis A. Simon, Supervising Architect. Mural in Lobby by Byron Ben Boyd.

Subject Matter: A. *Arrival of the First Train*.

Key to Drawings:

3. Elevation of end wall showing position of mural. Dimensions of mural 11′10″ wide x 9′11″ high.
4. Plan of Lobby.

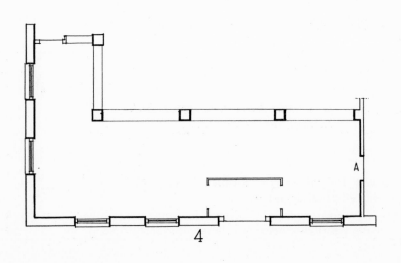

3

4

OYSTER BAY,
NEW YORK,
POST OFFICE

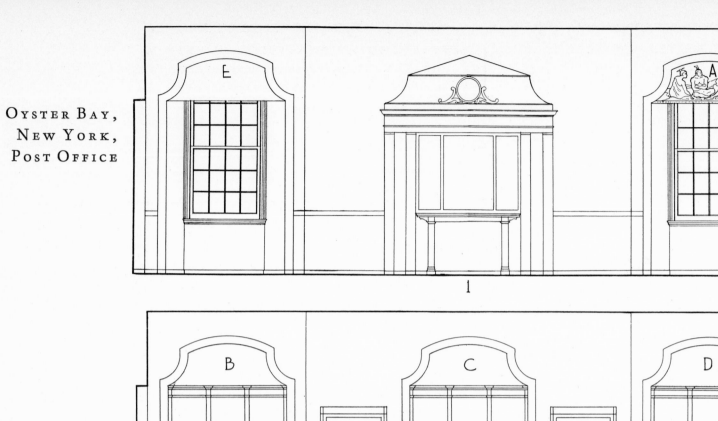

1

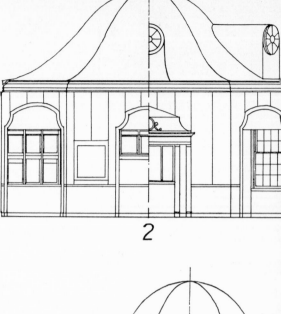

2

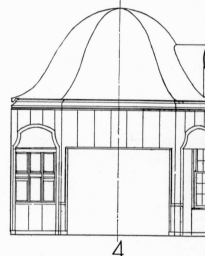

3

4

Oyster Bay, New York, Post Office

Architect: Lawrence Bottomley.

Murals in Lobby by Ernest Peixotto.

Subject Matter: *Historical Scenes in Oyster Bay:*

A. *William Leverich Discussing the Treaty with the Indians, 1653.*
B. *Washington at the Young's House, 1790.*
C. *James Caldwell, First Postmaster, and First Post Office, 1800.*

D. *Theodore Roosevelt at Sagamore Hill.*
E. *Springtime, Oyster Bay.*

Key to Drawings:

1. Elevation of entrance wall, showing positions of two mural panels. Dimensions of each panel 6' wide x 2'6" high.
2. Half elevation of long transverse section through lobby, showing elliptical domed ceiling.
3. Elevation of main screen wall, showing positions of three mural panels 6' wide x 2'6" high.
4. Half elevation of short transverse section through lobby, showing position of opening into corridor and elliptical domed ceiling.
5. Plan of Lobby.

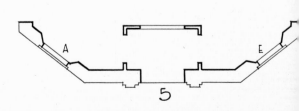

5

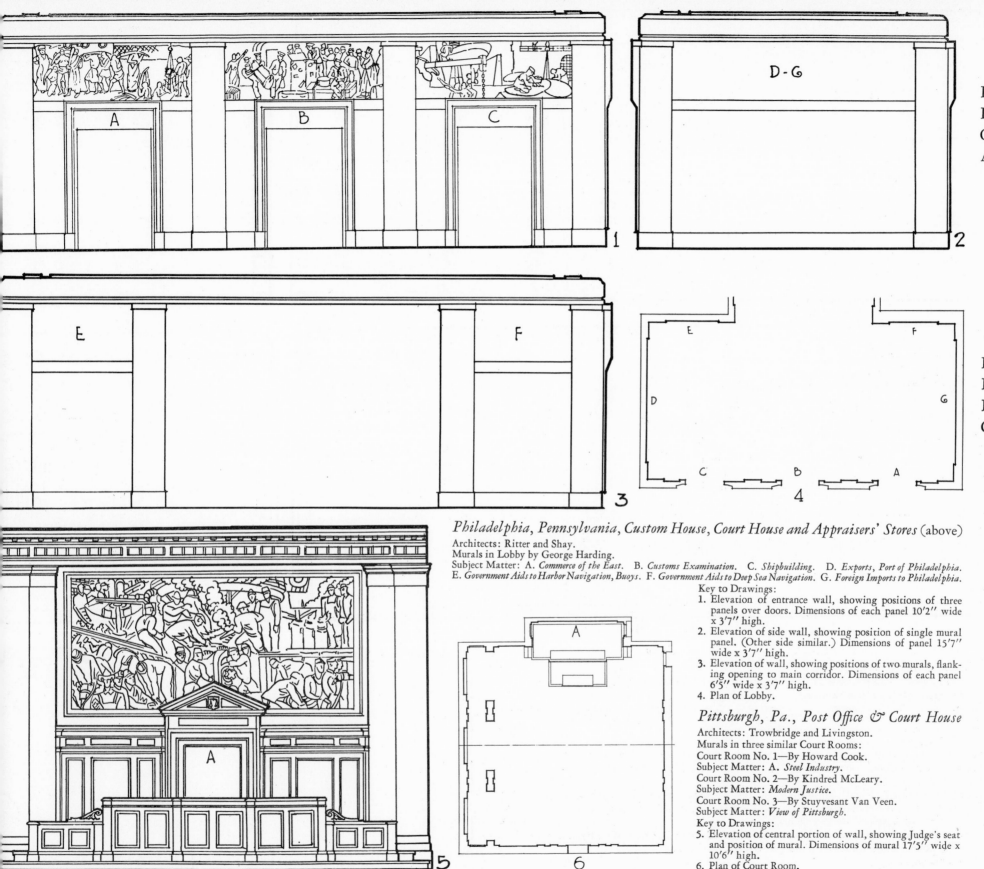

1

2

3

4

Philadelphia, Pennsylvania, Custom House, Court House and Appraisers' Stores (above)

Architects: Ritter and Shay.
Murals in Lobby by George Harding.
Subject Matter: A. *Commerce of the East.* B. *Customs Examination.* C. *Shipbuilding.* D. *Exports, Port of Philadelphia.*
E. *Government Aids to Harbor Navigation, Buoys.* F. *Government Aids to Deep Sea Navigation.* G. *Foreign Imports to Philadelphia.*
Key to Drawings:
1. Elevation of entrance wall, showing positions of three panels over doors. Dimensions of each panel 10′2″ wide x 3′7″ high.
2. Elevation of side wall, showing position of single mural panel. (Other side similar.) Dimensions of panel 15′7″ wide x 3′7″ high.
3. Elevation of wall, showing positions of two murals, flanking opening to main corridor. Dimensions of each panel 6′5″ wide x 3′7″ high.
4. Plan of Lobby.

Pittsburgh, Pa., Post Office & Court House

Architects: Trowbridge and Livingston.
Murals in three similar Court Rooms:
Court Room No. 1—By Howard Cook.
Subject Matter: A. *Steel Industry.*
Court Room No. 2—By Kindred McLeary.
Subject Matter: *Modern Justice.*
Court Room No. 3—By Stuyvesant Van Veen.
Subject Matter: *View of Pittsburgh.*
Key to Drawings:
5. Elevation of central portion of wall, showing Judge's seat and position of mural. Dimensions of mural 17′5″ wide x 10′6″ high.
6. Plan of Court Room.

5

6

259

1

2

3

4

Port Chester, New York, Post Office

Architects: Zoller & Muller.
Murals in Lobby by Domenico Mortellito, assisted by Gustavo Cenci.
Subject Matter: *Port Chester Pursuits:*

A. *Teacher.*	D. *Policeman.*	G. *Carpenter.*	J. *Old Port Chester.*	L. *Bolt and Nut Factory.*
B. *Grocer.*	E. *Postman.*	H. *Fireman.*	K. *Life Saver Factory.*	M. *Wharf.*
C. *Doctor and Nurse.*	F. *Cellist.*	I. *Baker.*		

Key to Drawings:
1. Elevation of entrance wall, showing positions of two lunettes and two larger panels flanking door. Dimensions of panel "M" 8′ wide x 10′ high. Dimensions of panel "L" 8′ wide x 14′ high.
2. Elevation of one end wall, showing positions of two lunettes over screen.
3. Elevation of wall opposite entrance, showing positions of lunettes over screen. Dimensions of all lunettes, 8′ wide x 4′ high.
4. Elevation of end wall showing positions of two large panels, broken by a door and a bulletin board. Dimensions of panels 8′ wide x 14′ high.
5. Plan of Lobby.

5

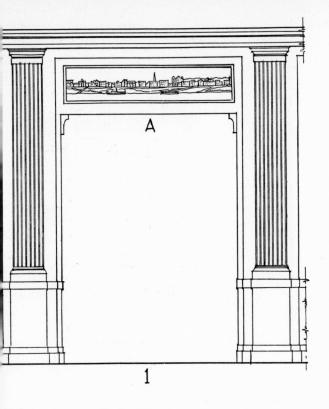

1

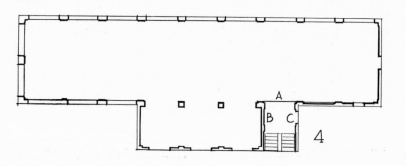

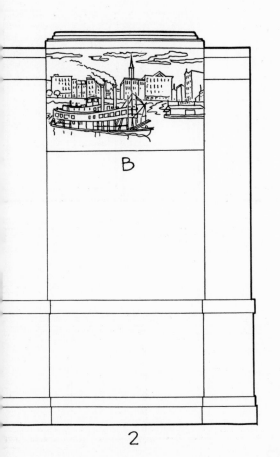

2

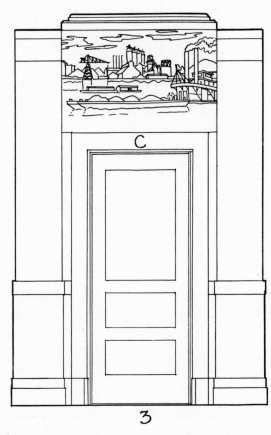

3

Portsmouth, Ohio, Post Office

Architect: S.A.O. Louis A. Simon, Supervising Architect.

Mural in Lobby by Clarence Carter.

Subject Matter: A. *Ohio River.*

Murals in Stairhall by Richard Zoellner.

Subject Matter: B. *Ferry Boat.*
C. *Coal Barge.*

Key to Drawings:

1. Elevation of opening from lobby to stairhall, showing position of mural. Dimensions of mural 7'2" wide x 1'7" high.

2. Elevation of wall in stairhall, showing position of mural. Dimensions of mural 4'7" wide x 3'1" high.

3. Elevation of wall in stairhall, showing position of mural over door. Dimensions of mural 4'7" wide x 3'1" high.

4. Plan of Lobby and Stairhall.

RATON, NEW MEXICO,
POST OFFICE

2

RAVENNA, OHIO,
POST OFFICE

1

4

3

5

Ravenna, Ohio, Post Office (upper right)

Architects: Good & Wagner.
Mural in Lobby by Clarence Carter.
Subject Matter: A. *Early Ravenna.*
Key to Drawings:
4. Elevation of end wall, showing position of mural. Dimensions of mural 11′ wide x 5′ high.
5. Plan of Lobby.

Raton, New Mexico, P.O.
(above)

Architect: S.A.O. James A. Wetmore, Acting Supervising Architect.
Murals in Lobby by Joseph A. Fleck.
Subject Matter:
A. *First Mail Coach Crossing Raton Pass.*
B. *Modern Mail.*
Key to Drawings:
1. Elevation of end wall, showing position of mural. Dimensions of mural 12′4″ wide x 7′6″ high.
2. Elevation of outside wall, showing position of mural. Dimensions of mural 4′ wide x 7′6″ high.
3. Plan of Lobby.

9

6

7

REDONDO BEACH,
CALIFORNIA,
POST OFFICE

Redondo Beach, California, Post Office (right)

Architect: S.A.O. Louis A. Simon, Supervising Architect.
All-over murals in Lobby by Paul Sample.
Subject Matter:
A. *Fishing From Redondo Dock.*
B. *Sheep Farming and the Ocean Near Redondo.*
C. *Excursion Train and Picknickers in the 90's.*
Key to Drawings:
6. Elevation of end wall, showing position of mural over screen. Dimensions of mural 12′ wide x 5′ high.
7. Elevation of end wall, showing position of mural over door and bulletin boards. Dimensions of mural 12′ wide x 5′ high.
8. Elevation of screen wall, showing position of mural. Dimensions of mural 36′ wide x 5′ high.
9. Plan of Lobby.

B

8

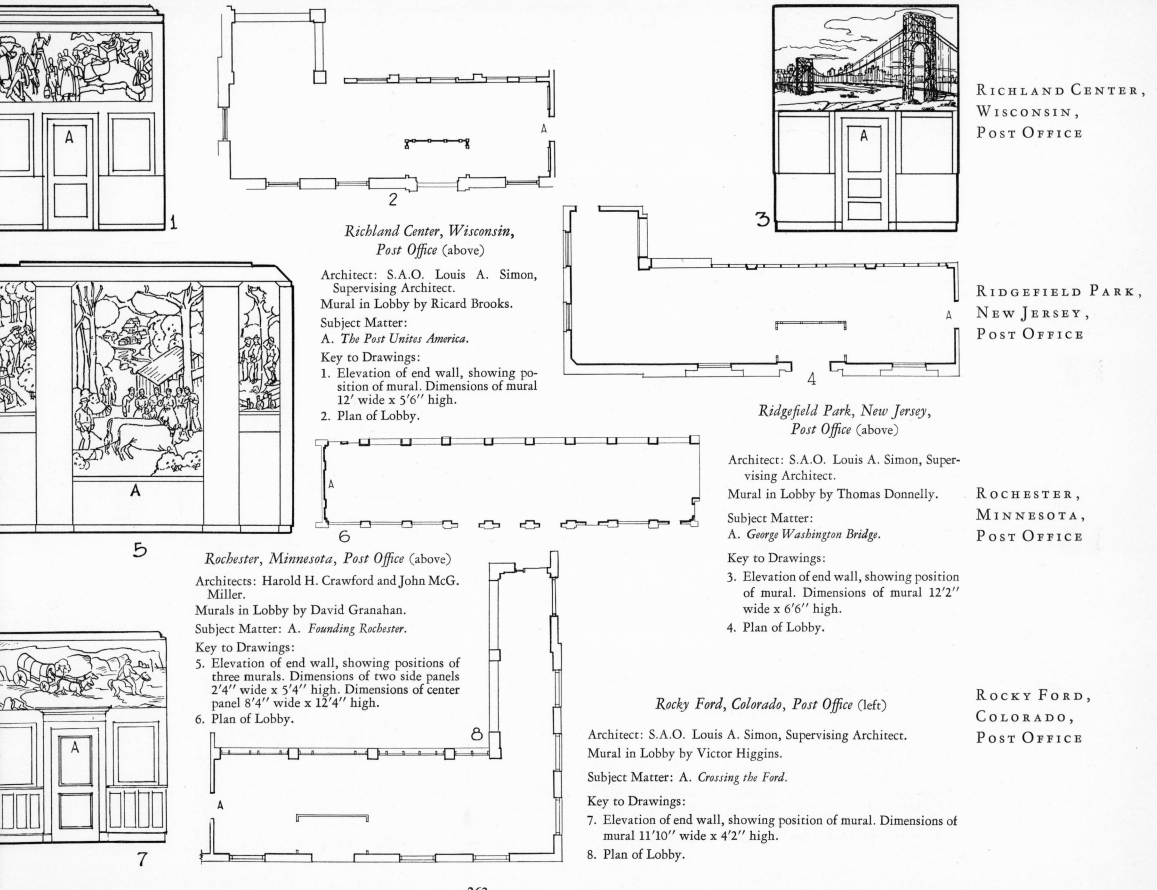

1

2

3

Richland Center, Wisconsin,
Post Office (above)

Architect: S.A.O. Louis A. Simon,
Supervising Architect.
Mural in Lobby by Ricard Brooks.

Subject Matter:
A. *The Post Unites America.*

Key to Drawings:
1. Elevation of end wall, showing position of mural. Dimensions of mural
12′ wide x 5′6″ high.
2. Plan of Lobby.

4

Ridgefield Park, New Jersey,
Post Office (above)

Architect: S.A.O. Louis A. Simon, Supervising Architect.

Mural in Lobby by Thomas Donnelly.

Subject Matter:
A. *George Washington Bridge.*

Key to Drawings:
3. Elevation of end wall, showing position
of mural. Dimensions of mural 12′2″
wide x 6′6″ high.
4. Plan of Lobby.

5

6

Rochester, Minnesota, Post Office (above)

Architects: Harold H. Crawford and John McG.
Miller.
Murals in Lobby by David Granahan.

Subject Matter: A. *Founding Rochester.*

Key to Drawings:
5. Elevation of end wall, showing positions of
three murals. Dimensions of two side panels
2′4″ wide x 5′4″ high. Dimensions of center
panel 8′4″ wide x 12′4″ high.
6. Plan of Lobby.

8

Rocky Ford, Colorado, Post Office (left)

Architect: S.A.O. Louis A. Simon, Supervising Architect.
Mural in Lobby by Victor Higgins.

Subject Matter: A. *Crossing the Ford.*

Key to Drawings:
7. Elevation of end wall, showing position of mural. Dimensions of
mural 11′10″ wide x 4′2″ high.
8. Plan of Lobby.

7

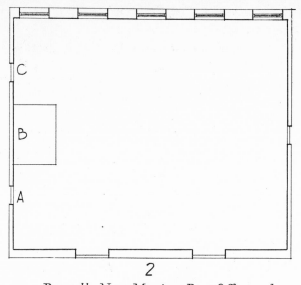

2

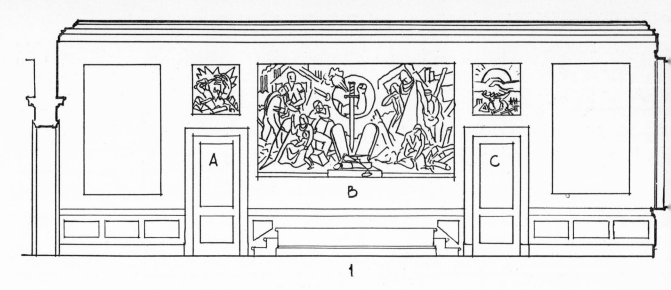

1

*Roswell, New Mexico, Post Office and
Court House* (above)

Architect: S.A.O. James Knox Taylor, Supervising Architect.
Murals in Court Room by Emil Bisttram.
Subject Matter: *Justice Tempered by Mercy:*
A. *Strife.*   B. (Left side) *Uphold the Right.*   C. *Cooperation.*
                    (Right side) *Prevent the Wrong.*

Key to Drawings:
1. Elevation of end wall, showing Judges' Bench and positions of
   three mural panels. Dimensions of center panel 13'6'' wide x 7'
   high. Dimensions of over-door panels 3' wide x 3'6'' high.
2. Plan of Court Room.

Rutland, Vermont, Post Office (right)

Architect: S.A.O. Louis A. Simon, Supervising Architect.
Murals in Lobby by Stephen Belaski, assisted by David Buckley and
Pierre Zwick.
Subject Matter: *Vermont History:*

A. *Ethan Allen and the Green*   E. *Benedict Arnold Commanding First*
   Mountain Boys.   *Naval Battle on Lake Champlain.*
B. *The Call to Unite.*   F. *The First Stroke for Vermont In-*
C. *The Beech Seal.*   *dependence—The Attack on the*
D. *Freedom of the First Slave in*   *James Breckenridge Farm in*
   the State of Vermont.   *Dorset.*

Key to Drawings:
3. Elevation of end wall, showing positions of three murals around
   office door. Dimensions of central panel, broken by door, 6'4''
   wide x 5' high. Dimensions of two flanking panels 4' wide x 11'
   high.
4. Elevation of end wall, showing positions of stairway and elevator
   door, with mural above it. Dimensions of mural 7' wide x 4'6'' high.
5. Elevation of outside wall, showing positions
   of murals flanking entrance doors. Dimensions
   of panels 8'6'' wide x 11' high.
6. Plan of Lobby.

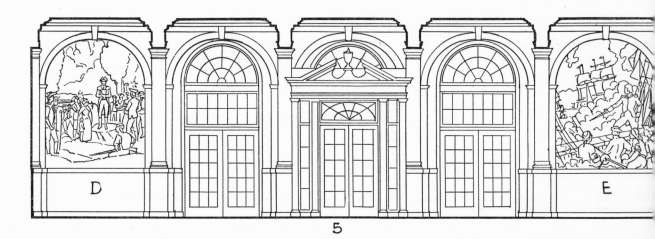

4

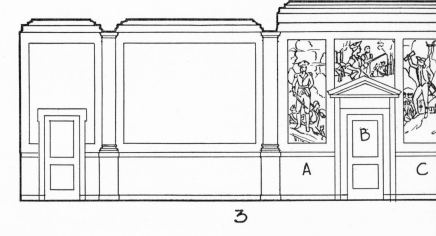

3

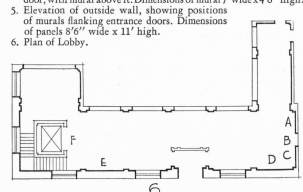

6

5

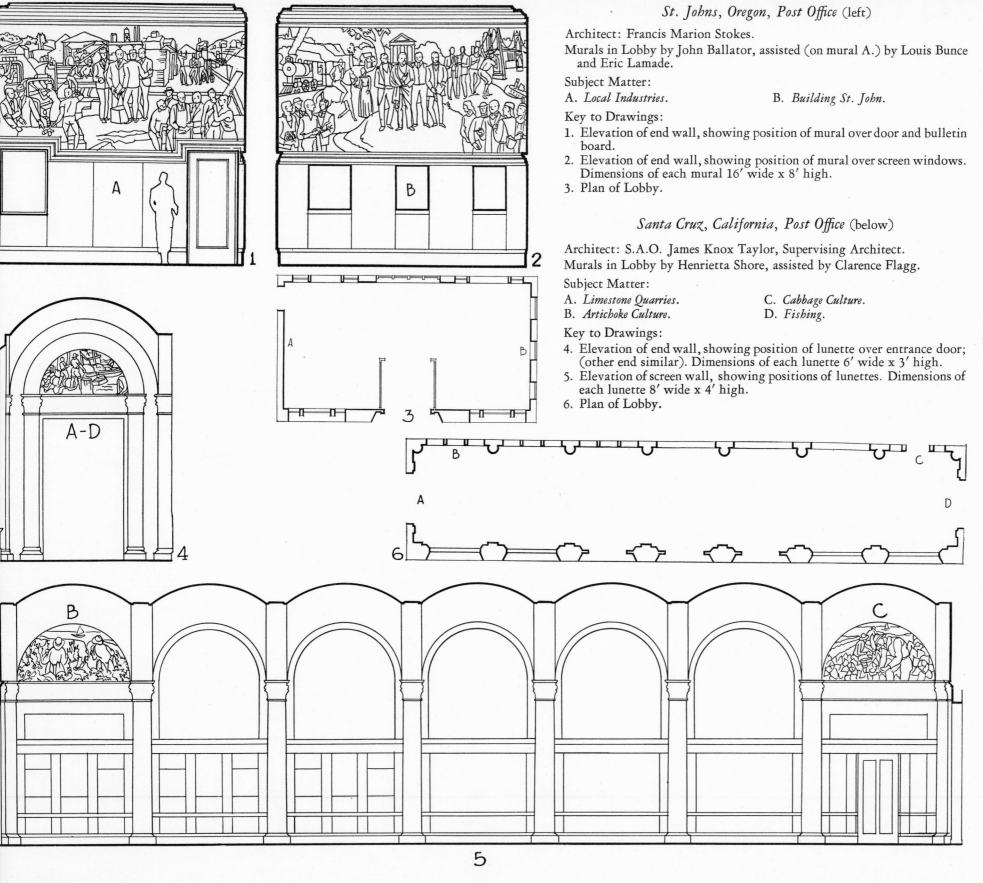

St. Johns, Oregon, Post Office (left)

Architect: Francis Marion Stokes.

Murals in Lobby by John Ballator, assisted (on mural A.) by Louis Bunce and Eric Lamade.

Subject Matter:

A. *Local Industries.*   B. *Building St. John.*

Key to Drawings:

1. Elevation of end wall, showing position of mural over door and bulletin board.
2. Elevation of end wall, showing position of mural over screen windows. Dimensions of each mural 16′ wide x 8′ high.
3. Plan of Lobby.

Santa Cruz, California, Post Office (below)

Architect: S.A.O. James Knox Taylor, Supervising Architect.

Murals in Lobby by Henrietta Shore, assisted by Clarence Flagg.

Subject Matter:

A. *Limestone Quarries.*   C. *Cabbage Culture.*
B. *Artichoke Culture.*   D. *Fishing.*

Key to Drawings:

4. Elevation of end wall, showing position of lunette over entrance door; (other end similar). Dimensions of each lunette 6′ wide x 3′ high.
5. Elevation of screen wall, showing positions of lunettes. Dimensions of each lunette 8′ wide x 4′ high.
6. Plan of Lobby.

ST. JOHNS, OREGON,
POST OFFICE

SANTA CRUZ,
CALIFORNIA,
POST OFFICE

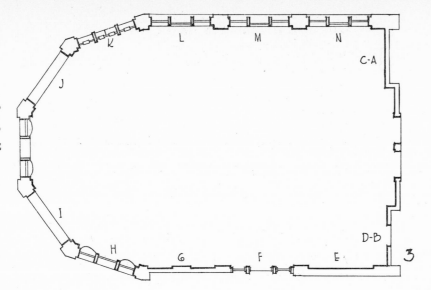

SARATOGA SPRINGS,
NEW YORK,
POST OFFICE

1

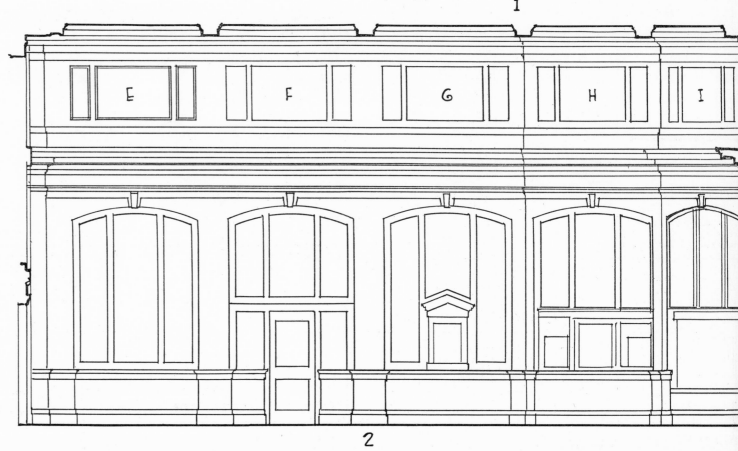

2

Saratoga Springs, New York,
Post Office

Architect: S.A.O. James Knox Taylor,
Supervising Architect.

Murals in Lobby by Guy Pène du Bois.

Subject Matter:

Large Panels A. and B. *Horse Racing*
Scene near Saratoga Springs.

Small Panels C. *Jockeys*. D. *Racing Crowd*.

10 additional smaller panels, of similar
subjects, as yet undetermined.

Key to Drawings:

1. Elevation of end wall, showing positions of two murals flanking entrance
door. Dimensions of murals 7′6″ wide
x 11′ high. Two small panels above
5′6″ wide x 3′4″ high, each.

2. Elevation of one-half of side wall of
Lobby, showing positions of small
panels.

3. Plan of Lobby.

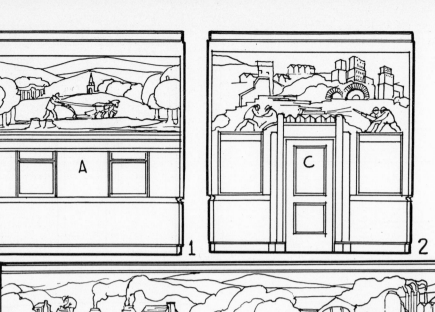

Scottdale, Pennsylvania, Post Office

Architect: S.A.O. Louis A. Simon, Supervising Architect.

All-over mural in Lobby by Harry Scheuch, assisted by Albert Shaffer.

Subject Matter: A, B, C. *Local Life and Industries.*

Key to Drawings:

1. Elevation of end wall, showing position of mural over screen windows. Dimensions of mural 12'6" wide x 5' high.

2. Elevation of end wall, showing position of mural over door and bulletin boards. Dimensions of mural 12'6" wide x 5' high.

3. Elevation of screen wall, showing position of mural. Dimensions of mural 36' wide x 5'6" high.

4. Plan of Lobby.

SCOTTDALE,
PENNSYLVANIA,
POST OFFICE

SEATTLE, WASHINGTON,
MARINE HOSPITAL

eattle, Washington, Marine Hospital

chitects: Bebb and Gould.

rals in Reception Room by Kenneth Callahan,
ssisted by Hovey Rich and Julius Twohy

ject Matter: *Marine Scenes:*

Radio.	F. *Steering Wheel.*
Painting.	G. *Sextant.*
Dock Scene.	H. *Marine Hall.*
Unloading.	I. *Engine Room.*
Life-Boat Drill.	J. *Ropes.*

w to Drawings:

, 7, 8, 9. Elevations of walls,
showing position of continuous mural broken by doors,
windows and a closet. Di-
mensions of room 26' wide x
42' long; murals 6' high
above wainscot.

Plan of Reception Room.

267

SELLERSVILLE,
PENNSYLVANIA,
POST OFFICE

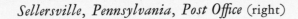

Sellersville, Pennsylvania, Post Office (right)

Architect: S.A.O. Louis A. Simon, Supervising Architect.

Mural in Lobby by Harry Sternberg.

Subject Matter: A. *Carrying the Mail.*

Key to Drawings:

1. Elevation of end wall, showing position of mural. Dimensions of mural 12′ wide x 5′8″ high.
2. Plan of Lobby.

Sheboygan, Wisconsin, Post Office

Architect: E. A. Stubenrauch.

Murals in Lobby by Schomer Lichtner.

Subject Matter:

A. *Primitive Indian Life.*	C. *The Pioneer.*	E. *Industry.*
B. *The Lake.*	D. *Industry.*	F. *Modern Life.*

SHEBOYGAN,
WISCONSIN,
POST OFFICE

Key to Drawings:

3. Elevation of end wall, showing position of mural over door. (Other end similar.) Dimensions of murals 14′6″ wide x 7′6″ high.
4. Part elevation of entrance wall, showing stairway and position of mural. Dimensions of mural 5′ wide x 7′6″ high.
5. Part elevation of entrance wall, showing positions of three murals. Dimensions of each mural 10′ wide x 7′6″ high.
6. Plan of Lobby.

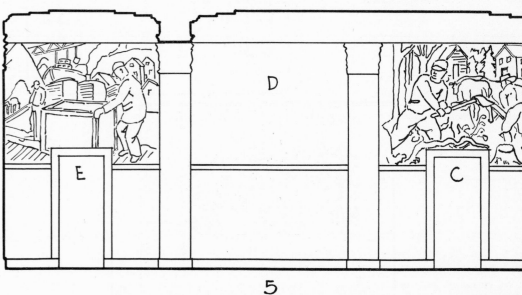

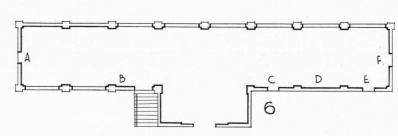

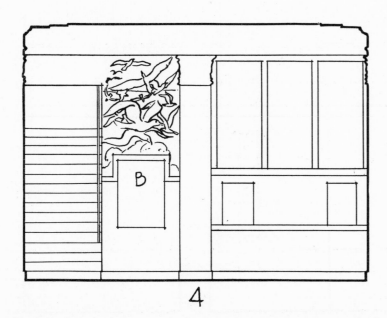

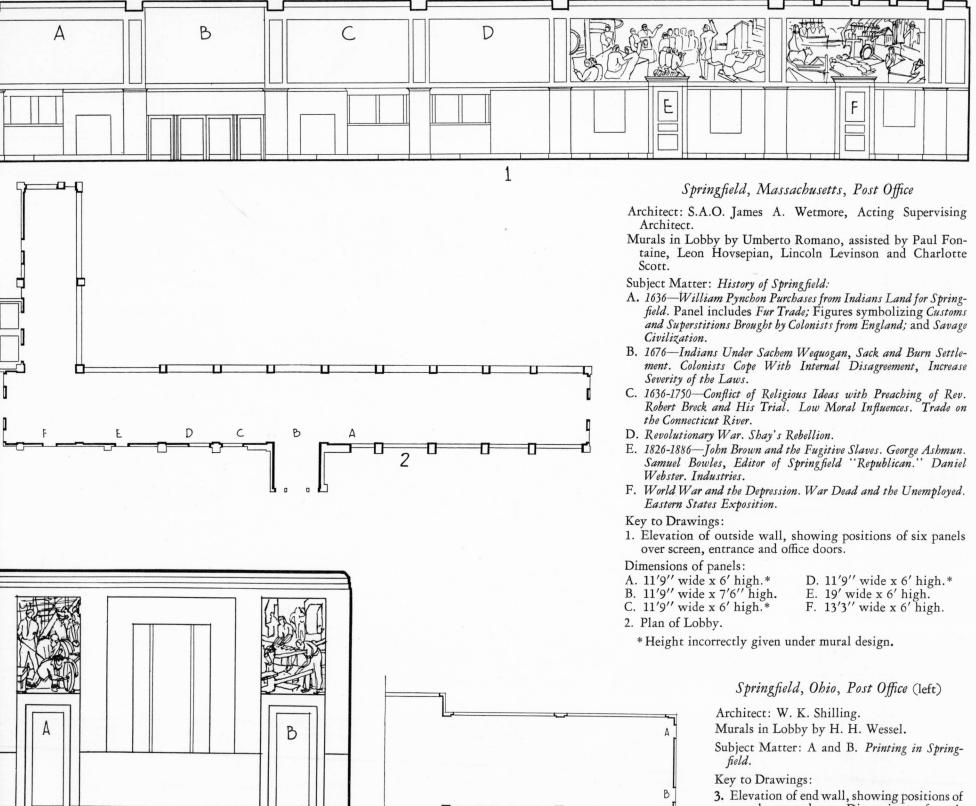

1

2

Springfield, Massachusetts, Post Office

Architect: S.A.O. James A. Wetmore, Acting Supervising
Architect.

Murals in Lobby by Umberto Romano, assisted by Paul Fon-
taine, Leon Hovsepian, Lincoln Levinson and Charlotte
Scott.

Subject Matter: *History of Springfield:*

A. *1636—William Pynchon Purchases from Indians Land for Springfield.* Panel includes *Fur Trade;* Figures symbolizing *Customs
and Superstitions Brought by Colonists from England;* and *Savage
Civilization.*

B. *1676—Indians Under Sachem Wequogan, Sack and Burn Settlement. Colonists Cope With Internal Disagreement, Increase
Severity of the Laws.*

C. *1636-1750—Conflict of Religious Ideas with Preaching of Rev.
Robert Breck and His Trial. Low Moral Influences. Trade on
the Connecticut River.*

D. *Revolutionary War. Shay's Rebellion.*

E. *1826-1886—John Brown and the Fugitive Slaves. George Ashmun.
Samuel Bowles, Editor of Springfield "Republican." Daniel
Webster. Industries.*

F. *World War and the Depression. War Dead and the Unemployed.
Eastern States Exposition.*

Key to Drawings:

1. Elevation of outside wall, showing positions of six panels
over screen, entrance and office doors.

Dimensions of panels:

A. 11'9'' wide x 6' high.*   D. 11'9'' wide x 6' high.*
B. 11'9'' wide x 7'6'' high.   E. 19' wide x 6' high.
C. 11'9'' wide x 6' high.*   F. 13'3'' wide x 6' high.

2. Plan of Lobby.

    *Height incorrectly given under mural design.

Springfield, Ohio, Post Office (left)

Architect: W. K. Shilling.

Murals in Lobby by H. H. Wessel.

Subject Matter: A and B. *Printing in Springfield.*

Key to Drawings:

3. Elevation of end wall, showing positions of
murals over doors. Dimensions of each
mural 4' wide x 6' high.

4. Plan of Lobby.

3

4

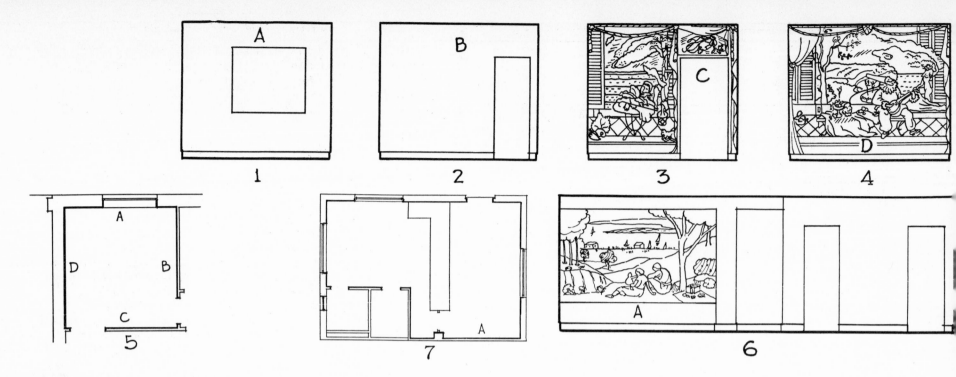

Stamford, Connecticut, P.W.A. Housing Project (above)

Architect: William J. Provoost, Chief Architect.

All-over mural scheme in Committee Room by Edna Reindel.

Subject Matter: A. B. C. and D. *Decorative Motives.*

Key to Drawings:

1-2-3-4. Elevations of four walls, showing position of continuous mural broken by doors and window. Dimensions of room 9′ wide x 10′ long; painted surface 8′6″ high above baseboard.

5. Plan of Committee Room.

Mural in the public space in the Main Office of the Administration Building, by Ann Brockman.

Subject Matter: A. *View of Stamford.*

Key to Drawings:

6. Elevation of wall opposite main entrance door, showing position of mural. Dimensions of mural 10′ wide x 6′ high.

7. Plan of Main Office.

Stockton, California, Post Office (below)

Architects: Bliss & Fairweather.

Murals in Lobby by Frank Bergman and Moya Del Pino.

Subject Matter:
A. *Mail and Travel by Stage Coach* (Del Pino).   B. *Mail Carriers of Today* (Bergman).

Key to Drawings:

8. Elevation of screen wall, showing positions of murals. Dimensions of murals 15′ wide x 8′6″ high.
9. Plan of Lobby.

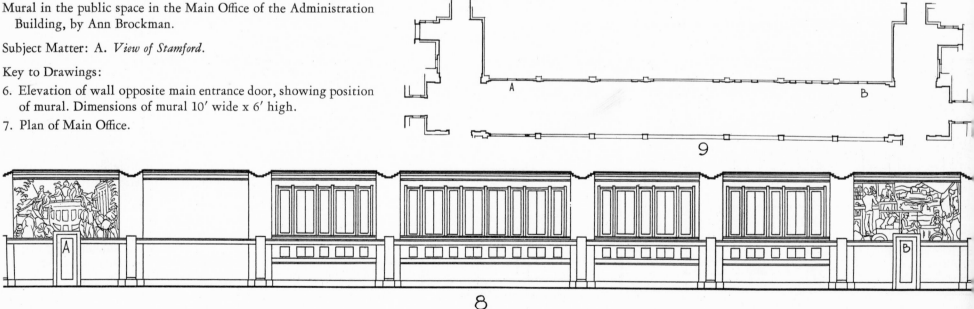

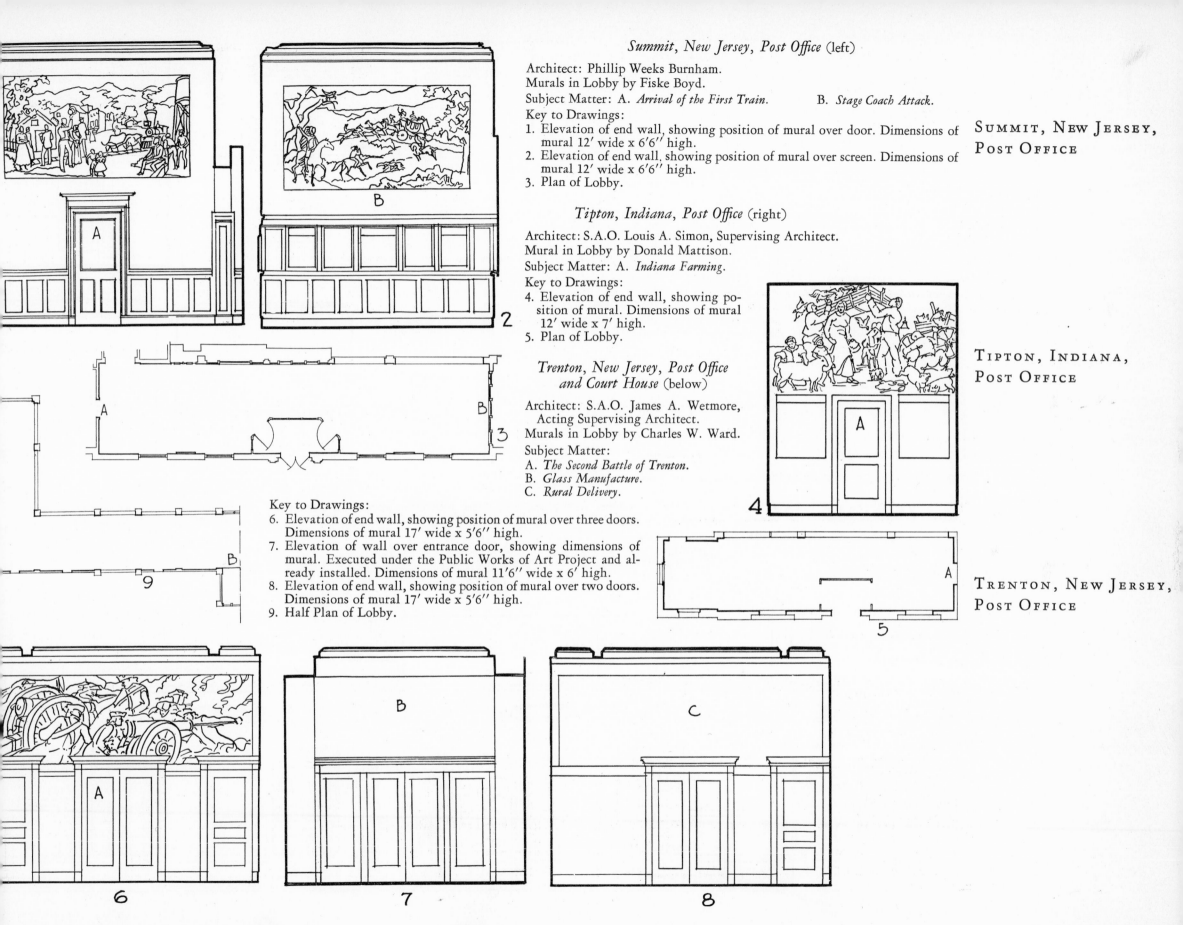

Summit, New Jersey, Post Office (left)

Architect: Phillip Weeks Burnham.
Murals in Lobby by Fiske Boyd.
Subject Matter: A. *Arrival of the First Train.*   B. *Stage Coach Attack.*
Key to Drawings:
1. Elevation of end wall, showing position of mural over door. Dimensions of mural 12′ wide x 6′6″ high.
2. Elevation of end wall, showing position of mural over screen. Dimensions of mural 12′ wide x 6′6″ high.
3. Plan of Lobby.

SUMMIT, NEW JERSEY, POST OFFICE

Tipton, Indiana, Post Office (right)

Architect: S.A.O. Louis A. Simon, Supervising Architect.
Mural in Lobby by Donald Mattison.
Subject Matter: A. *Indiana Farming.*
Key to Drawings:
4. Elevation of end wall, showing position of mural. Dimensions of mural 12′ wide x 7′ high.
5. Plan of Lobby.

TIPTON, INDIANA, POST OFFICE

Trenton, New Jersey, Post Office and Court House (below)

Architect: S.A.O. James A. Wetmore, Acting Supervising Architect.
Murals in Lobby by Charles W. Ward.
Subject Matter:
A. *The Second Battle of Trenton.*
B. *Glass Manufacture.*
C. *Rural Delivery.*

Key to Drawings:
6. Elevation of end wall, showing position of mural over three doors. Dimensions of mural 17′ wide x 5′6″ high.
7. Elevation of wall over entrance door, showing dimensions of mural. Executed under the Public Works of Art Project and already installed. Dimensions of mural 11′6″ wide x 6′ high.
8. Elevation of end wall, showing position of mural over two doors. Dimensions of mural 17′ wide x 5′6″ high.
9. Half Plan of Lobby.

TRENTON, NEW JERSEY, POST OFFICE

Vandalia, Illinois, Post Office (right)

VANDALIA, ILLINOIS, POST OFFICE

Architect: S.A.O. Louis A. Simon, Supervising Architect.

Mural in Lobby by Aaron Bohrod.

Subject Matter: *Old State Capitol, Vandalia.*

Key to Drawings:

1. Elevation of end wall, showing position of mural. Dimensions of mural 10'4" wide x 4' high.
2. Plan of Lobby.

Ventura, California, Post Office (below)

VENTURA, CALIFORNIA, POST OFFICE

Architect: Harold E. Burket.

All-over murals in Lobby by Gordon Kenneth Grant, assisted by Herman Cherry, Ellwood Graham and Howard Wertman.

Subject Matter: *Agriculture and Industries in Ventura:*

Citrus Fruit Industry:
A. Subject Matter Undetermined.
B. *Dairy.*
C. *Cultivating the Growth.*
D. *Picking the Fruit.*
E. *Packing the Fruit.*

F. *Horses.*
Bean Industry:
G. *Collecting the Beans.*
H. *Sorting and Putting Beans in Sacks.*
I. *Crushing.*

Oil Industry:
J. *Piping.*
K. *Pumping.*
L. *Putting into Cans for Retail.*

Key to Drawings:

3. Elevation of end wall, showing position of mural over screen. Dimensions of mural 15' wide x 7'6" high.
4. Elevation of end wall, showing position of mural, broken by door. Dimensions of mural 15' wide x 7'6" high.
5. Elevation of screen wall, showing positions of murals broken by nine grilles. Dimensions of painted surface, 82' wide x 7'6" high.
6. Elevation of outside wall, public lobby, showing positions of murals broken by door and windows. Dimensions of painted surface, 82' wide x 7'6" high.
7. Plan of Lobby.

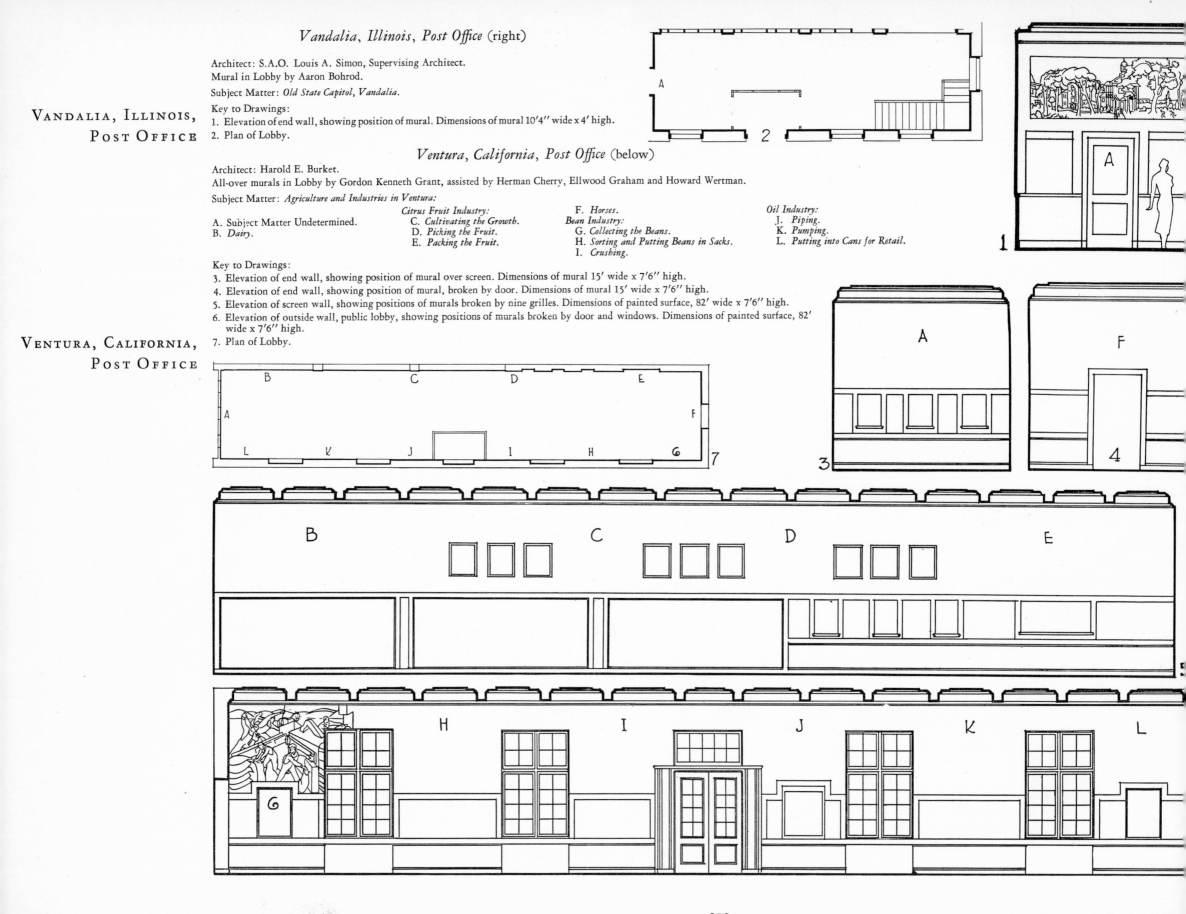

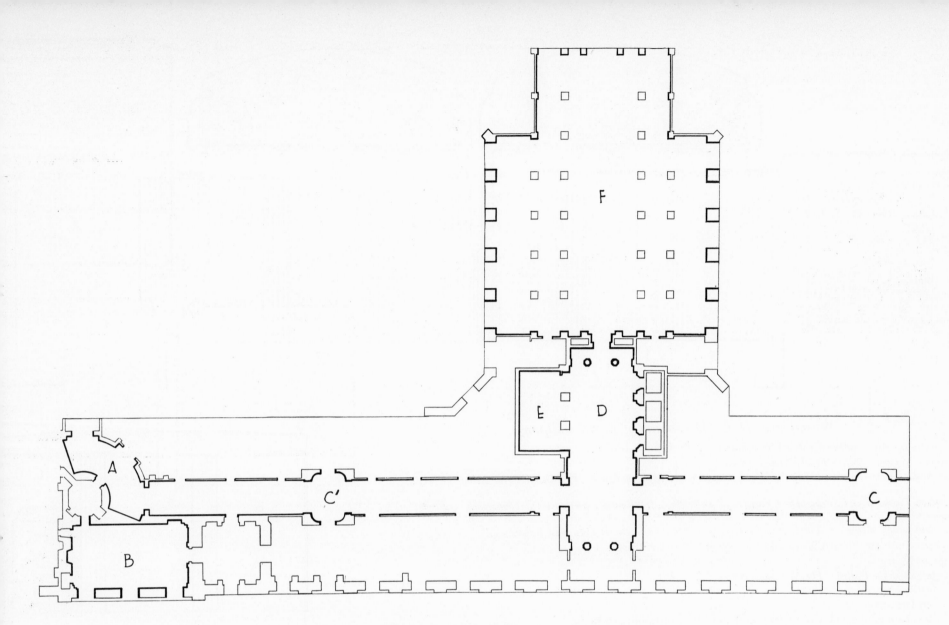

Washington, D. C., Department of Justice Building

Architects: Zantzinger and Borie.

Partial Plan of Fifth Floor, Department of Justice Building, showing positions of
murals by the following artists, which are being, or have been, executed:

Letters to the right of artists' names refer to locations of murals indicated on plan:

Louis Bouché	A.	George Biddle	E finished.
Leon Kroll	B.	Maurice Sterne	F.
Henry Varnum Poor C & C' finished.		(Boardman Robinson, murals in main	
John Steuart Curry D.		stairway from first to second floor).	

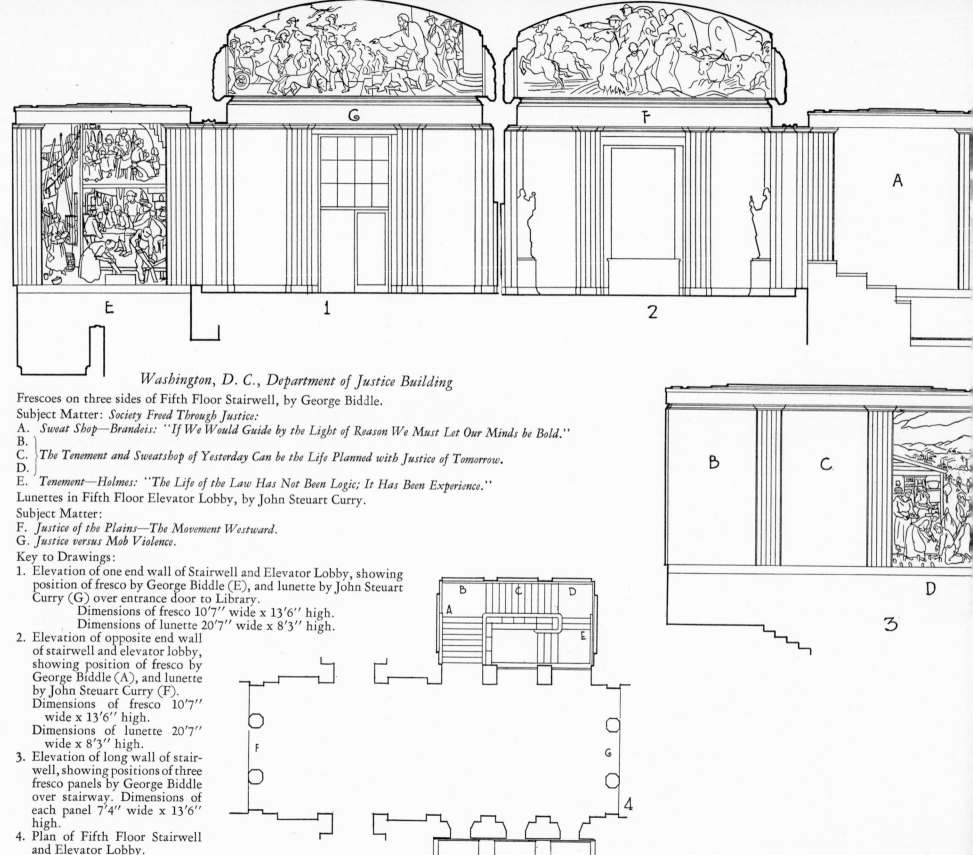

Washington, D. C., Department of Justice Building

Frescoes on three sides of Fifth Floor Stairwell, by George Biddle.

Subject Matter: *Society Freed Through Justice:*

A. *Sweat Shop—Brandeis: "If We Would Guide by the Light of Reason We Must Let Our Minds be Bold."*

B.
C. } *The Tenement and Sweatshop of Yesterday Can be the Life Planned with Justice of Tomorrow.*
D.

E. *Tenement—Holmes: "The Life of the Law Has Not Been Logic; It Has Been Experience."*

Lunettes in Fifth Floor Elevator Lobby, by John Steuart Curry.

Subject Matter:

F. *Justice of the Plains—The Movement Westward.*
G. *Justice versus Mob Violence.*

Key to Drawings:

1. Elevation of one end wall of Stairwell and Elevator Lobby, showing position of fresco by George Biddle (E), and lunette by John Steuart Curry (G) over entrance door to Library.
    Dimensions of fresco 10'7" wide x 13'6" high.
    Dimensions of lunette 20'7" wide x 8'3" high.

2. Elevation of opposite end wall of stairwell and elevator lobby, showing position of fresco by George Biddle (A), and lunette by John Steuart Curry (F).
    Dimensions of fresco 10'7" wide x 13'6" high.
    Dimensions of lunette 20'7" wide x 8'3" high.

3. Elevation of long wall of stairwell, showing positions of three fresco panels by George Biddle over stairway. Dimensions of each panel 7'4" wide x 13'6" high.

4. Plan of Fifth Floor Stairwell and Elevator Lobby.

1

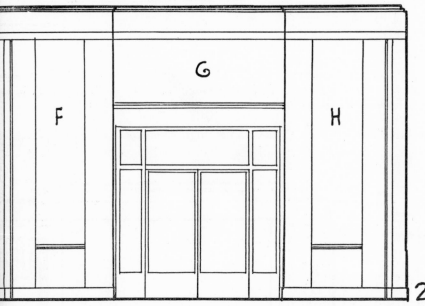

2

3

Washington, D. C., Department of Justice Building

Murals in curved space outside Attorney General's Office, by Louis Bouché, assisted by Charles Bateman.

Subject Matter: *Violent and Peaceful Functions of the Department of Justice:*

A. *Violent Functions of the Department of Justice:*

  A Typical Court House Scene in a Small American Community.
  Crimes on the High Seas.
  Crimes on Indian Reservations.
  Alcoholic Beverage Violations.
  Sabotage.
  Gangsters—Racketeering.
  Seaboard Fortifications.
  Espionage.
  A Prison Building—Kidnapping.
  A Board of Parole.
  U. S. Supreme Court Building.
  The Capitol.

B. *An Arrest.*
C. *American Eagle and Symbols of Justice.*
D. *Immigration Scene.*

E. *Peaceful Functions of the Department of Justice:*

  Radio Act.
  Safety Appliance Act.
  Aeronautics.
  Labor—Industry.
  Interstate Commerce.
  National Banking Act.
  Postal Laws.
  Pure Foods Act.
  Meat Inspection Act.
  Indian Lands and Affairs.

F.
G. *Symbols of Justice.*
H.

Key to Drawings:

1. Elevation (extended) of curved space directly outside Attorney General's Office, showing positions of murals. Dimensions of total area, broken by door, 48′ wide x 11′ high.

2. Elevation (extended) of wall opposite door to Attorney General's Office, showing positions of mural panels. Two side panels 3′ wide x 11′ high. Central panel 9′ wide x 11′ high.

3. Plan of Corridor.

WASHINGTON, D. C.,
DEPARTMENT OF
JUSTICE BUILDING

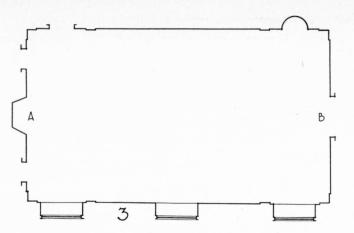

Washington, D. C., Department of Justice Building

Murals in the Attorney General's Private Office, by Leon Kroll.
Subject Matter:
A. *Triumph of Justice.*　　　　B. *Defeat of Justice.*
Key to Drawings:
1. Elevation of end wall, showing position of lunette over fireplace.
2. Elevation of end wall, showing position of lunette over entrance door.
　Dimensions of lunettes, 21′8″ wide x 8′6″ high.
3. Plan of Lobby.

Murals in two identical breaks in Corridor on Fifth Floor, by Henry Varnum Poor.
Break C—*Bureau of Lands and Customs.* A. *Unloading.* B. *Examination and Customs.* C. *Surveying New Lands.*—*Bureau of Prisons.* D. *Imprisonment.* E. *Vocational Training.* F. *Relea*
Break C′—*Crime Prevention.* A′. *Anti-Trust Division.* B′. *Kidnapping.* C′. *Bureau of Investigation.* D′. *Tennessee Valley Authority.* E′. *Symbols of Justice.* F′. *Gold Case.*
Key to Drawings:
4. Elevation of one side of break, showing office door and positions of three mural panels. Dimensions of flanking panels 3′ wide x 13′6″ high. Dimensions of central panels 6′ wide x 4′ high.
5. Elevation of opening from break to corridor, showing positions of two narrow panels flanking opening.
6. Ground Plan of Break (other break similar).

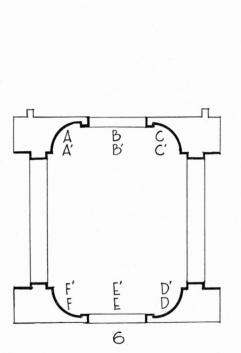

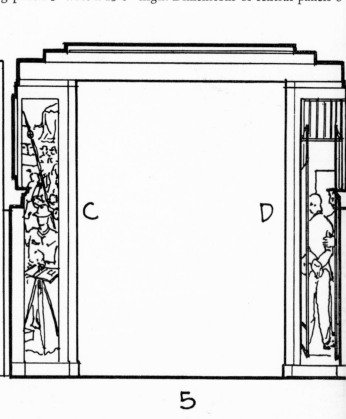

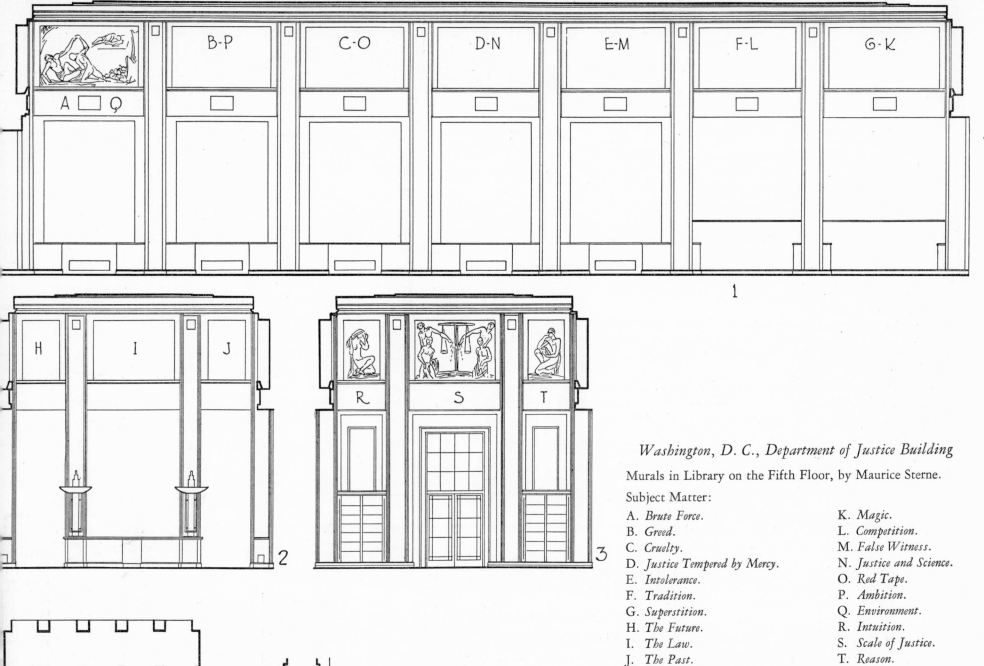

Washington, D. C., Department of Justice Building

Murals in Library on the Fifth Floor, by Maurice Sterne.

Subject Matter:

A. *Brute Force.*	K. *Magic.*
B. *Greed.*	L. *Competition.*
C. *Cruelty.*	M. *False Witness.*
D. *Justice Tempered by Mercy.*	N. *Justice and Science.*
E. *Intolerance.*	O. *Red Tape.*
F. *Tradition.*	P. *Ambition.*
G. *Superstition.*	Q. *Environment.*
H. *The Future.*	R. *Intuition.*
I. *The Law.*	S. *Scale of Justice.*
J. *The Past.*	T. *Reason.*

Key to Drawings:

1. Elevation of one side wall, showing openings into lower part of Library and positions of mural panels. (Other side similar.) Dimensions of panels, each, 10′ wide x 6′ high.

2. Elevation of one end wall, showing positions of murals over delivery desk.

3. Elevation of opposite end wall, showing positions of three murals over entrance doors.

   Dimensions of four flanking panels 3′ wide x 6′ high.
   Dimensions of two central panels 8′ wide x 6′ high.

4. Plan of Library.

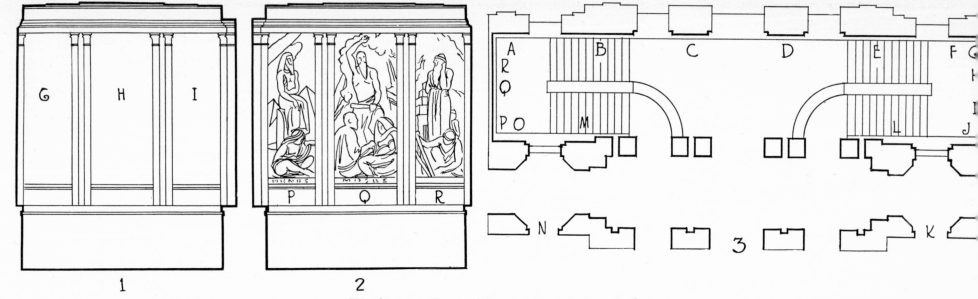

1

2

Washington, D. C., Department of Justice Building

Murals in Main Stairhall from First to Second Floor, by Boardman Robinson.

Subject Matter: *Great Codifiers of the Law*:

A. *Coke.*	C. *Blackstone.*	E. *Constitution.*	G. *Gaius.*	I. *Justinian.*	K. *Christ.*	M. *Holmes.*	O. *Grotius.*	Q. *Moses.*
B. *Magna Charta.*	D. *Marshall.*	F. *Kent.*	H. *Solon.*	J. *Henry II.*	L. *Bracton.*	N. *Socrates.*	P. *Menes.*	R. *Hammurabi.*

Key to Drawings:

1, 2. Elevations of end walls of main stairway, showing positions of six mural panels. Dimensions of four flanking panels 3'11" wide x 12'6" high; two central panels 5'7" wide x 12'6" high.

3. Plan of stairhall and corridor on second floor.

4. Elevation of outside wall, showing positions of six mural panels between windows. Dimensions of four flanking panels 3'11" wide x 12'6" high; two central panels 10'4" wide x 12'6" high.

5. Elevation of inside wall, showing three central openings from stairway to corridor, and two lateral openings to corridor flanked by four panels. Dimensions of four flanking panels 3'11" wide x 12'6" high. Also showing positions of two small panels (K and N) on wall in corridor behind lateral openings. Dimensions of two small panels 5'6" wide x 5'3" high. (The drawing is found on the following page.)

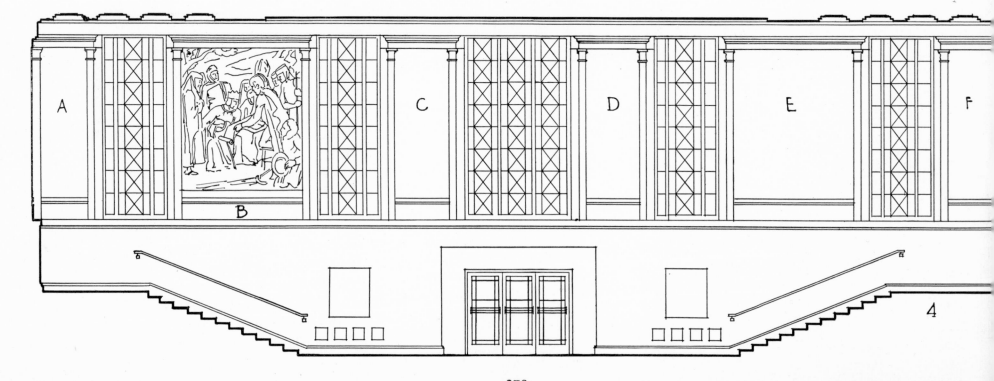

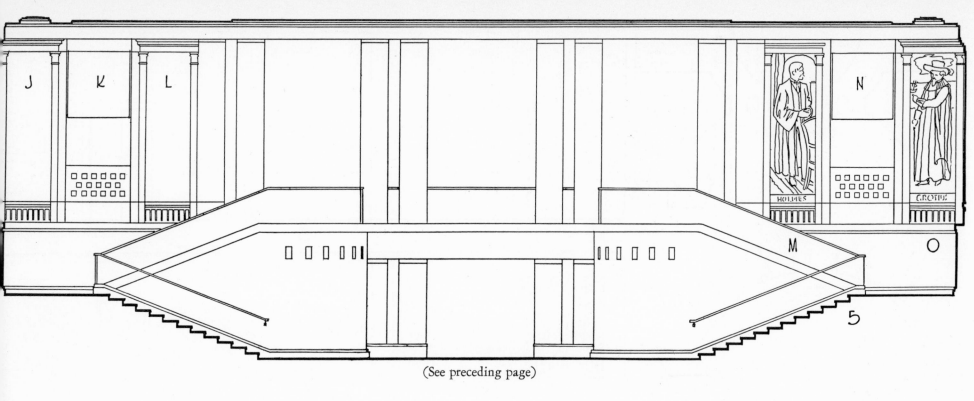

(See preceding page)

WASHINGTON, D.C.,
POST OFFICE DEPART-
MENT BUILDING,
BENJAMIN FRANKLIN
POSTAL STATION

Washington, D. C., Post Office Department Building

Architects: Delano and Aldrich.
Mural in Entrance Vestibule to the Benjamin Franklin Postal Station, by Tom Lea.

Subject Matter: A. *Texas Farm—Penetration of Isolation by Post.*

Key to Drawings:

6. Elevation of end wall, showing position of mural. Dimensions of mural 6′ wide x 11′6″ high.
7. Plan of Vestibule and Half Plan of Lobby.

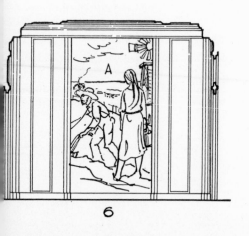

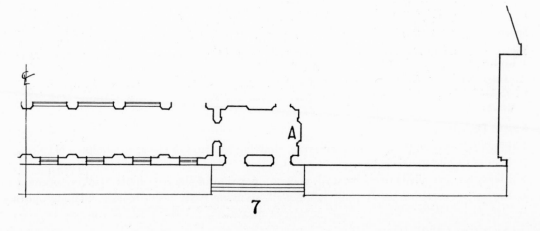

Washington, D. C., Post Office Department Building

Architects: Delano and Aldrich.

Murals in North and South Elevator Lobbies on five floors, at either side of the central opening of the building. The Lobbies are similar except for a slight difference of ceiling height on each floor. One plan elevation is being used for all. Murals are located as follows:

SOUTH LOBBY

Seventh Floor *Karl Free*

Two panels, each, 13'6'' wide x 6'6'' high.
A. *French Explorers and Indians.*
B. *Arrival of Mail in New Amsterdam.*

Sixth Floor *George Harding*

Two panels, each, 13'6'' wide x 6' high.
A. *Franklin and His Administration of the Philadelphia Post Office.*
B. *Carrying of Dispatches in the Revolution.*

Fifth Floor *Ward Lockwood*

Two panels, each, 13'6'' wide x 6' high.
A. *Opening of the Southwest.*
B. *Building of the Railroads in the West.*

Fourth Floor *Alfred Crimi*

Two panels, each, 13'6'' wide x 7' high.
A. *Post Office Work Room.*
B. *Transportation of Mail.*

Second Floor *Rockwell Ke[nt]*

Two panels, each, 13'6'' wide x [6'] high.
The Colonies:
A. *Mail Service in Puerto Rico.*
B. *Mail Service in Alaska—D[og] Sleds and Air Mail.*

NORTH LOBBY

Seventh Floor *William Palmer*

Two panels, each, 13'6'' wide x 7' high.
A. *Stage Coach Attacked by Bandits.*
B. *Covered Wagon Attacked by Indians.*

Sixth Floor *Doris Lee*

Two panels, each, 13'6'' wide x 6' high.
A. *Country Post.*
B. *General Store and Post Office.*

Fifth Floor *Frank Mechau*

Two panels, each, 13'6'' wide x 6' high.
A. *Pony Express.*
B. *Dangers of the Mail.*

Fourth Floor *Reginald Marsh*

Two panels, each, 13'6'' wide x 7' high.
A. *Sorting Mail.*
B. *Transfer of Mail from Liner to Tugboat.*

Second Floor *Eugene Sava[ge]*

Two panels, each, 13'6'' wide x [?] high.
A and B. *The Post as a Connecti[ng] Thread in Human Life.*

Key to Drawings:

1. Plot Plan of part of Post Office Building, showing location of elevator lobbies—(N) North Lobby, (S) South Lobby.
2. Plan of One Elevator Lobby.
3. Elevation (extended) of lobby wall, showing position of elevator doors, flanking opening to circular staircase.
4. Elevation (extended) of elevator lobby wall, showing positions of murals, flanking opening to corridor.

*Sketches not yet complete[d]

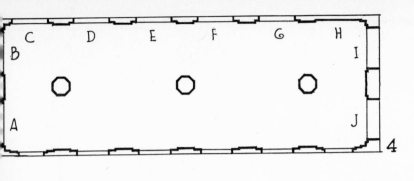

Washington, D.C., Treasury Department, Procurement Division, Building

Architect: S.A.O. Louis A. Simon, Supervising Architect.

Murals in Lobby by Harold Weston, assisted by Phillip F. Bell.

Subject Matter:

Wall to the left of entrance.

Branch of Supply:

A. *Fuel Depot.*   B. *Loading Platform.*

Small predella panels underneath:

Pipe Lines.	*Carving.*
Heating.	*Brick and Plaster Work.*
Elevators.	*Painting.*
Bids for Contractors.	

Wall directly opposite entrance:

Construction:

C. *Surveying (California).*   F. *Steel Superstructures (New York).*

D. *Pouring Concrete (Middle West).*   G. *Brick Work (New England).*

E. *Steel Foundations (Washington, D.C.).*   H. *Roofing (Florida).*

Wall to the right of entrance:

Architecture:

I. *Recent Buildings Built by the Treasury.*

J. *Older Buildings Built by the Government.*

Small predella panels underneath:

Piping.
Architectural Designing, Draughting Room.
Mimeographing.
Map of the United States, Showing Location of Work Being Done.
Multigraphing.
Making Blue-prints.
Filing.

Key to Drawings:

1. Elevations of two end walls, showing positions of murals interrupted by column.
2. Dimensions of each mural 20'5" wide x 10' high.
3. Elevation of wall opposite entrance, showing positions of six murals over elevator doors. Dimensions of each mural 6' wide x 8'6" high.
4. Plan of Lobby.

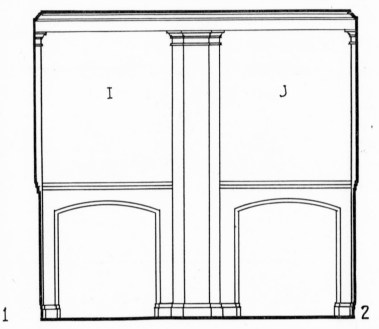

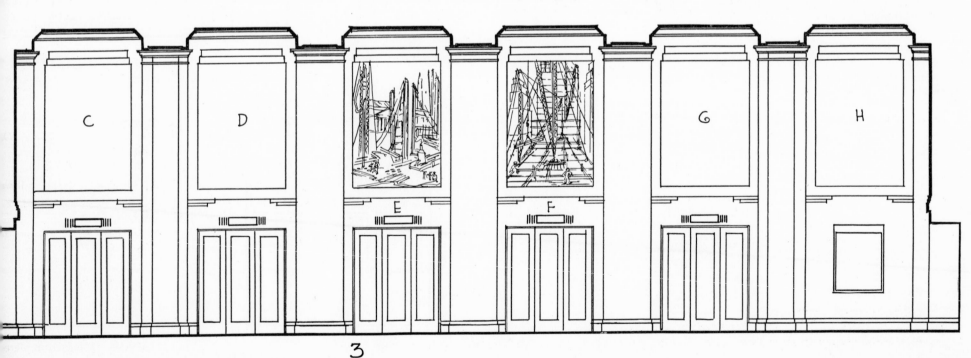

WHITE RIVER JUNCTION, VERMONT, POST OFFICE

White River Junction, Vermont, Post Office (right)

Architect: S.A.O. Louis A. Simon, Supervising Architect.

Mural in Lobby by Douglass Crockwell.

Subject Matter: A. *Industries of Vermont.*

Key to Drawings:

1. Elevation of end wall, showing position of mural. Dimensions of mural 16′ wide x 6′6″ high.
2. Plan of Lobby.

Wichita, Kansas, Post Office and Court House (below)

Architect: S.A.O. Louis A. Simon, Supervising Architect.

Murals in Lobby by Richard Haines and Ward Lockwood.

Subject Matter:

A. *Kansas Farming* (Haines).   B. *Pioneers in Kansas* (Lockwood).

Key to Drawings:

3. Elevation of one end wall showing position of mural. (The other end is similar.) Dimensions of each mural 10′6″ wide x 4′7″ high.
4. Half Plan of Lobby.

WICHITA, KANSAS, POST OFFICE AND COURT HOUSE

Woodland, California, Post Office (below)

Architect: S.A.O. Louis A. Simon, Supervising Architect.

Murals in Lobby by George Harris.

Subject Matter:

A and B. *Farm Life.*

Key to Drawings:

5. Elevation of end wall, showing position of mural over door and bulletin boards.
6. Elevation of end wall, showing position of mural over screen. Dimensions of each mural 12′ wide x 5′ high.
7. Plan of Lobby.

WOODLAND, CALIFORNIA, POST OFFICE

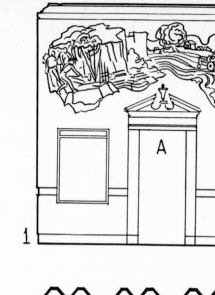

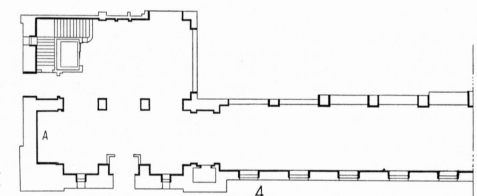

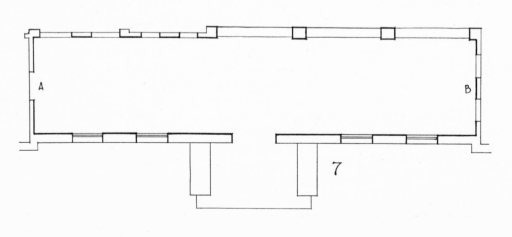

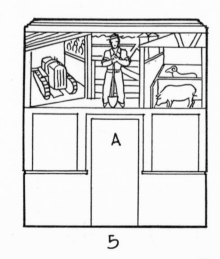

THE TREASURY DEPARTMENT ART PROGRAM
By EDWARD BRUCE

UNDER THE Constitution (Article I, Section 8, Paragraph 17) Congress was given power to exercise exclusive legislation over all places required for "needful buildings," purchased with the consent of the legislature of the state where such properties were to be located. Control of the construction of federal buildings was entrusted to the President. Washington, Jefferson and Jackson often personally selected the most skilful architects available. Later, while the building activities of the Federal Government were not definitely coordinated until the 1830's, there are indications that Congress consistently entrusted the Secretary of the Treasury with the duty of purchasing sites and constructing adequate Federal buildings, which were built under the supervision of a local commission. This in turn was appointed by the Secretary, with local architects and superintendents.

In July, 1836, Robert Mills was appointed "Federal Architect" by Andrew Jackson, in order to design certain Federal buildings, including the Treasury, for which Congress had appropriated funds. Mills occupied this position until 1842, during which time he designed, besides the Treasury, the Patent Office and the old Post Office, and had general charge of the erection of buildings situated outside of Washington.

In 1853 a uniform method for the construction of public buildings was adopted by Secretary Guthrie to organize a "Construction Branch of the Treasury Department." An officer from the Engineer Corps of the Army was detailed by the Secretary of War and assigned to duty in charge of this Branch.

With the development of the country, there was a steady growth in the work of this new Construction Branch. In 1886 the following statement was reported: "The question very naturally arises as to what had become of the officer known as the 'Engineer in Charge,' and who had made the annual reports from 1853 to 1861, inclusive. A careful search has been made for this missing official, but he appears to have not only vacated his office, but to have taken his official robes with him, and his disappearance is surrounded with such profound mystery that no trace of the causes leading to his disappearance were found. We are left to conjecture. It is presumed than when the Civil War commenced, the officers of the War Department found ample scope for their legitimate operations in the arts of war. The arts of peace were then left to the tender mercies of civil experts, and the 'Engineer in Charge' has never found his way back."

Later, in 1871, the first appropriation was made, definitely placing public construction under the Supervising Architect of the Treasury Department. The activities of this office became increasingly important, particularly after the passage of the Public Building Act of May, 1926. This program included the development of the "Triangle Area" in Washington and construction of needed Federal buildings throughout the country, much necessary building having been neglected after the war.

Procurement Division

IN JUNE, 1933, the President authorized the creation of a Procurement Division in the Treasury Department, and in November appointed Rear Admiral Christian Joy Peoples as Director. He was charged with "the function of determination of policies and methods of procurement, warehousing and distribution of property, facilities, structures, improvements, machinery, equipment, stores and supplies."

The various activities which were joined to form the Procurement Division were formerly under an Assistant Secretary of the Treasury. For convenience and control the work of the Division was divided into two main working parts: The Branch of Supply, and the Public Buildings Branch.

The principal functions of the latter, by order of the Secretary of the Treasury, are as follows:

The collection and preparation of data and estimates for submission to Congress as a basis for the legislative authorization of public building projects;

The acquisition of lands for Federal building sites, including the taking of proposals therefor, the inspection of various properties offered, and the making of contracts for the purchase of such sites;

The preparation of drawings, estimates and specifications for public building construction, including the taking of proposals and the entering into contracts for such construction;

The supervision (through a field force) of the performance of contracts for construction, rebuilding, expanding and repairing of public buildings;

The operation, repair and maintenance of all public buildings outside the District of Columbia under control of the Treasury Department, including the employment and supervision of the custodial forces for such buildings, also supplying furniture and equipment therefor.

The repair and preservation of all public buildings, formerly under control of the Treasury Department, which were transferred to the Post Office and Interior Departments under the provision of Executive Order No. 6166.

Under the two Emergency Acts of 1933-35, Congress appropriated funds to the Treasury Department for public building construction and it has been concerned in building these new projects authorized by the Emergency Acts, as well as in completing the 1926 Program, an architectural undertaking of impressive proportions.

The drawings, specifications and estimated costs for the proposed buildings are prepared in the office of the Supervising Architect, Louis A. Simon. Bids taken for the construction are sent to a Board of Award, which makes recommendations to the Assistant Director of Procurement.

When a project reaches the construction stage, it is handled by the Supervising Engineer's office in collaboration with that of the Supervising Architect.

District Engineer Offices

IN ORDER to facilitate the handling of the execution of projects in the field, and for close control of repairs and maintenance, eight district offices were created instead of the former number of six. These are given definite authority in connection with construction problems, and are located in Boston, New York, Washington, D. C., Chicago, Atlanta, Kansas City, Missouri, Dallas and San Francisco.

Construction has been speeded up and made more efficient because of this reorganization of the field forces. It permits quicker decisions from the inspection engineers in adjusting difficulties and greater understanding of local labor regulations. In July, 1934, 32% of the projects lagged more than 10% behind normal progress—in December of the same year after the reorganization, only 14% of the projects were in this category.

Design Committee

IN ORDER to obtain the private architect's point of view, and to secure the best possible designs for public buildings, a committee of architectural consultants meets once a week to discuss and pass on the work being released by the Division. This Committee now consists of Charles Z. Klauder, of Philadelphia; Aymar Embury, II, of New York; Philip B. Maher, of Chicago; Henry Shepley, of Boston; and the Supervising Architect. These architects review the drawings by members of the Supervising Architect's Office, those by consulting architects working in Washington, and those by private architects having contracts for public buildings.

As the work of the Treasury Department Art Program is concerned with the decoration of Federal buildings, its place is obviously in the office of the Supervising Architect, where cooperation between the architects, painters and sculptors employed by the Program can be developed to its highest point.

The Treasury Department has become one of the greatest, if not the greatest, architectural client and producer in the world and its architectural activities affect communities of every size from coast to coast. It has had, as one of its traditional duties, supervision of most Federal architecture and has incidentally been concerned with murals and sculpture in public buildings. The present program is the first one completely organized to combine painting and sculpture with architecture in a coherent production unit. This cooperation between the three great arts is what gives this program its essential character of permanence and its social and educational force.

Public Works of Art Project

FOLLOWING IS A brief account of the procedure used, and a summary report of what has actually been accomplished by this Program, the idea of which came out of the Public Works of Art Project, initiated on December 8, 1933, under a grant from the Civil Works Administration to the Treasury Department. The Public Works of Art Project was organized as an employment program for artists at craftsmen's wages, under the direction of Edward Bruce and Forbes Watson. Besides the Washington administrative organization, the country was divided into sixteen regions, each in charge of a volunteer committee which selected and employed artists and supervised the work in their region. The disinterested and efficient help of these six hundred volunteer men and women who served on the various regional and state sub-committees was of the utmost importance to the success of the Project.

Artists were selected on the basis of professional qualifications and need of employment. The "American Scene" was suggested as subject matter, but not insisted upon, the utmost freedom of expression being allowed. 15,663 works were executed, consisting of a number of murals and many paintings, sculptures, water colors, and prints, augmented by iron work, pottery, weaving, woodcarving, and work in other mediums. The collection belongs to the Federal Government, and its various items have been allocated to institutions supported, in part or in whole by taxes. A double purpose already has been served by placing these works of art in public buildings. They have added interest to the buildings and have valuably increased the fame of the artists who made them.

Section of Painting and Sculpture

THE SUCCESS of this initial cooperation between the Government and the artists, which officially terminated on June 30, 1934, led to the formation of the permanent Section of Painting and Sculpture, created by the Secretary of the Treasury, Henry Morgenthau, Jr., on October 16, 1934, for the decoration of the new buildings being erected under the large building program. The chief objectives of the work of the Section are defined by the Secretary's order:

(1) *To secure suitable art of the best quality available for the embellishment of public buildings.*

(2) *To carry out this work in such a way as will assist in stimulating, as far as practicable, development of art in this country and reward what is regarded as the outstanding talent which develops.*

(3) *So far as consistent with a high standard of art, to employ local talent.*

(4) *To endeavor to secure the cooperation of people throughout the country interested in the arts and whose judgment in connection with art has the respect of the Section in selecting artists for the work to be done and criticism and advice as to their production.*

(5) *In carrying out this work, to make every effort to afford an opportunity to all artists on the sole test of their qualifications as artists and, accordingly, to encourage competitions wherever practicable.*

The Section is concerned with the decoration of Federal Buildings under the Treasury Department: post offices, court houses, marine hospitals, etc., in process of being built. Only those buildings for which money is available under their own building funds, and which have suitable spaces for murals and sculpture, offer opportunities for the initiation of competitions.

The plans of all new buildings are studied by a member of the Section of Painting and Sculpture; spaces and decorative suggestions are then discussed with the architect of the building. When suitable spaces occur, a monetary reservation is set aside from the building fund. The expenditure of this reservation is authorized by the Director of Procurement, for a mural painting or a piece of sculpture, if it has not been necessary to use it in the construction of the building. The amount of money reserved for painting and sculpture, or both, is estimated at approximately one per cent of the building's cost.

Local Competitions

WHEN THE money has become available, the Section invites an expert with taste and discrimination, an artist who does not wish to enter the competition, a museum director, the head of an art association who lives in the vicinity of the building in question, or some other expert, to act as chairman of a committee to run the competition. The chairman is

sent a letter of instruction, a form announcement which specifies the amount of money, the size of the space, the scale of sketches, where and when they are to be submitted. He is asked to appoint a jury consisting of the architect of the building and one or two other persons. The chairman goes over this form announcement with his committee, fills in the dates, etc., makes suggestions and returns it to Washington. This corrected announcement is mimeographed in quantity and returned, with group of blueprints. The competition is announced. The local committee notifies directly the artists known to them and, through the local press and otherwise, informs all artists in their region of the forthcoming competition. The competitors submit anonymous designs usually after a designing period of three months.

The following is an example of a form announcement:

deal with the Post, local history, past or present, local industry, pursuits or landscape, the committee feels of important that the artist realize that the central idea it the Postal Service is communication, by which experiences, ideas, and goods are shared throughout the civilized world. This element of communication, the committee believes, need not be represented by the more obvious symbols of aeroplanes, trains, packet ships, etc., but might take on great dramatic and human significance. The Post Office, moreover, is the one concrete link between every community of individuals and the Federal Government, and in addition to mail service, through such departments as postal savings, money orders, etc., functions importantly in the human structure of the community. As distinguished and vital a conception as possible along such lines is desired.

The artist agrees to make such revision of his competition designs as will be necessary for approval by the Director of Procurement.

The artist who receives the commission will be required to pay all expenses in connection with the execution and installation of this work.

The sum of $2,000.00 will be paid for the mural in three separate installments.

The first installment, $600.00, will be payable after formal approval by the Director of Procurement of the design; which design shall thereupon become the property of the Government; and after the successful competitor has signed the contract for execution of the mural.

The second installment, $500.00, will be payable when in the opinion of the Director the mural is one-half complete.

The balance, $900.00, will be payable after the mural is completed, installed and approved by the Director and a negative and one print, 8" x 10", showing the mural installed, are furnished.

The artist will be required to furnish a bond of $500.00 for the faithful performance of his contract.

The medium and the quality of the materials to be used by the artist must be approved by the local committee and by the Director of Procurement.

The designs should be submitted, carrying charges prepaid or delivered in person, not later than October 1, 1936, at the Worcester Art Museum, Worcester, Mass.

The artists are required to furnish their designs in a 3" scale (i. e., 3" to the foot) and an architectural rendering in the scale of 1" to the foot with colors and materials of the interior simply indicated, in order to show the designs in their architectural setting.

The designs should give as clear an idea as possible as to how the proposed mural will look when completed. It would be advisable to look at the space itself before designing. Each design must be mounted or carried out on board sufficiently stiff to remain flat, with a border not greater than 4" at its widest point. Designs should be submitted without glass.

The design should not be signed. It should be accompanied with a plain, sealed envelope, enclosing the artist's name and address. These envelopes will be carefully numbered when received with the same number as the designs they accompany, and will remain unopened until after selection of the best design.

In other words, the local committee will submit all designs,

with the sealed envelopes unopened, to the Section of Painting and Sculpture, Procurement Division, Treasury Department, with its recommendations.

This is an open competition and is not limited to those artists invited. Any artist resident of or attached to the States of Maine, New Hampshire, Vermont, Massachusetts, Rhode Island, and Connecticut, who wishes to may enter.

Any artist may submit as many designs as he desires. Should he submit more than one design he should remember to send a sealed envelope, with his address, with each entry.

Artists submitting outstanding designs not actually used in this building will be seriously considered for appointment to do murals for other buildings in the program of the Section of Painting and Sculpture.

If, however, no designs are submitted which are of sufficient merit to justify a recommendation by the Section of Painting and Sculpture, no contracts will be awarded, and all designs will be returned to the artists.

Awards

THE COMMITTEE discusses these sketches and sends a letter of recommendation on the sketches, designated by number, to Washington. The designs are studied by the members of the Treasury Department Art Projects for a week or ten days.

The desire of the Washington office is to keep the Program as decentralized as possible and to encourage local recommendations, thus stimulating the artist's interest in the community as well as the community's interest in him. In practice, few local decisions have been reversed. In every case these reversals have been thoroughly discussed with the local committee before the announcement has been made; but the final responsibility of the decision rests with the recommendation of the Section of Painting and Sculpture to the Director of Procurement. The policy of the Section has been to develop regional art and artists as much as this is consistent with the obtaining of good art.

After the winning design has been selected, and not until then, the envelopes are opened, and the names of the contestants revealed. The Section submits its recommendations to the Supervising Architect. If he approves of the choice made, the Director of Procurement makes a final approval and the artist is given a Government contract to execute the finished mural or sculpture.

Exhibitions

FROM THE first, the Section has encouraged exhibitions of designs and models submitted in competition, believing that such exhibitions would serve two purposes: they would show both the public and the artists exactly what the Section was doing and awaken the interest of different communities in the work, while they would make clear to the competing

artists how different individuals solved the mural problem and wherein they failed or succeeded.

Payments and Supervision

THE PRICE of the murals is estimated from ten to twenty dollars a square foot. This rate was decided upon after conference with a number of experienced artists, who felt it was a fair and just rate. The usual time allowed an artist under contract is two years, but this allowance is flexible and may be extended. The quality of the work, as it progresses, is supervised by the local chairman, with whom the Section has a contract for a small fee, varying from fifty to two hundred dollars for current expenses, such as postage, expressage, telephone calls, telegrams, and travel. During the three months of a competition and the six months to two years duration of the artist's contract, the chairman is called upon for various incidental services. His fee is obviously a nominal sum and does not represent adequate payment for the work or interest of this public spirited citizen. It is intended to pay incidental expenses. This service virtually becomes a voluntary one which has been of inestimable value to the successful working of the project.

First National Competition

THE LARGEST and most important undertaking which was available when the Section of Painting and Sculpture began, was to obtain murals and sculpture for the Post Office and Justice Department Buildings in Washington, D. C. It was decided to consider these two buildings as one project. After conferences with the officials concerned, with Messrs. Delano and Aldrich and Messrs. Zantzinger and Borie, and with the Chairman of the Commission of Fine Arts, the painting and sculpture was divided into twelve painting and fourteen sculpture units for one building, and ten painting units for the other.

As a result of these discussions, an Advisory Committee to the Section of Painting and Sculpture, composed of twenty-one experts from all parts of the country, was appointed. This committee was composed of the following members:

John S. Ankeney, Formerly Director of the Dallas Museum of Art, Dallas, Texas; C. L. Borie, Jr., Architect, Justice Department Building; Homer S. Cummings, Attorney General of the United States; Frederick A. Delano, Chairman, National Planning Board; William A. Delano, Architect, Post Office Department Building; James A. Farley, Postmaster General of the United States; Robert Harshe, Director, Chicago Institute of Art, Chicago; Walter S.

Heil, Director, M. H. de Young Memorial Museum, San Francisco; Anna Hyatt Huntington, Sculptor; Bancel La Farge, Painter; Henry Allen Moe, Secretary, Guggenheim Memorial Foundation, New York City; Charles Moore, Chairman, Commission of Fine Arts, Washington, D. C.; William Milliken, Director, Cleveland Museum of Art, Cleveland, Ohio; C. Powell Minnigerode, Director, Corcoran Gallery of Art, Washington, D. C.; Ernest Peixotto, Formerly President, Society of Mural Painters; Duncan Phillips, Founder of Phillips Memorial Gallery, Washington, D. C.; Henry Schnakenberg, Painter; Eugene Speicher, Painter; Justice Harlan F. Stone, Justice, United States Supreme Court; Francis Taylor, Director, Worcester Museum of Art, Worcester, Mass.; Harry Wehle, Curator of Painting, Metropolitan Museum of Art.

Attorney General Cummings, Postmaster General Farley and Frederick A. Delano acted as ex-officio members of the committee and took no part in the selection of the artists who were appointed or invited to compete.

Without conferring together, these gentlemen sent to the Section their individual lists of the twenty-two painters and fourteen sculptors whom they considered the outstanding artists in this country for this work. These lists were handed in confidentially.

A large number of artists throughout the country received one or more votes, but a group of eleven painters and two sculptors stood out in receiving at least three more votes than any of the other artists mentioned. With the approval of the architects of the buildings, these artists were recommended by the Section of Painting and Sculpture to the Director of Procurement for appointment. These artists were:

Painters: Thomas Benton, George Biddle, John Steuart Curry, Rockwell Kent, Leon Kroll, Reginald Marsh, Henry Varnum Poor, Boardman Robinson, Eugene Savage, Maurice Sterne, and Grant Wood (who resigned on account of previous commitments).
Sculptors: Paul Manship and William Zorach.

All the other artists who received a minority vote were invited to a national competition for the remaining eleven mural and twelve sculptural spaces. This list was amplified by additional names.

Painters were invited to compete, being divided into nearly equal groups. To each group specific subject matter was suggested.

107 sculptors had been suggested by the Advisory Committee and by the Section of Painting and Sculpture. It was felt that it would be unfair to ask so many individuals to make scale models for these twelve statues. Consequently, each sculptor was written to and asked to send in photographs of his work, if he were interested in competing. This comprehensive photographic material was reviewed by a jury, consisting of

Paul Manship, Maurice Sterne, and William Zorach. They recommended forty-eight sculptors to the Section of Painting and Sculpture, who were divided into units of four. Each group was invited to compete for one of twelve statues of mail carriers, the period and classification of each carrier being specified.

A jury of six painters: Leon Kroll, Bancel La Farge, Jonas Lie, Ernest Peixotto, Henry Schnakenberg, and Eugene Speicher, and three sculptors: Alice Decker, Paul Manship, and William Zorach, as well as the architects of the buildings: Messrs. William Adams Delano and Charles L. Borie, together with executives of the Section of Painting and Sculpture, spent three days examining 315 designs, submitted by 142 painters and sixty-two sculpture models submitted by fifty sculptors for the Post Office Department Building, together with ninety-one designs submitted by fifty-five painters for the Justice Department Building. The designs by the following artists were awarded the work in competition:

Painters: Alfred Crimi, Karl Free, George Harding, Ward Lockwood, Frank Mechau, and William C. Palmer. Two other artists were appointed: Doris Lee and Tom Lea, and both were asked to re-design.

Sculptors: Stirling Calder, Gaetano Cecere, Chaim Gross, Arthur Lee, Oronzio Maldarelli, Berta Margoulies, Attilio Piccirilli, Concetta Scaravaglione, Carl L. Schmitz, Louis Slobodkin, Heinz Warneke, and Sidney Waugh.

Besides the winners of this competition, eighty-two artists were invited to design murals for other post offices, as a result of good designs submitted in the competition, and sixteen sculptors were offered commissions.

This combination of competitions and appointments seems to be a fair method and lessens the speculative chances of the artists who enter the competitions of the Section. It enables a non-winning artist who has submitted good sketches to receive a commission. In other words, the competitions under the Section of Painting and Sculpture are not for a single job. Fine sketches result in a definite appointment, whenever the space is available.

Activities, October 16, 1934, to July 31, 1936

FORTY-SEVEN local competitions; fifty-one contracts awarded (this does not include the non-relife master artists who were appointed to T.R.A.P. mural assignments as a result of good sketches submitted in competitions); six national competitions held, three mural and three sculpture; sixty-two contracts awarded; forty-nine artists working on tentative projects; eighty-nine artists under contract; twenty-four completed projects; 1,852 artists have competed; 3,147 sketches have been submitted in competitions.

The Treasury Relief Art Project

ON JULY 25th, 1935, the Treasury Relief Project was formed by a grant of $530,784 a cated to the Treasury Department by the Wo Progress Administrator for the decoration of Fed buildings. At approximately the same time the Wo Progress Administration initiated its comprehens relief program for artists under the name of the Fed Art Project, under the direction of Holger Cahill.

The fund allocated to the Treasury Relief Art Pro is administered strictly according to the relief paym rules of the Works Progress Administration, un which the "going wage" varies from $69 to $10 month with all materials supplied, the average artist being $89 for ninety-six hours work. The Wo Progress Administration has allowed a twenty-five cent. non-relief exemption. The work produced is Federal buildings, old or new, which have no mo available under the building funds for murals or scu ture, but which have suitable spaces. Only artists w can meet Federal building mural and sculpture star ards are eligible to work on this Project, even wh they are on relief.

The total employment is 328, with 259 relief and six nine non-relief. The personnel of the Project consists practising, professional artists, with the exception three supervisors: Mrs. Alice M. Sharkey, of New Yo City; Mrs. Elizabeth S. Lane, of Boston; and Bern Roufberg, of Los Angeles. The supervisors intervi artists, handle negotiations with the National Emplo ment Service, discuss various projects with the artis architects and advisors, and help them in any way pos ble. They check the progress of the projects and ke the central office informed of developments.

All payrolls, except in California, New York C and Illinois, are made up in Washington, D. C. T checks are mailed twice a month directly to the artis

At the inception of the Project, lists of relief arti were requested from local advisors, and a number artists so recommended, or whose work was known this office, were placed on the Treasury Relief A Project. At the same time a number of non-relief mas artists were appointed in key localities, where grou of unemployed artists existed. Many of these non-rel appointments were made as a result of good sketch submitted in the competitions initiated by the Secti of Painting and Sculpture.

There are a great many buildings, both old and new, u der control and supervision of the Treasury Departmen Procurement Division. For this reason Federal building with suitable spaces for murals or sculpture, are like to be situated within a fifty mile radius of the home o relief or non-relief artist trained to meet the requiremen

A letter of appointment is written to the artist selected, including the instructions and rules of the project, the wages and hours, the procedure for obtaining assistants, and the method of filling out requisitions for materials. The central office also fills out a requisition form to the local employment office, requesting the services of the particular artist. If the master artist wants an assistant, one is secured. At the same time the master artist is sent a blueprint of the building for which he is to design murals, and a travel order. He or she is allowed two trips to the site of the building, if this should be necessary.

The central office confers with the architect of the building, asking for his advice and cooperation, and the artist meets him and discusses the mural problem with him. The architect also keeps in touch with the progress of the sketches. Both technical advice and information on local subject matter have been given by different members of the community. Architects, artists, and museum directors have helped with constructive criticism, while members of local art societies, of the Chamber of Commerce, of historical societies, have generously placed their knowledge of local history and subject matter at the disposal of the artists. As in the case of the Advisory Chairman to the Section of Painting and Sculpture, the voluntary help given by disinterested men and women has been absolutely essential to the success of the Project.

When the plan of the mural or sculpture has been thoroughly discussed locally, the artist sends in his suggested subject matter, and the architect and adviser send in their reports to the central office.

The designs vary from single panels to large and important all-over murals. The sketches, in the case of mural paintings, are worked out in the scale of 1½″ to 1′. Very often a full size detail is included. In sculpture, a plaster model for a free-standing figure at approximately a 2″ scale, or an outline drawing for a bas-relief, is submitted. The period allowed for designing is flexible and varies from six weeks to four, or more, months. When the preliminary sketches have been approved and discussed by the artist, the architect, and the adviser, they are sent to this office and are either recommended for approval to the Director of Procurement by the Executives of the Treasury Department Art Program and the Supervising Architect, or are returned to the artist for further development. The procedure of discussion and approval of sketches by the central office is handled in precisely the same manner as in the anonymous competitions initiated by the Section of Painting and Sculpture.

Sometimes an artist has been supplied with two or three assistants in designing large mural schemes. In some cases, he does not employ assistants until the sketches have been approved, and he is ready to work on the full size. The number of assistants varies from one to six. This is an optional matter with the master artist, who may have as many as he can use with efficiency. Most of the work is done in studios. In many cases, working space has been donated by museums or Federal departments. In a few cases, the work is done directly on the walls.

When the sketches have been finally approved, and not until then, the materials for projects are purchased through regular Procurement Division procedure. The New York storeroom has charge of this procedure for the entire country, with the exception of California.

The majority of the work done under the Project consists of murals and sculpture for post offices and court houses under the Treasury Department, but there has also been considerable cooperation with other Federal departments in obtaining for them mural painting, sculpture, posters, portraits, screens and easel paintings. This work will be reproduced in future volumes.

How Individual Paintings Are Distributed

THE PROJECT has not confined itself to painting of murals. It has engaged artists from all parts of the country to do water colors, small oils, gouaches, and prints. These depict local scenes, landscapes, figure compositions, and historical buildings. When completed the pictures are sent to the Washington office, and there held in reserve for exhibitions and future allocations. To give some idea of the eventual placing of these pictures, the following list of buildings and institutions to which they have already been or will be allocated, is submitted:

DISTRICT OF COLUMBIA WELFARE BOARD:
The Welfare Board receives individual pictures for the National Training School for Girls.

FEDERAL OFFICES:
Pictures are hung in the offices of executives and legislators, and have already stimulated a greater interest in the work of American artists among government workers. These pictures naturally are seen by a wide and varied audience.

HOWARD UNIVERSITY:
A group of easel paintings by negro artists is being reserved for this Federal University, which is under the Interior Department.

TREASURY DEPARTMENT:
(a) NARCOTIC FARM, LEXINGTON, KENTUCKY:
Individual pictures are sent to the Farm to decorate and make more agreeable the rooms of the patients.
(b) LEPER COLONY, CARVILLE, LOUISIANA:
Pictures are sent to the Colony to decorate the rooms of the individual cottages in which the patients live.
(c) MARINE HOSPITALS:
In addition to the murals being done in various marine hospitals, a considerable number of individual pictures are sent to them for the adornment of their rooms.

STATE DEPARTMENT:
A number of pictures are being sent to Unites States Embassies and Legations.

Framing Shop

THE INDIVIDUAL pictures are framed in a shop attached to the central office. This shop also has made a number of screens for the State Department and is executing a series of architectural models which on occasion will be used for exhibition purposes.

Traveling Exhibitions

FROM THE individual pictures five groups of twenty-four pictures each are being sent to various museums and art societies throughout the country. The exhibitions are available to all such institutions, but the transportation between each place must be paid for by the museums or societies holding the exhibitions.

Cooperation with Other Departments

FROM ITS inception it has been the aim of the Treasury Department Art Program to cooperate in every feasible way with all other departments of the Government, believing that by so doing it would not only be carrying out the true spirit of Government, but it would also be creating new opportunities for artists and bringing them to a wider and more general public. The number and types of projects thus carried out have greatly increased since the inception of the Treasury Relief Art Project. They are too numerous to be set down in detail, and once more we have recourse to listing examples of our cooperative efforts. The following list will give a general idea of the work, and all those who wish further detailed information, can secure it in reports and bulletins which will be sent upon request.

DEPARTMENT OF AGRICULTURE—BUREAU OF PUBLIC ROADS:
Easel paintings depicting the development of bridge construction in the United States will be used for educational exhibitions and to stimulate interest in good highway construction.

DEPARTMENT OF COMMERCE—CENSUS BUREAU:
Posters for the Texas Centennial Exhibition have

been made, portraying the various activities and services of the Census Bureau.

DEPARTMENT OF THE INTERIOR—P.W.A. HOUSING DIVISION:

Mural painting and sculpture is being carried out for Housing Projects in Harlem, New York City; Stamford, Connecticut; Chicago, Illinois; Langston Terrace, Washington, D. C.; Old Harbor Village, Boston, Massachusetts; Whiskey Island, Cleveland, Ohio; and Camden, New Jersey.

DEPARTMENT OF JUSTICE—INDUSTRIAL REFORMATORY:

The Industrial Reformatory in Chillicothe, Ohio, is using the services of an artist in making color and design studies for the interior painting of offices and social rooms. The material is supplied for the Reformatory. The same artist is making stencilled friezes with decorative designs for the purpose of enlivening the rooms through a type of decoration sufficiently mechanical to enable the inmates to help carry them out, and thereby teaching them the trade of stencilled decoration. In addition, this artist is also starting a class in commercial art. This project is of educational and social importance.

POST OFFICE DEPARTMENT:

Twenty-four posters for the Christmas display were executed by one artist, with four assistants. This project has been continued for the execution of a second group of twenty-four posters.

STATE DEPARTMENT:

Copies of famous portraits of distinguished Americans have been executed for Embassies and Legations. Five artists are engaged in making screens for the State Department.

TREASURY DEPARTMENT:

(a) PROCUREMENT DIVISION:

Murals are being completed in the lobby of the building depicting construction and activities of the Procurement Division; a portrait plaque of Robert Mills, the Architect of the Treasury Department and other famous buildings, has been made; a carved monument to the same architect was designed and will be put up by the Federal Architect's Society; fifty murals for post offices and court houses, ranging from one panel to large all-over designs, and ten sculpture projects for post offices and court houses, ranging from over-door figures to large groups, are partially completed.

(b) UNITED STATES COAST GUARD:

Murals are being executed for the Coast Guard Academy at New London, Connecticut, with accurate technical representation of the history of shipping and its relation to the Coast Guard; the Coast Guard has supplied two wooden doors and a lectern, which are now being carved; the Officers' Mess and Recreation Room

in the St. Petersburg, Florida, Coast Guard Air Station is being decorated with murals related to the history of flying. A marble plaque for the gates is also being done by the same artist.

(c) PUBLIC HEALTH SERVICE:

A series of portraits of former Surgeon-Generals is being done; also murals for Seattle, Washington, and Louisville, Kentucky, Marine Hospitals; decorative carved panels for the Louisville Hospital; murals for the Nurses' Home, Buffalo, New York. Batiks for seven marine hospitals are being carried out by a master designer, with seventeen assistants, the materials being supplied by the hospitals.

WAR DEPARTMENT:

For this Department artists have undertaken busts of Orville and Wilbur Wright for the Aeronautical Museum of the Wright Flying Field, Dayton, Ohio; paintings depicting important incidents in flying history in the same museum; maps showing the Illinois region for the private office of the General in Charge in the Chicago Post Office; decorative panels for the Officers' Mess at Fort Sheridan, Illinois.

Projects, July 25, 1935, to July 31, 1936

SEVENTY-ONE mural projects (sixty-seven master artists, fifty-six assistants); twenty-seven sculpture projects (twenty-seven master artists, twenty-one assistants); twenty-three appointments as result of Section of Painting and Sculpture Competitions; 108 easel painters; forty-nine artists receiving miscellaneous employment; 328 artists employed (259, Relief, and sixty-nine, Non-relief); five projects completed; 3,355 easel paintings received; 477 easel paintings allocated; 138 easel paintings in traveling exhibitions.

Personnel

THESE TWO Treasury Projects work in close cooperation. They are both under the general direction of Edward Bruce, Chief of the Section of Painting and Sculpture, and Forbes Watson, Adviser. The personnel of these two sections is as follows:

Edward B. Rowan, Superintendent, Inslee A. Hopper, Assistant Superintendent, Section of Painting and Sculpture; Olin Dows, Chief, Henry La Farge, Assistant, Treasury Relief Art Project.

Appointments and recommendations on work submitted are discussed by this group and sent to the Supervising Architect and thence to the Director of Procurement for final approval.

The personnel further includes:

Maria Ealand, Assistant, Section of Painting and Sculpture; Cecil H. Jones, Assistant Chief, Treasury Relief Art Project.

Bulletin

ALL COMPETITIONS, and other activities of t program, are announced in a Bulletin, edited Forbes Watson, which appears periodically a is being sent free to approximately 5,300 artists and p sons interested in art. There have been ten issues to da It has full information as to competitions under the S tion and appointments under both the Section and t Treasury Relief Art Project. It contains articles of ge eral interest and policy and has short biographie sketches of winning artists. It is intentionally no critical and is an organ of information and reportir

Correspondence

AN EXTENSIVE correspondence concerning ge eral art matters is carried on with artists a persons interested. Much general advice a technical information finds its way both in and out this office, which acts as a sort of clearing house.

Photographs

THE TREASURY Department Art Projects ha on file photographs of the work of some 3,2 American artists. This file is composed of phot graphs made under the Public Works of Art Project, sketches submitted to the Section and the Treasu Relief Art Project, of much of the mural work bei done under the W.P.A. Art Project, and by reprodu tions of work collected through outside sources or giv by individual artists. This great file is being added continuously and promises to be most comprehensiv It is invaluable both to the Treasury Department A Projects and to any person interested in investigati the work of contemporary American artists.

Exhibitions

BESIDES THE exhibitions of competition sketche held by the local chairman and the traveli exhibitions of easel paintings and prints, t Treasury Department Art Projects held a small exhil tion of winning designs at the Cosmopolitan Club New York during November, 1935, following a som what larger one at the Corcoran Gallery of Art in Was ington, D. C., in October. A more comprehensive exl bition of winning designs, models, and finished mura was held in the Whitney Museum of American Art in Ne York from October 6 to November 6, and at the Corcor. Gallery of Art in Washington beginning November 1 1936, the exhibition's scope was again increased.

Conclusion

THE TREASURY Department Art Program resolves itself into a necessarily disinterested attempt to secure in the fairest way possible the [be]st work of American artists. Although begun because [of] the depression, and made possible partly by relief [fun]ds, it has demanded work of quality, and in the com[pet]itions under the Section of Painting and Sculpture, [s]ections are unaffected by relief needs.

The two separate projects, whose operation I have [de]scribed above, are part of the Office of the Supervisnig [Ar]chitect, Louis A. Simon, who supervises the design[in]g and construction of all buildings built by the Treas[ur]y Department. Under the guidance of the Director of [Pr]ocurement, Admiral Christian Joy Peoples, one of the [lar]gest contemporary building programs is proceeding. [Th]e art program has been possible because of the co[op]eration of these two officials.

The acquisition of works of painting and sculpture [for] public buildings is in the tradition of all civilized [na]tions. It is fitting that the Federal Buildings of the [Un]ited States should be decorated by American artists. The anonymous competitions by which most of this [wo]rk is chosen functions well because they are believed [in] by artists who feel that the system is fair. It is flex[ib]le enough to meet individual needs.

No artists have been appointed to execute murals [fr]om winning sketches which they have been unable to [ca]rry out satisfactorily. The mural paintings and statues [ha]ve usually been better executed than the winning [sm]all scale sketches. Here the double check by the local [co]mmittee and the Washington office has obviated the [sn]ap acceptance of a "slicked up," unsound sketch.

The same general policy of local and national anony[m]ous competitions will be continued; the advice of [ar]tists and experts sought. Fewer local competitions [wi]ll be held, but for larger sums, and the period for de[si]gning and the geographical region will be extended. Since the initiation of the program fifty-three com[pe]titions have been held and 113 contracts awarded. [Se]venty-three appointments to the Treasury Relief Art [Pr]oject were made as a result of sketches submitted in [co]mpetition. Forty-nine artists are working on designs [wh]ich on approval will result in contracts. These facts [ma]ke it clear that the competitions are not for single [jo]bs, but that artists who have submitted outstanding [de]signs are considered for further appointments. New [an]d vital problems, raised by the decorating of public [bu]ildings, are stimulating to painters and sculptors who [en]joy their craft and are definitely within the scope of [th]e contemporary spirit of American art. A number of [pa]inters have preferred more important schemes at a [lo]wer rate to a smaller undertaking at a higher rate.

This interest in the jobs themselves is shown by the case of one young artist who, being on relief, and working on sketches for a Post Office near his home town, was offered a private commission paying considerably more than his relief wages. Although his sketches had not been approved, he refused the job and turned it over to his assistant. The private employment was not lost, but the master artist was too interested to exchange this work for the Government for a private commercial job. This is one of many cases offering young artists a chance to show their mettle.

In solving these mural and sculptural problems for their Government, and fellow citizens, it is fair to suppose that artists are becoming more conscious of the society of which they are a part, and that they are being brought into closer cooperation with their neighbors. This in itself is an innovation in the United States and recalls the great ages in art, when an artist worked as a master craftsman for and with a group on civic problems which interested everyone in the community.

Such voluntary cooperation with the members of the community is clearly shown in the case of the two well known artists, who have been working on murals for the Treasury Department Art Program. One painter did a series of incidents relating to the whaling industry which, when published in sketch form, received some criticism on technical details from old whalers. The artist then made a series of studies, welcoming the criticism of these authorities on his revised drawings. He produced results satisfactory to the whalers and artistically as successful as the first sketches.

Another, while working on his murals for a Post Office, received a number of criticisms from engineers in that department during the progress of the mural, particularly concerning the angle of the mail chute. They explained that after scientific experimentation it was found that a thirty degree angle was the only practical angle at which a circular chute could be graded. If a greater angle of descent is made, the mail is injured; if a lesser, the chutes work ineffectively. These suggestions the artist followed and incorporated in his final designs.

I believe that the attitude of these two artists is something of an innovation. In both the artist's and the public's point of view toward mural painting there is developing a greater sense of reality.

In spite of localized subject matter, however, I can detect no genuine tendency toward regional expression, although there are certain areas which a particular painter's or teacher's point of view has greatly influenced. Outstanding talent has been found in unexpected places—but as often as not it is sophisticated. Among younger painters, there is a tendency towards the objective—toward a realism and design. They want to have their work understood by an observant American public.

The growth of our correspondence files gives every indication that the Treasury Department Art Program is making the public more widely conscious of art and is bringing it into closer contact with the artists. Fine murals, concerned with the locality and by artists of the region, placed in public buildings, stimulate local culture. Through these wall pictures, everyday scenes, familiar objects, industries, etc., achieve a new dignity. (Even the occasional differences of opinion on work produced are in this sense healthy.)

Local Historical Societies, Chambers of Commerce, and other public bodies often request work which the Department is unable to supply. They have generously given valuable suggestions on subject matter, and general treatment to individual artists, sometimes making it possible to amplify the work originally proposed.

One painter who had been working on sketches for a Post Office discussed the general treatment with a large group of local authorities, both before and after finishing his preliminary studies. The Mayor and this group were so pleased with the results and with the intelligent handling of their township's history that they are trying to raise a sum from the locality to add three panels to those under contract with the Department.

An aroused public interest in murals may profoundly affect the interior of our public buildings. With the leadership and cooperation of the more intelligent architects, who are designing suitable spaces and using wall paintings, a new school is gradually appearing—and our public walls are being enhanced. Owing to a government attitude toward the artist which encourages him to be free to express himself in his own way and owing to the painting and sculpture opportunities flowing naturally from an enlightened and coordinated building plan, results that benefit the artists and increase the value and beauty of Federal buildings must inevitably follow.

The service to the public that the art projects render is clearly seen, again, in the allocation of pictures to hospitals. The fact that in the major Federal Hospitals, and particularly in the Leper Colony at Carville, Louisiana, the patients can choose pictures for their rooms and wards, adds a pleasant note to their enforced stay.

In the case of the educational work being undertaken in Chillicothe, where a master artist has charge of a group of over twelve inmates, the educational service and development in the teaching of a specialized trade to those who are talented is of inestimable value.

The money spent on this Project has produced a social worth which is impossible to estimate. In actual money values, as well as in a permanent spiritual value, I believe that the Government has received much more than it has spent. There is no doubt that some of this work will be what is known as "great." Almost all of it will be an addition to our faith and our civilization.

DAMS, BERTRAND R.,

WEBSTER CITY, IOWA

Winner of competition for mural in the Dubuque, Iowa, Post Office.

1907, BORN, November 29, Webster City, Iowa. Studied taxidermy with local taxidermist. 1925—Enrolled in a commercial art correspondence course. 1928—Entered University of Iowa, where he majored in art and economics. 1934—Began work on Iowa State College Library murals as assistant, under Public Works of Art Project. Has worked in most mediums, with exception of lithography and fresco. Has prepared plaster casts for bronze tablets and modelled heads.

DAMS, KENNETH M.,

TAOS, NEW MEXICO

Appointed to design mural for the Goodland, Kansas, Post Office, as result of quality of sketches submitted in National Competition for decoration of the Post Office Department Building, Washington, D.C.

1897, BORN, August 6, Topeka, Kansas. 1912—Began study of art in high school. Also studied under George M. Stone, a local artist. 1916—Entered Chicago Art Institute. 1919—Studied at Art Students' League, New York, under George Bridgman, Eugene Speicher and Maurice Sterne; also at Summer Art School, Woodstock, New York, under Andrew Dasburg. 1921—Went to France and spent some months in Paris in various sketch classes. Painted landscapes in south of France, later returning to Paris. Spent some months in Italy studying frescoes of Giotto, Piero della Francesca and Masaccio. 1924—Painted in Taos, New Mexico. Revisited France, but soon returned to Southwest. 1934—Worked under Public Works of Art Project. Has exhibited in national exhibitions and held several one-man shows. Work owned by Los Angeles Museum; Mulvane Art Museum, Topeka, Kansas; University of New Mexico; Honolulu Academy of Fine Arts; Kansas State Agricultural College; San Francisco Art Museum. Awards: Denver Art Museum, Denver, Colorado, 1928—Honorable Mention for Oil Painting; Denver Art Museum, 1930—Honorable Mention for Graphic Arts; Print Club of Philadelphia, Fourth Exhibition of American Lithography—First Honorable Mention; Art League of New Mexico, 1932—Purchase Prize; Corcoran Gallery of Art, Fourteenth Biennial Exhibition—Fourth W. A. Clark Prize and Honorable Mention Certificate.

ALBRIZZIO, CONRAD A.,

3217 North Boulevard

BATON ROUGE, LOUISIANA

Appointed to design mural for De Ridder, Louisiana, Post Office, as result of quality of sketches submitted in National Competition for murals in the Justice Department Building, Washington, D. C.

1894, BORN, October 20, New York City. 1911—Studied architectural drawing, Cooper Union night classes. 1912—Employed as draughtsman. 1918—Studied at Beaux Arts under Frederick Hirons. 1919—Employed as draughtsman and designer in New Orleans. 1923—Studied at Art Students' League, New York, under Luks and Du Mond. Worked as designer. Studied in Paris and traveled in Europe. Learned fresco in Rome, Italy, under Professor Venturini Paperi, and studied at American Academy; also at Fontainebleau School, France. 1931—Commissioned to execute frescoes for Governor's reception room and court rooms for Louisiana State Capitol. 1932—Studied fresco and encaustic, Pompeii, Italy. 1933—Taught in Public School, New York. Work includes murals for Richmond Hill High School, under Public Works of Art Project, and for Church of St. Cecilia, Detroit, Michigan. Organized Fresco Guild. 1936—Became a member of the faculty of the Fine Arts Department of Louisiana State University in Baton Rouge, where he now teaches and paints.

BALLATOR, JOHN R.,

1966 S.W. 4th Avenue

PORTLAND, OREGON

Winner of competition for mural in the St. Johns, Oregon, Post Office, and appointed to design a second mural in the same building.

1909, BORN, February 7, Portland, Oregon. 1928—Studied painting and sculpture at University of Oregon under Kenneth Hudson and Harry Camden. 1929—Entered Yale School of Fine Arts. Studied sculpture under Robert G. Eberhart, and painting under Edwin C. Taylor, Eugene Savage and Deane Keller. 1934—B.F.A. from Yale. Collaborated in executing seven panel mural in oil for Nathan Hale School, New Haven, Connecticut, under Public Works of Art Project, having at different times about seven assistants. In October, supervised a mural undertaking for Franklin High School, Portland, Oregon, consisting of one panel in oil and two over-door panels in tempera. Has painted number of portraits and pictures for private individuals, receiving commissions both in the East and in Portland, Oregon.

BARANCEANU, BELLE,

1715½ 29th Street

SAN DIEGO, CALIFORNIA

Selected to design mural for the La Jolla, California, Post Office.

Born Chicago, Illinois. Studied at Minneapolis School of Art and in Chicago. Pupil of Richard Lahey, Morris Davidson, Cameron Booth and Anthony Angarola. Painted and taught in Chicago, where she was member of Chicago Society of Artists and served on Board of Directors, Chicago No-Jury Society of Artists. Has exhibited at Art Institute of Chicago, Los Angeles Museum, Kansas City Art Institute, John Herron Art Institute of Indianapolis, Nebraska Art Association, Des Moines Association of Fine Arts, and San Diego Fine Arts Gallery. Has painted four murals, including one in Palace of Education, Balboa Park, and one, which was executed in true fresco in the San Diego Fine Arts Gallery Garden.

BELASKI, STEPHEN J., 58 Williams Street
BELLOWS FALLS, VERMONT

Selected to design murals for the Rutland, Vermont, Post Office.

1909, BORN, March 25, New York City. 1924—While still at high school was employed as show-card writer in department store, working after school hours and on holidays. Also enrolled in International Correspondence Schools, Scranton, Pennsylvania. Studied at Vesper George School of Art in Boston. Won a school scholarship for free tuition for one year, and later won foreign scholarship for three months study at Fontainebleau School, France. Studied with Jean Despujols, André Strauss and Gaston Balande. Work includes group of murals for foyer, Bellows Falls High School; large mural executed for the American Legion, Bellows Falls; and a number of paintings commissioned by various private individuals.

BERGMAN, FRANK, 58 Santa Barbara Avenue
SAN FRANCISCO, CALIFORNIA

Winner of competition for mural in the Stockton, California, Post Office.

1898, BORN, August 6. Studied at National Academy, Vienna, for seven years. 1924—Exhibited at Kuenstlerhaus, Vienna. Worked with Josef Urban and Willy Pogany, New York. Has exhibited at Architectural League, New York; Chicago Art Institute; Los Angeles Museum; Palace of Legion of Honor, San Francisco; and annual exhibitions of San Francisco Art Association. Work includes mural executed under Public Works of Art Project; murals: San Francisco Board of Education; two well-known steamships (won in local competition); and for a number of buildings in San Francisco, including the Sir Francis Drake Hotel, the San José Pacific Loan Association and a number of other prominent buildings.

BIDDLE, GEORGE,
CROTON-ON-HUDSON, NEW YORK

Appointed to design frescoes in the Fifth Floor Stairwell, Department of Justice Building, Washington, D. C.

1885, BORN, January 19, Philadelphia, Pennsylvania. Educated at Groton School and Harvard College, receiving A.B. in 1908 and L.L.D. in 1911. Studied one year at Julian's Academy, Paris, and two years at Pennsylvania Academy of Fine Arts. Served two years during World War; was in action at Second Battle of Marne, St. Mihiel, Meuse Argonne; became Acting Assistant Chief of Staff, First Army Corps. Wrote and illustrated "Green Island," Coward McCann, 1930. Published articles in Scribner's, Creative Arts, American Magazine of Art, Parnassus, and The Arts. Paintings owned by Whitney Museum, New York; Pennsylvania Academy of Fine Arts; Dallas Museum. Lithographs and arts and crafts work in Kaiser Friederich Museum, Berlin; Museo d'Arte Moderna, Venice; Chicago Art Institute; Boston Museum; John Herron Art Institute; California Palace of Legion of Honor; Public Library, New York City; Museum of Modern Art, New York City. Former Vice-President, Society of Painters, Sculptors and Gravers; President, Society of Mural Painters. 1936—Studied fresco technique under Olle Nordmark.

BISTTRAM, EMIL, Box 4
TAOS, NEW MEXIC

Selected to design murals for the Roswell, New Mexico, CourtHouse

1895, BORN, April 7, Hungary. 1906—Came to America; was naturalized o reaching majority. Studied in night classes, National Academy c Design, Cooper Union and New York School of Fine and Applie Art. Became commercial artist, and opened an art service whic employed from eighteen to twenty men. Was Associate Instructc New York School of Fine and Applied Art, and later taught for fiv years at Master Institute, Roerich Museum, New York. 1931—Wc Guggenheim Fellowship award for study of fresco abroad. Worke for short time with Diego Rivera in Mexico. 1932—Founded Ta School of Art, Taos, New Mexico.

BOHROD, AARON, 2406 N. Clark Stre
CHICAGO, ILLINO

Winner of competition for mural in the Vandalia, Illinois, Po Office.

1907, BORN, November 21, Chicago, Illinois. Studied two years at Chicago A Institute; two years at Art Students' League, New York, und John Sloan, Boardman Robinson and Kenneth Hayes Miller. 1936 Won Guggenheim Fellowship award in creative painting. Wo owned by Chicago Art Institute and Whitney Museum of Americ Art, New York. Awards: Clyde M. Carr Prize, 1933; Joseph Eise drath Prize, 1934; William H. Tuthill Prize, 1934; Watson F. Bla Prize, 1935; Chicago Artists' Prize, 1935.

BOUCHÉ, LOUIS, 155 East 89th Stre
NEW YORK CI

Selected to design murals for space outside of the Attorney Genera Office, Department of Justice Building, Washington, D. C.

1896, BORN, March 18, New York City. 1910 to 1915—Studied in Paris w Desvailliers, Lucien Simon, Prinet and Bernard Naudin; Atelie Colarossi, La Grande Chaumière and L'Ecole des Beaux Arts. 1§ to 1916—Studied at Art Students' League, New York, with ! Mond and Luis Mora. Has exhibited in American and Europe shows and held one-man exhibitions. Work owned by New Yc University Gallery of Living Art, Phillips Memorial Galle Whitney Museum of American Art, Ferdinand Howald Collecti and private collectors. Has executed decorations for Radio C Music Hall, New York City, and various private residences. Me ber, Society of Painters, Sculptors and Gravers, also an act member of the National Society of Mural Painters.

BOYD, BYRON BEN, 304 42nd Str
DES MOINES, IO

Appointed to design mural for the Osceola, Iowa, Post Office, result of quality of sketches submitted in National Competition decoration of the Post Office Department Building, Washington, D

1889, BORN, January 22, Wichita, Kansas. Attended public schools, Den Colorado. Studied painting in high school under Jean Manhe and under various instructors in schools and universities. University of Colorado for three years; Northwestern University for one year, receiving A.B. Four years later received M.A. in architecture from Columbia University. 1914—Moved to Des Moines. Became designer in architectural firm. 1916—Organized firm of Boyd and Moore and practiced architecture for fourteen years, building some of most important structures in Iowa. During World War headed division designing submarine bases, Navy Department, Bureau of Yards and Docks. Continued architectural practice until 1926, meantime painting as an avocation. Attended National Academy for two seasons, later studying with Henry Leith Ross and Henry Hensche. Painted during extended trips to Europe, Africa and the Near East. Has exhibited in galleries and museums in New York City, Boston, Philadelphia, Washington, Chicago, cities of the Middle West and Southwest, and in most national exhibitions.

OYD, FISKE,   55 Hobart Avenue
SUMMIT, NEW JERSEY

Winner of competition for murals in the Summit, New Jersey, Post Office.

95, BORN, Philadelphia, Pennsylvania. 1913 to 1916—Studied at Pennsylvania Academy of Fine Arts under Grafley, Garber, Pearson and Breckinridge. 1921 to 1924—Studied at Art Students' League, New York, under John Sloan, Boardman Robinson and Kenneth Hayes Miller. Has held one-man exhibitions in leading galleries in New York and Boston. Painted landscapes under Public Works of Art Project. Awarded Woodblock Prize, Philadelphia Print Club, 1931. Represented by woodcuts and etchings in Print Collection of Metropolitan Museum; Whitney Museum of American Art; New York Public Library; Boston Museum of Fine Arts; John Herron Art Institute, Indianapolis; Addison Gallery of American Art, Andover, Massachusetts; paintings in Phillips Memorial Gallery, Washington, D. C.; Whitney Museum of American Art; Newark Museum. Was one of the painters exhibiting regularly with the group which came into prominence soon after the famous "Armory" show.

OYNTON, RAY,   20 Del Mar Avenue
BERKELEY, CALIFORNIA

Selected to design murals for the Modesto, California, Post Office.

83, BORN, Iowa. 1904—Studied at Chicago Academy of Fine Arts under William P. Henderson, John W. Norton and W. J. Reynolds. Since leaving, has worked entirely by himself. 1913—Moved to Spokane, Washington, where he did first mural decoration in that city. 1914—Moved to California. 1917—Made first experiments in fresco. Has taught drawing and painting at University of California since 1920, and fresco at California School of Fine Arts, San Francisco, since 1927. Work includes mural painting for Council Chamber, Spokane City Hall; lunette for dining room in a San Francisco hotel; ceiling in Mills College, Oakland, California; and frescoes and murals for various private and public buildings, including California School of Fine Arts, University of California Faculty Club, and Coit Memorial. Has exhibited continuously for last twenty years.

BRITTON, EDGAR,   645 North Michigan Avenue
CHICAGO, ILLINOIS

Winner of competition for mural in the East Moline, Illinois, Post Office.

1901, BORN, April 15, Kearney, Nebraska. 1921—First worked with small group in Cedar Rapids, Iowa, drawing and painting landscapes. Moved to Chicago; spent several years studying and working with Edgar Miller, using many mediums. Executed series of nine panels in tempera for Deerfield-Shields High School, Highland Park, Illinois, under Public Works of Art Project. Is now completing six frescoes for Bloom Township High School, Chicago Heights, Illinois. Has exhibited at Chicago Art Institute, Whitney Museum of American Art and Brooklyn Museum, New York.

BROCKMAN, ANN,   Harbor View Cottage
ROCKPORT, MASSACHUSETTS

Selected to design mural for the Stamford, Connecticut, P. W. A. Housing Project.

1898, BORN, Alameda, California. Studied at Art Students' League, New York, with John Sloan and Gifford Beal. Has exhibited extensively.

BROOKS, RICARD,   3725 Odana Road
MADISON, WISCONSIN

Appointed to design mural for the Richland Center, Wisconsin, Post Office, as result of quality of sketches submitted in competition for decoration of the Rochester, Minnesota, Post Office.

1894, BORN, Haverhill, Massachusetts. Spent early life in Montana. Attended Virginia Military Institute. Studied at Boston Museum School, five years; Art Students' League, New York; and various night classes in drawing. Served twenty months in France during World War. Has worked for commercial painters, assisted mural painters, and done some easel painting. 1929 to 1933—Worked and studied abroad. Has exhibited in National Academy and Architectural League Shows, New York. Work includes decoration of public buildings in New York, Montreal and the Middle West; collaborated with Eric Gugler, Architect, on maps and ceiling decoration, State Board of Education Building, Harrisburg, Pennsylvania.

BROWNE, ALDIS B.,   c/o United States Coast Guard Academy
NEW LONDON, CONNECTICUT

Appointed to design murals for the New London Coast Guard Academy, as result of quality of sketches submitted in competition for decoration of the New London Post Office.

1907, BORN, August 2, Washington, D. C. 1928—Entered Yale School of Fine Arts, studying under Taylor, Savage and York; spent one year in tempera class. 1934—B.F.A. from Yale. Worked under Public Works of Art Project. Did two panels for Fairhaven Junior High School in collaboration with Vincent Mondo. Interested in water color, imaginative composition and decoration. His work further includes portraits which have been carried out in various mediums.

BUNN, WILLIAM L.,   852 Newell Avenue
MUSCATINE, IOWA

Winner of competition for mural in the Dubuque, Iowa, Post Office.

1910, BORN, May 29, Muscatine, Iowa. 1933—B.A. in Graphic and Plastic Arts, University of Iowa. 1934—Made summer tour with own Punch and Judy Puppet Theatre in rural Iowa and Missouri, performing in town squares, sketching meanwhile. Returned to University of Iowa; became Graduate Assistant in Dramatic Arts. Engaged for two years in art and technical activities of University Theatre; studied mural design under Grant Wood. Holds Carnegie Fellowship in Art; assisting in designing frescoes for University theatre.

CALLAHAN, KENNETH,   440 25th Street, North
SEATTLE, WASHINGTON

Appointed to design murals for the Seattle, Washington, Marine Hospital, as result of quality of sketches submitted in competition for decoration of the St. Johns, Oregon, Post Office.

1907, BORN, Seattle, Washington. Attended University of Washington. Worked at odd jobs and as merchant sailor, giving all his spare time to painting. 1930—Art critic for Seattle Town Crier; later for Seattle Times. 1932—Went to Mexico. 1933—Worked at Seattle Art Museum. 1934—Painted first mural, using logging industry as subject matter; this mural later purchased and given to Seattle Art Museum.

CAMPBELL, CHARLES,   7426 Detroit Avenue
CLEVELAND, OHIO

Selected to design murals for the P. W. A. Housing Project at Cleveland, Ohio.

1905, BORN, August 27, Dayton, Ohio. Drew from early childhood. Attended Cleveland Art School for five years. Has worked independently since, painting mostly in oils. Work owned by Cleveland Museum of Art.

CARROLL, ORVILLE,   718 East 6th Street
NEW ALBANY, INDIANA

Appointed to design murals for the reception room of the Louisville, Kentucky, Marine Hospital, as result of quality of sketches submitted in competition for the lobby of the same building.

1912, BORN, February 18, New Albany, Indiana. Grandson of John Carroll of Cork, Ireland, able cabinet maker. Sketched with father, James Carroll, at early age. 1926—Received Art Scholarship, Louisville Conservatory of Music. Studied at Louisville Art Center, where he taught Crafts and Design 1934-1935. Has executed sheet metal and concrete reliefs, wood carvings, lithographs, and a variety of craft work. Work includes four mural panels for Louisville Library.

CARTER, CLARENCE H.,   2074 East 107th Street
CLEVELAND, OHIO

Winner of competition for mural in the Ravenna, Ohio, Post Office, and winner also of competition for the Portsmouth, Ohio, Post Office.

1904, BORN, March 26, Portsmouth, Ohio. Attended Cleveland School of Art. Later studied with Hans Hoffman in Capri; visited galleries in Italy, Sicily, Belgium, London and Paris. Has exhibited in almost all large museums and exhibitions in this country. Work owned by Cleveland Museum of Art; Brooklyn Museum; Whitney Museum of American Art, New York; William Rockhill Nelson Gallery, Kansas City. Awards: Cleveland Museum of Art—First Prize Annual May Show, twelve times. Executed two large mural panels for the Cleveland Auditorium, one of the most ambitious decorative plans which was carried out by a coordinating group of artists under Public Works of Art Project.

CHAMBERLAIN, NORMAN S.,   245 South 26th Street
HERMOSA BEACH, CALIFORNIA

Appointed to design murals for the Huntington Park, California, Post Office, as result of quality of sketches submitted in competition for decoration of the Beverly Hills, California, Post Office.

1887, BORN, March 7, Grand Rapids, Michigan. Studied for seven years in local school of art. 1910—Studied and painted in the Hague, Holland. Later devoted himself to decorative work and mural design. Gave up painting for seven years, working in various trades. 192? Moved to California, where he resumed painting. Executed architectural studies for a private client. Went to France, and worked a year. On returning to United States, spent some time in Taos, New Mexico, studying Indian ceremonials and making designs for murals. Worked under Public Works of Art Project. Work includes two murals executed for Riverside High School as well as the mural installed in First National Bank, Pasadena.

CHRISTIAN, GRANT W.,   1851 North Pennsylvania Avenue
INDIANAPOLIS, INDIANA

Appointed to design murals for the Indianapolis, Indiana, Post Office, as result of quality of sketches submitted in competition for decoration of the Louisville, Kentucky, Marine Hospital.

1911, BORN, July 17, Edinburgh, Indiana. Brought up on farm near Edinburgh, where he attended high school. Won scholarship and completed four years training at John Herron Art Institute, Indianapolis. 1933—Received one-year scholarship, Pennsylvania Academy of Fine Arts. 1934—Awarded Thouron Prize in composition from that institution. 1934—Returned to Herron Institute, studying under Donald Mattison and Henrik Martin Mayer. Through this course of study he became interested in mural decoration.

COOK, HOWARD N.,   547 Hill Street
SEWICKLEY, PENNSYLVANIA

Winner of competition for mural in the Pittsburgh, Pennsylvania, Post Office and Court House.

1901, BORN, July 16, Springfield, Massachusetts. Studied painting in high school and later at Art Students' League, New York. Spent several years drawing and painting in France, Turkey, China, Central America and United States; work published in Survey Graphic, Century and Forum Magazines. Entirely self-taught in woodcutting and etching. 1932—Received Guggenheim Fellowship for a year's work in Mexico; Fellowship subsequently renewed for year's travel and work in United States. Interested in study of characteristic types of American people. Besides etchings, woodcuts, and water colors, work includes fresco for hotel in Tasco, Mexico; two frescoes in Court House, Springfield, Massachusetts, under Public Works of Art Project; many small frescoes on moveable panels. Has exhibited in galleries in New York, Denver, Santa Fe and Springfield. Work mainly in black and white. Prints belong to a number of museum collections both in this country and Europe.

COVEY, ARTHUR,   R.F.D. No. 2
                                    TORRINGTON, CONNECTICUT

Winner of competition for mural in the Bridgeport, Connecticut, Post Office.

1877, BORN, Bloomington, Illinois. Moved with family to Wisconsin and then into Kansas. 1893—Drove team for father in Cherokee strip opening, where he helped get 480 acres under cultivation. First professional work, newspaper assignment, making drawings of American subjects for Indianapolis News and Cleveland Press. 1899 to 1903—Studied at Chicago Art Institute, with Vanderpoel. 1904—Studied with Frank Duveneck and Gari Melchers. Went to Munich, where he received first honors and became pupil of Karl Marr. 1905 to 1908—Worked in London as assistant to Frank Brangwyn and instructor in London School of Art. 1913—Executed eight panels for Panama Pacific Exposition, as assistant to the late Robert Reid. Work includes three murals for Wichita, Kansas, Library; murals for Lord and Taylor's Department Store, New York; large frieze for Filene's Department Store, Boston; murals for building in Kohler, Wisconsin; decoration of two wards for Orthopedic Hospital, Orange, New Jersey; ceiling of Squibb Building, New York; War Memorial panels; studies for Worcester Auditorium. Has been Director of Department of Mural Decoration, which operates under the National Academy of Design, for the past four years.

CRIMI, ALFRED D.,   1986 Belmont Avenue
                                        THE BRONX, NEW YORK

Winner of competition for murals in the Post Office Department Building, Washington, D. C.

1900, BORN, December 1, Italy. 1911—Came to America. 1916—Attended evening classes in drawing, painting and composition, National Academy of Design, New York. Studied modelling at Beaux Arts Institute. 1925—Received Tiffany Fellowship. 1928—Painted two murals for St. Roch Church, Staten Island, New York. 1929—Visited art centers in France. Studied fresco and Pompeian encaustic under Professor Venturini Paperi in Rome, where he won first prize; also studied woodcutting under Professor Giuliani. 1931—Sent to Portland, Oregon, by firm of New York decorators as consultant to architects remodelling a department store. Did work in Royal York Hotel, Toronto, and in many public and private buildings for same firm. 1934—Painted oils and small frescoes under Public Works of Art Project. Went to Key West under F.E.R.A.; painted two fresco panels for Open Air Tropical Aquarium. At present painting fresco

for Harlem Hospital, New York City. Has exhibited at National Academy of Design; Sesqui-Centennial in Philadelphia, 1926; International Littoriale, Bologna, Italy, 1921; International Water Color Show, Brooklyn Museum, 1931; Chicago Art Institute and many other collective exhibitions. Has held number of one-man exhibitions in galleries and museums in New York City, San Francisco, and Portland, Oregon. Awards: National Academy of Design, 1919—Second Prize in Drawing; 1920—First Prize in Drawing; First and Second Prizes in Composition. Money Prizes at Chaloner National Monthly competitions for drawings from life.

CROCKWELL, DOUGLASS,
                                        GLENS FALLS, NEW YORK

Appointed to design mural for the White River Junction, Vermont, Post Office, as result of quality of sketches submitted in National Competition for decoration of the Post Office Department Building, Washington, D. C.

1904, BORN, Columbus, Ohio. 1926—Received B.Sc. degree, Washington University School of Commerce and Finance; studied art half-time, St. Louis School of Fine Arts, last two years of college. 1926—Studied at American Academy of Art, Chicago. 1927 to 1931—St. Louis School of Fine Arts. 1929 and 1930—European travel. Studied in St. Louis under Carpenter, Wuerpel, Goetsch, Ludwig, Berninghaus; in Chicago, under Weismann and Manoir. Has exhibited at St. Louis Artists' Guild, 1929, 1930, 1931, 1932; Chicago Art Institute Annual Exhibition, 1931; Kansas City Art Institute, 1931; Pennsylvania Academy Annual Exhibition, 1935; Public Works of Art Exhibitions, Corcoran Gallery and Museum of Modern Art. Awards: Two foreign traveling Fellowships, St. Louis Art Alliance; Crunden Prize for Best Figure Painting, St. Louis Artists' Guild Show, 1931; St. Louis Chamber of Commerce Prize for Best Industrial Painting, which was exhibited in the Artists' Guild show, 1932.

CSOSZ, JOHN,   3711 Euclid Avenue
                                            CLEVELAND, OHIO

Selected to design murals for the University Center Station, Cleveland, Ohio, Post Office.

1897, BORN, October 2, Budapest, Hungary. 1910—Came to America. 1916—Enrolled in Cleveland School of Art. Won scholarship in pictorial arts, also Amsden Prize for Illustration. After graduating from school, set out as free lance artist, also teaching at various settlement houses. 1923—Sold several pictures at Annual Exhibition of Cleveland Artists, which enabled him to continue studies. 1924—Traveled in Europe; returned to United States and taught at Akron Art Institute. 1925—Returned to Cleveland, where he executed a number of commissions. 1929—Instructor, Cleveland Business Men's Art Club. 1935—Instructor, Federal Adult Education Art classes. Work includes painting for University Club, Akron, Ohio; series of etchings of the city for large Cleveland bank; series of historical illustrations of steel industry; portrait for Cleveland Medical Library; mural decorations for Church of Holy Ghost, Cleveland;

decoration for main courtroom, Cleveland Juvenile Court; panels for Kirk Junior High School, under Public Works of Art Project. Paintings owned privately and by Cleveland Public School. Award: Cleveland Museum—Honorable Mention, Water Color.

CURRY, JOHN STEUART,   Box 261
                                          WESTPORT, CONNECTICUT

Appointed to design murals for the Department of Justice Building, Washington, D. C.

1897, BORN, November 14, Dunavant, Kansas. Pupil of Norton, Reynolds, Shoukhieff. Work owned by Addison Gallery of American Art, Andover, Massachusetts; University of Nebraska; Kansas State College; Whitney Museum of American Art, and Metropolitan Museum, New York. Has executed murals *Comedy* and *Tragedy* for Westport, Connecticut, High School. Awards: Purchase Prize, Northwest Print Makers, Fifth Annual Exhibition, 1933; Second Prize, Thirty-first International Exhibition, Carnegie Institute, 1933. Member Art Students' League, New York.

DALSTROM, GUSTAF,   649 Kemper Place
                                              CHICAGO, ILLINOIS

Winner of competition for mural in the Gillespie, Illinois, Post Office.

1893, BORN, January 18, Gothland, Sweden. Studied at Chicago Art Institute; pupil of George Bellows, Randall Davey. Member Chicago Society of Artists, Chicago No-Jury Society, Chicago Society of Etchers. Awards: Peterson Prize, Scandinavian American Exhibition, Chicago, 1929; Gold Medal, Chicago Society of Artists; Publication Prize, Chicago Society of Etchers, 1934.

DE DIEGO, JULIO,   511 Grant Place
                                              CHICAGO, ILLINOIS

Selected to design murals for the Officers' Mess Hall, Army General Hospital, Fort Sheridan, Illinois.

1900, BORN, May 9, Madrid, Spain. 1915—Apprentice to theatrical scenery painter. 1919—Enlisted in Spanish Army. 1921—First trip to Paris. 1924—Came to America. Earned living doing fashion designs, illustrations, cartoons, decorations for churches and cabarets. 1928—Returned to Spain; studied etching and lithography in Escuela de Artes Graficas, Madrid. Has exhibited in Madrid, Paris, New York, Chicago, Milwaukee, Dallas and other cities. Awards: Chicago Art Institute—Martin B. Cahn Prize and Honorable Mention, 1935.

DEL PINO, MOYA,   31 Presidio Terrace
                                        SAN FRANCISCO, CALIFORNIA

Winner of competition for mural in the Stockton, California, Post Office.

1891, BORN, March 3, Priego, Cordova, Spain. 1902—Apprentice to Carlos Mouton, religious painter of Cordova Sierras, who supplied peas-

ants with paintings in exchange for supplies. 1904—Studied Granada; entered workshop of Laterre, religious painter, gilder an sculptor; attended life class, School of Arts and Crafts, evening 1907—Studied at National School of Fine Arts, Madrid; pupil Degrain and Sorolla; won prizes and traveling scholarship. Becam active in Spanish Post-impressionist group. 1915—Illustrate books, modern woodblock. Copied entire collection of Velasque 1925—Exhibited in Philadelphia, Brooklyn, and San Francisc 1933—Worked under Public Works of Art Project. Work includ murals in Coit Tower, San Francisco, under Public Works of A Project; Merchants Exchange Club, San Francisco; Chapel, Bilba Spain; Aztec Brewing Company, San Diego; Cereal Products Cor pany Building, San Francisco. Work owned by Palace of Legion Honor, San Francisco; San Francisco Museum of Art; Museum Fine Arts, Barcelona; and private collectors.

DONNELLY, THOMAS,   Box 9
                                            VALHALLA, NEW YOR

Selected to design murals for the Mount Kisco, New York, an Ridgefield Park, New Jersey, Post Offices, as result of quality sketches submitted in National Competition for decoration of t. Post Office Department Building, Washington, D. C.

1893, BORN, Washington, D. C. Took drawing as a major subject in high schoc After graduation worked for three years in Art Departments Washington Post and Washington Times; studied in night clas Corcoran School of Art, Washington. 1915—Studied for year at A Students' League, New York, under George Bridgman and Lu Mora; won scholarship for painting. Eighteen months in Arm during World War, one year with A. E. F. 1918 to 1922—Worked daytime; studied in night class, Art Students' League, under Joh Sloan. 1922—Traveled in England and France with George Picke visiting museums and drawing. Has been represented in nation exhibitions of past ten years. Worked under the Public Works Art Project. Work owned by Whitney Museum of American Ar Dartmouth College, and private and public collections. Represente in White House, Commerce Building, House Office Building, I terior Building and Foreign Affairs Commission, Washington, D. Former member, Board of Control, Art Students' League; memb of the Board of Directors of the Salons of America, 1933-35; Me ber, Society of Painters, Sculptors and Gravers.

DRIGGS, ELSIE,
                          NEW HOPE, BUCKS COUNTY, PENNSYLVANI

Selected to design murals for the P.W.A. Harlem Housing Projec New York City.

1898, BORN, West Hartford, Connecticut. Studied at Art Students' League, Ne York, under Bridgman, Luks, Sterne; worked in Rome and Antic with Sterne. Has exhibited in New York galleries. Work owned Whitney Museum of American Art; Barney Collection, Ya Howald Collection, Columbus, Ohio; and various private collecto

DU BOIS, GUY PENE,   3 Washington Square
NEW YORK CITY

Selected to design murals for the Saratoga Springs, New York, Post Office.

1884, BORN, Brooklyn, New York. Studied Chase School, New York; pupil of William M. Chase, Robert Henri, Kenneth Hayes Miller, Frank V. Du Mond. Work owned by Metropolitan Museum; Whitney Museum of American Art; Museum of Modern Art; Newark Museum; Milwaukee Museum; Los Angeles Museum; Brooklyn Institute of Arts and Sciences; Cleveland Museum of Art; Detroit Institute of Art; Addison Museum, Andover, Massachusetts; Institute of Fine Arts, San Diego, California; Phillips Memorial Gallery, Washington, D. C.; Pittsburgh Athletic Club; Gallery of Living Art, New York. Awards: Purchase Prize, Los Angeles Museum; Harris Silver Medal, Chicago Art Institute, 1930; Second Altman Prize, National Academy of Design, 1936. Has written extensively on painting.

FLECK, JOSEPH A.,
TAOS, NEW MEXICO

Selected to design mural for the Raton, New Mexico, Post Office.

1893, BORN, Vienna, Austria. Studied Royal Academy, Vienna, under Professors Tichy and Bacher; School of Graphic Art and Industry, Vienna. 1922—Entered United States; became American citizen, 1927. Has exhibited at all national exhibitions and Carnegie International. Work owned by Kansas City Public Library; Municipal Collection of St. Joseph, Missouri; War Museum, Richmond, Virginia; Fort Worth Museum of Fine Arts, Fort Worth, Texas; Breckinridge Museum, San Antonio, Texas; Museum of Fine Arts, Houston, Texas; Vanderpoel Collection, Chicago; McKey Collection, Rockford, Illinois. Awards: Kansas City Art Institute, 1923—Received Bronze Medal, receiving Silver Medal in 1929, and Honorable Mention in 1934; Chicago Art Institute, 1927—Rosenwald Prize.

FORBES, HELEN K.,   1405 Montgomery Street
SAN FRANCISCO, CALIFORNIA

Winner of competition for mural in the Merced, California, Post Office.

1891, BORN, February 3, San Francisco, California. Studied Hopkins Institute of Art, San Francisco School of Fine Arts; pupil of Armin Hansen, three years; Akademie der Bildenden Kunste, Munich, under Professor Groeber; fresco technique under Professor Doerner; painted with André L'Hôte, Paris, and Ernest Leyden, Holland; painted in Mexico, 1926. 1928 to 1930—President, San Francisco Society of Women Artists. 1931—Taught at University of California. Has exhibited extensively in California museums. Work includes murals for Fleischhacker Memorial Mothers House, under Public Works of Art Project; for San Francisco Young Women's Christian Association; and for various private residences. Represented in San Diego Museum, San Francisco Museum, Mills College. Awards: San Francisco Society of Women Artists, 1930—First Prize; Sacramento, California, State Fair, 1934—First Prize; San Francisco Society of Women Artists, 1934—First Award, Water Color.

FOSTER, GERALD S.,   23 Stoneleigh Park
WESTFIELD, NEW JERSEY

Winner of competition for mural in Freehold, New Jersey, Post Office, and selected to design mural for Cranford, New Jersey, Post Office.

1900, BORN, September 30, Westfield, New Jersey. 1921—Studied New York School of Fine and Applied Art. 1923—Graduated from Princeton University. Studied at National Academy of Design and Art Students League. 1928—Completed training under Curran, Jones, Olinsky, Auerbach-Levy, and Ipsen. 1933 to 1934—Instructor in Fine Arts, Rhode Island State College Summer School. Has exhibited oils, etchings and drawings: Chicago Art Institute International, Whitney Museum of American Art Biennial, Chicago World's Fair. Executed oils and etchings under Public Works of Art Project. Member Princeton Architectural Association, Westfield Art Association (President 1931), South Country Art Association, Art Center of the Oranges, Plainfield Art Association. Awards: Art Center of the Oranges, 1934-1935: First and Second Awards, Black and White. Represented in the White House Collection.

FOY, FRANCES,   649 Kemper Place
CHICAGO, ILLINOIS

Winner of competition for mural in the East Alton, Illinois, Post Office.

Born Chicago, Illinois. Studied at Chicago Art Institute, night classes, under George Bellows, and independently abroad. 1921—Member, Board of Directors, Chicago No-Jury Society. Served on P.W.A.P. Technical Committee, 1934. Has exhibited in Chicago Art Institute Annual Exhibitions, and other local and national exhibitions, including the "10 Artists" in Chicago. Has had numerous one-man shows. Awards: Chicago Society of Artists Gold Medal, 1929; Marshall Fuller Holmes Prize, 1929; Jules F. Brower Prize, 1931; Frank G. Logan Prize, 1932.

FREE, KARL R.,   14 West 8th Street
NEW YORK CITY

Winner of competition for murals in the Post Office Department Building, Washington, D. C.

1903, BORN, May 16, Davenport, Iowa. Draughtsman for utilities company for three years. Studied, night school, Tri-City Art League, Davenport, under Herman More; won scholarship to Art Students' League, New York, where he studied three years under Joseph Pennell, Allen Tucker, Boardman Robinson, and Kenneth Hayes Miller. 1924—Worked in studio of Ezra Winter. 1928—Illustrated Thirteenth Edition of Encyclopedia Brittanica. Traveled abroad. Has exhibited at Whitney Studio Galleries; Corcoran Gallery; Chicago Art Institute; Colorado Springs Art Center; Whitney Museum of American Art. Work owned by Whitney Museum of American Art, Davenport Municipal Art Gallery, and various private collectors. Member, Society of Painters, Sculptors and Gravers, and Art Student's League, New York. Has been for a number of years the Curator of Graphic Arts, Whitney Museum of American Art.

FREUND, HARRY LOUIS,   501 South Third Road
CLINTON, MISSOURI

Selected to design murals for the Clinton, Missouri, Post Office.

1905, BORN, September 16, Clinton, Missouri. Studied Missouri University Art Department, under J. S. Ankeney; St. Louis School of Fine Arts; Washington University; pupil of E. H. Wuerpel, Gustave Goetsch, and Fred Carpenter. 1929—Won travel scholarship; studied at Colarossi Academy, Paris, under Henry Moriset. 1931—Assistant to Bradshaw Crandell, illustrator, New York. 1932 to 1933—Worked as illustrator, New York. 1933—Carried out murals for State of Missouri, Chicago Exposition Hall of States. 1934—Worked under Public Works of Art Project. Has exhibited at leading Midwestern art exhibitions. Work owned by St. Louis School of Fine Arts; Department of Labor Offices, Washington, D. C.; Kansas City Public Schools; Independence, Missouri, County Court House; Clinton, Missouri, Public Schools; Clinton Public Library.

GARDNER, WALTER,   722 Sansom Street
PHILADELPHIA, PENNSYLVANIA

Appointed to design murals for the Honesdale, Pennsylvania, Post Office, as result of quality of sketches submitted in competition for decoration of the Philadelphia Custom House and Appraisers' Stores.

1902, BORN, May 7, Liverpool, England. Educated in private schools, England. 1919—Came to United States. 1921—Studied at Pennsylvania Academy of Fine Arts. Received Cresson Traveling Scholarship. Worked under Public Works of Art Project. Awarded Purchase Prize, Wanamaker's Regional Art Exhibition, September, 1934.

GONZALES, XAVIER,   5121 St. Charles Avenue
NEW ORLEANS, LOUISIANA

Selected to design murals for the Hammond, Louisiana, Post Office.

1898, BORN, February 15, Almeria, Spain. Studied at Art Institute of Chicago. Teacher of painting and design, Newcomb Memorial College School of Art. Work includes murals for the War and Peace Auditorium, San Antonio, Texas; Dallas Museum of Fine Arts; and State Teachers College, Alpine, Texas. Received award: International Mural Competition, Los Angeles, California, 1930.

GRANAHAN, DAVID M.,   2122 Lyndale Avenue, South
MINNEAPOLIS, MINNESOTA

Selected to design murals for the Hopkins, Minnesota, Post Office. Later won competition for mural in the Rochester, Minnesota, Post Office.

1909, BORN, July 31, Litchfield, Minnesota. Studied art in high school. Studied at Minneapolis School of Art, under Kopietz and Mitchell; won scholarships and studied abroad. Post-graduate work, Minneapolis School of Art; summer session, Chicago Art Institute. Employed by Public Works of Art Project. Work includes series of murals for Gateway Building, Minneapolis. Illustrated two books—"101 Best Stories of Minnesota," "The Philosophy of a Politician." Has

exhibited extensively in Illinois, Wisconsin, and Minnesota. Awards: Second Prize, Twin City Exhibition, 1931; First Prize, Twin City Exhibition, 1932. Van Derlip Scholarship, 1932.

GRANT, GORDON KENNETH,
SANTA BARBARA, CALIFORNIA

Selected to design murals for the Ventura, California, Post Office

1908, BORN, January 21, Berkeley, California. Studied drawing California School of Fine Arts, San Francisco; Arts and Crafts School, Berkeley; studied architecture, University of California. Worked for Albert Herter, James Monroe Hewlett, D. Putnam Brinley, New York. Studied Indian dances and songs, New Mexico. Designed decorations for New Mexico Art Museum. Has been employed as designer, silversmith and blacksmith.

GREITZER, JACK J.,   1763 Page Avenue
CLEVELAND, OHIO

Winner of competition for mural in the Cleveland, Ohio, Post Office

1910, BORN, March 18, New York City. Graduate Cleveland School of Art. Studied abroad. 1934—Employed by Public Works of Art Project, executing murals for Cleveland Public Auditorium. Has exhibited extensively in many museums and galleries in the United States. Work owned by Pennsylvania Academy, Philadelphia; Cleveland Museum of Art; and numerous private collectors. Award: Cleveland Museum, First Prize in Oil Painting, 1931 and 1934.

GROPPER, WILLIAM,
CROTON-ON-HUDSON, NEW YORK

Selected to design murals for the Freeport, New York, Post Office

1897, BORN, December 3, New York City. Pupil of George Bellows and Robert Henri. Studied at New York School of Fine and Applied Art, under Howard Giles. Has drawn many cartoons and illustrations for national publications and metropolitan newspapers. Illustrated books; author of three books. Work includes murals for Schenley Corporation and Hotel Taft. Member, Mural Painters Society; Society of Painters, Sculptors and Gravers; American Newspapermen's Guild; American Artists' Congress. Received many awards.

HAINES, RICHARD,   885 Fifth Avenue
MARION, IOWA

Winner of competition for mural in the Wichita, Kansas, Post Office, and selected to design mural for the Cresco, Iowa, Post Office

Born Iowa; lived on farm and worked in North woods and harvest fields. Pupil of Edmund Kopietz and Glen Mitchell, Minneapolis School of Art; John Norton, Chicago. Won traveling scholarship; studied fresco under St. Hubert, composition under Despujols, Fontainebleau School, France. Work includes two murals for West High School, Denver, Colorado; seven panels in South High School, Minneapolis; two mural decorations in private residences.

HARDING, GEORGE, 1231 Montgomery Avenue
WYNNEWOOD, PENNSYLVANIA

Winner of competition for murals in the Philadelphia Custom House and Appraisers' Stores, and in National Competition for decoration of Post Office Department Building, Washington, D. C.

1882, BORN, October 2, Philadelphia, Pennsylvania. Pupil of Howard Pyle, Pennsylvania Academy of Fine Arts. Made drawings and wrote articles for Harper's Magazine. Traveled with Newfoundland Sealing Fleet, and in Arabia, Australia, New Guinea and China. Captain of Engineers, one of official artists with A.E.F. during World War. Instructor in illustration and fresco painting, Pennsylvania Academy of Fine Arts. Has executed numerous mural decorations. Member of Corcoran Biennial Jury, 1935.

HARRIS, GEORGE, 402 Jackson Street
SAN FRANCISCO, CALIFORNIA

Selected to design murals for the Woodland, California, Post Office.

1913, BORN, January 24, San Francisco, California. Pupil California School of Fine Arts, fresco and mural decoration under Ray Boynton, drawing and sculpture under Ralph Stackpole. Observed Diego Rivera working on fresco in that school. Employed by Public Works of Art Project, assisting in executing fresco in Coit Tower, San Francisco. Has assisted Victor Arnautoff and Ralph Stackpole in carrying out mural decorations; and conducted life drawing classes.

HIGGINS, VICTOR,
TAOS, NEW MEXICO

Appointed to design mural for the Rocky Ford, Colorado, Post Office, as result of quality of sketches submitted in National Competition for decoration of the Post Office Department Building, Washington, D.C.

1884, BORN, June 28, Shelbyville, Indiana. Studied at Chicago Art Institute; Chicago Academy of Fine Arts; Academie de la Grande Chaumière, Paris; and with H. Von Hyeck, Munich. Represented in Chicago Art Institute; Pennsylvania Academy of Fine Arts; Corcoran Gallery of Art, Washington, D. C.; Butler Art Institute, Indiana; Chicago Municipal Gallery; Terre Haute, Indiana, Art Association. Awards: Palette and Chisel Club, Chicago, 1914—Gold Medal; Chicago Municipal Art League Prize, 1915; Martin B. Cahn Prize, Chicago Art Institute, 1915; Edward B. Butler Prize, 1916; Second Logan Medal, Chicago Art Institute, 1917; First Altman Prize (Figure), National Academy of Design, 1918; John C. Shaffer Prize, 1928; First Altman Prize (Landscape), National Academy of Design, 1932.

HOLMER, JOHN F., 3302 Elland Avenue
CINCINNATI, OHIO

Appointed to design murals for the Cincinnati, Ohio, Post Office, as result of quality of sketches submitted in competition for decoration of the Louisville, Kentucky, Marine Hospital.

Born Cincinnati, Ohio. Received early training under father, who was a church decorator. Pupil of Duveneck, Meakin, Barnhern, Cincinnati Art Academy. Traveled extensively in Europe. Work includes decoration of St. Paul's Church, Cincinnati, Ohio; Taft Auditorium, Columbus, Ohio; various other public buildings. Has worked in many mediums, including lithograph, etching, water color, fresco, woodcut, stained glass, murals, sculpture, architectural design, etc. Taught at Cincinnati Art Academy, Ohio Mechanics Institute, Chicago Academy of Fine Arts. Awards: Prix de Rome, 1921—Honorable Mention; 1921—Chaloner Prize, given for monthly competitions in drawing, painting and composition, open to art students under thirty years of age.

HOUSER, LOWELL, 918 Wilson Avenue
AMES, IOWA

Winner of competition for mural in the Ames, Iowa, Post Office.

1903, BORN, Chicago, Illinois. Studied at Chicago Art Institute; independent study in Mexico, Aztec work in museum and modern fresco. Joined staff of Carnegie Institute, Yucatan; copied Mayan frescoes and bas reliefs under direction of Jean Charlot. Cruised for year with sailor archaeologist. Did book illustration. Joined archaeological expedition in Canyon del Muerto, Arizona. Designed in pennant factory. Taught painting, Art Students' Work Shop, Des Moines. Employed by Public Works of Art Project, worked under Grant Wood executing murals for Iowa State College. Has exhibited in a New York Gallery, and at various International Water Color and Wood Engraving Shows, Chicago Art Institute.

KASSLER, CHARLES, II, 3129 Sunset Boulevard
LOS ANGELES, CALIFORNIA

Winner of competition for murals in the Beverly Hills, California, Post Office.

1897, BORN, September 9, Denver, Colorado. Studied at Church School of Art, Chicago, and Chicago Art Institute. 1922 to 1924—Instructor in Art, The Atelier, Denver, Colorado, branch of Beaux Arts Institute. Founded, with John Thompson, painter, and Robert Garrison, sculptor, Chappell School of Art, Denver. Member of Faculty, Art Department, University of Denver. Studied abroad, doing considerable research, and studying fresco with noted French painter. Has exhibited widely. Work includes frescoes for Los Angeles Public Library under Public Works of Art Project, and Fullerton District Junior College, Fullerton, California.

KNIGHT, FREDERIC, 4 West 15th Street
NEW YORK CITY

Selected to design murals for the Johnson City, New York, Post Office.

1898, BORN, October 29, Philadelphia, Pennsylvania. Educated in public schools, Scranton, Pennsylvania. Awarded State Scholarship, Pennsylvania Museum and School of Industrial Art, Philadelphia. Worked in advertising art. Work includes mural paintings for Catholic Medical Mission Society, New York. Represented in Rockefeller Collection, Dartmouth College; Whitney Museum of American Art; Woodstock Art Association and private collections. Award: Woodstock Art Association, 1931—Best painting by an artist under thirty-five.

KOSTELLOW, ALEXANDER J.,   6 Ellsworth Place
                                        PITTSBURGH, PENNSYLVANIA

Volunteered to carry out mural designed by the late T. Frank Olson, for the Jeannette, Pennsylvania, Post Office.

1897, BORN, December 25, Persia. Studied at Art Students' League and National Academy of Design, New York; pupil of Vaclav Vytacil, Anthony Angarola. Member, Kansas City Society of Artists, Pittsburgh Art Association. Professor of Painting and Decoration, College of Fine Arts, Carnegie Institute of Technology, Pittsburgh, Pennsylvania. Awards: Art Institute of Pittsburgh—Smith Memorial Prize for Figure Painting; International Exhibition of Painting, Carnegie Institute, 1933—Honorable Mention.

KROLL, LEON,   39 West 67th Street
                                            NEW YORK CITY

Appointed to design murals for the Justice Department Building, Washington, D. C.

1884, BORN, December 6, New York City. Started painting and drawing at an early age, winning prizes at school. Worked at night for two years in Public Library; studied art in daytime. Studied at National Academy of Design; won all prizes competed for. Awarded traveling scholarship. 1906—First exhibited at National Academy of Design. 1910—First one-man show. Became Instructor at the Academy. 1913—Exhibited at Armory Exhibition, New York. 1931—President, American Society of Painters, Sculptors and Gravers. 1935—Retrospective exhibition at Carnegie Institute, Pittsburgh. Work owned by most of the large museums and galleries in the United States, including Metropolitan Museum of Art and The Whitney Museum of American Art. Awards: Salmagundi Club, New York, Annual Exhibition, 1912—Porter Prize; Pan Pacific Exposition Department of Fine Arts, 1915—Bronze Medal; Chicago Art Institute, First Logan Prize and Purchase Prize, 1919—Honorable Mention; National Academy of Design, 1921—Thomas B. Clarke Prize; Wilmington Society of Fine Arts, 1921—First Prize; National Academy of Design, 1922—First Altman Prize; Philadelphia Street Exposition, 1924—First Prize; Chicago Art Institute, 1924—Potter Palmer Gold Medal; Carnegie Institute, 1925—Honorable Mention; Pennsylvania Academy of Fine Arts, 1927—Temple Gold Medal; Rhode Island Art Association, 1929—First Prize; National Arts Club, 1930—Maida Gregg Memorial Prize; Pennsylvania Academy of Fine Arts, 1930—Beck Gold Medal; Indianapolis Art Institute, 1930—Purchase Prize; Pan American Exposition Department of Fine Arts, 1931—First Prize; National Academy of Design, 1932 and 1935—First Altman Prize; Carnegie Institute International, 1936—First Prize.

LA FARGE, THOMAS S.
                                    MOUNT CARMEL, CONNECTICUT

Winner of competition for mural in the New London, Connecticut, Post Office.

1904, BORN, Paris. Lived abroad until 1915. One year at Harvard College. Studied under Eugene Savage. Worked on church decorations with father, Bancel La Farge. Served apprenticeship in stained glass building; studied mosaic laying. Work includes fresco and decorations in the Pediatric Lobby, New York Hospital; St. Andrew's Church, Southampton; altar piece for church, Foxon, Connecticut; Portrait of Jeremiah Atwater, Middlebury College, Middlebury, Vermont. In collaboration with Bancel La Farge—decoration of Trinity College Chapel, Washington, D. C.; frescoes for St. Paul Seminary, and windows for St. Paul Cathedral, St. Paul, Minnesota.

LAHEY, RICHARD,   505 South Lee Street
                                        ALEXANDRIA, VIRGINIA

Appointed to design mural for the Brownsville, Pennsylvania, Post Office, as result of quality of sketches submitted in National Competition for decoration of the Post Office Department Building, Washington, D. C.

1893, BORN, June 23, Jersey City, New Jersey. Pupil of Robert Henri and George Bridgman, Art Students' League. During World War was in Navy Camouflage Division. Taught at Minneapolis School of Fine Arts and Art Students' League. Present Principal, Corcoran School of Art, Washington, D. C. Has exhibited in numerous exhibitions throughout the country. Represented in museums by paintings, water colors and etchings. Awards: Chicago Art Institute, 1925—Tuthill Prize for Water Color; Pennsylvania Academy of Fine Arts, 1929—Gold Medal. Member, Society of Painters, Sculptors and Gravers; Salons of America; American Fine Arts Society.

LAMAN, THOMAS,   767 North Point Street
                                        SAN FRANCISCO, CALIFORNIA

Selected to design murals for the Eureka, California, Post Office and Court House.

1905, BORN, September 23, Walla Walla, Washington. Studied at Portland Art Academy, one year; worked and studied with Ralph Stackpole and Edgar Walter. Work includes architectural sculpture for Oregon State College; memorial sculpture for Children's Home, San Francisco; mural decoration in tempera for S.E.R.A.; sculpture in wood and stone for private clients. Winner of three scholarships and several prizes, California School of Fine Arts.

LAMBDIN, ROBERT L.,   Greenacre Lane
                                        WESTPORT, CONNECTICUT

Winner of competition for mural in the Bridgeport, Connecticut, Post Office.

1886, BORN, October 7, Dighton, Kansas. Studied at Read Art School, Denver, Colorado; Kansas City Art Institute, under Charles A. Wilimovsky. Worked in studio of commercial artist, and later on Rocky Mountain News and Denver Republican. Feature illustrator, Kansas City Star. Taught newspaper illustration. Worked in oil, pen and ink, and other mediums, and illustrated for various magazines. Has designed theatrical scenery. Executed murals for Saugatuck Elementary School, Westport, Connecticut, under Public Works of Art Project.

LEA, TOM, 1400 Nevada Street
EL PASO, TEXAS

Winner of competition for mural in the Post Office Department Building, Washington, D. C.

1907, BORN, July 11, El Paso, Texas. Studied at Chicago Art Institute. Assisted John Norton on mural decorations for buildings in Chicago, St. Paul and Birmingham. 1930—Studied great murals of Italy. Taught drawing and painting, Studio School of Art, Chicago. Studied and painted in New Mexico two years; attached to Staff, Laboratory of Anthropology, Santa Fe. Work includes murals for private residences in Chicago, El Paso, and Santa Fe; murals for public buildings of South Park Commission, Chicago; two panels for College Library, Mesilla Park, New Mexico, under Public Works of Art Project; mural for Public Library, Las Cruces, New Mexico; murals for West Texas Room, State of Texas Building, Dallas, Texas.

LE BRUN, FREDERICO, 3 Washington Square
NEW YORK CITY

Appointed to design murals for the New York City Post Office Annex, as result of quality of sketches submitted in National Competition for decoration of the Department of Justice Building, Washington, D. C.

1900, BORN, December 10, Naples, Italy. Studied at a technical school four years; attended night classes, Naples Academy. Worked for short period with decorator. 1923—Came to America. Did commercial art work; returned to Italy to study. Instructor, Art Students' League, New York. Work includes paintings, frescoes and many drawings. Winner of Guggenheim Scholarship, 1935.

LEE, DORIS,
WOODSTOCK, NEW YORK

Winner of competition for murals in the Post Office Department Building, Washington, D. C.

1905, BORN, February 1, Aledo, Illinois. Pupil of Anthony Angarola, Arnold Blanch, and Ernest Lawson. Has exhibited in leading galleries of the country. Member Woodstock Art Association. Work owned by Rhode Island School of Design. Has won several prizes.

LEECH, HILTON,
SARASOTA, FLORIDA

Winner of competition for mural in the Chattanooga, Tennessee, Court House.

1906, BORN, October 13, Bridgeport, Connecticut. Pupil of George Pearse Ennis. Member, American Water Color Society; Salmagundi Club; Florida Federation of Art. Instructor, Ringling School of Art, Sarasota, Florida. Awards: New York Water Color Club, 1930—Purchase Prize; Florida Federation of Art, First Prize, Water Color.

LICHTNER, SCHOMER, 2619 North Downer Avenue
MILWAUKEE, WISCONSIN

Selected to design murals for the Sheboygan, Wisconsin, Post Office.

1905, BORN, March 18, Peoria, Illinois. Studied at State Teachers College, Milwaukee, under Gustave Moeller; Chicago Art Institute; National Academy of Design; Art Students' League, under Boardman Robinson. Studied history of art, University of Wisconsin. Has exhibited locally and at Carnegie International, Chicago Art Institute, and Art Center, New York. Executed murals under Public Works of Art Project. Winner of awards and prizes at local exhibitions.

LOCKWOOD, WARD,
TAOS, NEW MEXICO

Winner of competition for murals in the Post Office Department Building, Washington, D. C., and winner also of competition for mural in the Wichita, Kansas, Post Office.

1894, BORN, September 22, Atchison, Kansas. Studied at University of Kansas; Pennsylvania Academy of Fine Arts; Academy Ranson, Paris. Studied painting independently abroad. Member, Fellowship of Pennsylvania Academy of Fine Arts; Exhibiting Member, Foundation of Western Art, Los Angeles. Work includes murals in Kansas City Country Club, Taos County Court House. Represented in Whitney Museum of American Art and private collections. Awards: Chicago Art Institute, 11th Annual Water Color Exhibition, 1931—Logan Prize; California Palace of Legion of Honor, 1932—Purchase Prize, Water Color; Denver Art Museum, 1932—Honorable Mention.

LONG, FRANK W.,
BEREA, KENTUCKY

Appointed to design murals for the Louisville, Kentucky, Post Office, as result of quality of sketches submitted in competition for decoration of the Louisville, Kentucky, Marine Hospital.

1906, BORN, May 7, Knoxville, Tennessee. Studied at Chicago Art Institute; Pennsylvania Academy of Fine Arts; Julian's Academy, Paris. Has exhibited at galleries in Chicago, New Orleans and Knoxville, Tennessee, also in American Federation of Arts Traveling Shows, Print Club of Philadelphia, Brooklyn Museum, Columbus Gallery of Fine Arts, Toledo Museum, Chicago Art Institute. Work includes murals in Library, University of Kentucky, and in private residences. Published "Herakles" and "The Twelve Labors," a series of wood-cuts with explanatory text. Under Public Works of Art Project executed murals in Berea College, Kentucky.

McCOSH, DAVID, 967 Patterson Street
EUGENE, OREGON

Appointed to design mural for the Kelso, Washington, Post Office, as result of quality of sketches submitted in National Competition for decoration of the Post Office Department Building, Washington, D.C.

1903, BORN, Cedar Rapids, Iowa. Studied at Chicago Art Institute; graduated with traveling scholarship; studied abroad. 1929—Director of

Municipal Art Museum School, Davenport, Iowa. Won Tiffany Foundation Fellowship. Taught lithography, Chicago; lithography and painting, Storm City Art Colony, Iowa. Instructor in drawing and painting, University of Oregon. 1933—One-man exhibition in Chicago. Represented in Whitney Museum of American Art, Cedar Rapids Art Association, and other collections. Work includes mural for Century of Progress Exposition, Chicago.

McLEARY, KINDRED, Carnegie Institute of Technology
PITTSBURGH, PENNSYLVANIA

Winner of competition for mural in the Pittsburgh, Pennsylvania, Post Office and Court House.

1901, BORN, December 3, Weimar, Texas. Studied architecture, University of Texas. Worked four months in Joseph Urban's studio; assisted in decoration of Ziegfeld Theatre ceiling, New York. Assisted Jacques Carlu, French architect, in executing murals for a Boston hotel. Work includes decoration for private residence, Austin, Texas.

MANGRAVITE, PEPPINO, 281 Rye Beach Avenue
RYE, NEW YORK

Appointed to do murals for Hempstead, New York, Post Office, as result of quality of sketches submitted in competition for decoration of the Post Office Department Building, Washington, D. C.

1896, BORN, June 28, Lipari, Italy. Studied at Art Students' League; Cooper Union, New York. Has written articles on art and art education for The Arts, Progressive Education, American Magazine of Art, etc. Art Director, Ethical Culture Schools, New York. Work owned by Phillips Memorial Gallery and Corcoran Gallery of Art, Washington, D. C.; Whitney Museum of American Art, New York.

MARSH, REGINALD, 4 East 12th Street
NEW YORK CITY

Appointed to design murals for the Post Office Department Building, Washington, D. C.

1898, BORN, Paris, France. Son of well known painter, Frederic Dana Marsh; early association with artists. 1920—Graduated from Yale. 1922 to 1925—Staff artist, New York Daily News, New Yorker Magazine, Illustrator, etc. Pupil of Kenneth Hayes Miller, du Bois, Luks, Sloan, Sergeant Kendall. Studied fresco under Olle Nordmark; now studying sculpture under Mahonri Young. Represented in many museums, including Metropolitan and Whitney, New York, and private collections. Winner of prizes for painting and etching.

MATTISON, DONALD M., John Herron Art Institute
INDIANAPOLIS, INDIANA

Appointed to design mural for the Tipton, Indiana, Post Office, as result of quality of sketches submitted in competition for decoration of the Rochester, Minnesota, Post Office.

1905, BORN, April 24, Beloit, Wisconsin. Studied at Yale Art School, under Eugene F. Savage; also at American Academy in Rome. Member,

Society of Mural Painters; Grand Central Art Galleries; Indianapolis Art Club. Director of John Herron Art School, Indianapolis. Work includes mural for Museum of the School of Fine Arts, Yale University, New Haven; Cities Service Building, New York. Awards: Prix de Rome, 1918; Indianapolis Art Association, 1935.

MAYER, HENRICK MARTIN, 2845 North Pennsylvania Street
INDIANAPOLIS, INDIANA

Winner of competition for murals for the Louisville, Kentucky, Marine Hospital, and winner also of competition for the Lafayette, Indiana, Post Office.

1908, BORN, December 24, Nashua, New Hampshire. 1927—Graduated from Manchester Institute of Arts and Sciences. Studied under Maud Briggs Knowlton. Worked in studio of Willy Pogany, assisting him in painting murals. 1931—B.F.A., Yale University. Won William Wirt Winchester Fellowship for travel in Europe. 1932—Worked in studio of Austin Purves, Jr., designing and executing murals for Cosmolitan Club, New York. Instructor of composition and drawing, Cooper Union, New York. Assistant to Director and Instructor in Drawing, John Herron Art School, Indianapolis. Member, Society of Mural Painters; Indiana Artists Club. Award: Hoosier Salon, Chicago, 1935—Daughters of Indiana Prize.

MAYS, PAUL,
BRYN ATHYN, PENNSYLVANIA

Winner of competition for murals in the Norristown, Pennsylvania, Post Office.

1888, BORN, Cheswick, Pennsylvania. Pupil of Henry Keller, William M. Chase, Kenneth Hayes Miller, Charles Hawthorne, John Johansen; studied at Heatherley School, London; Colarossi's, Paris. Worked as assistant to New York mural painter. Painted landscapes in Cornwall, Brittany, and on the Mediterranean; exhibited abroad. Illustrated "Autobiography of Benjamin Franklin" by José Pijoan. Work includes murals for theatres in Los Angeles; mural decorations under Public Works of Art Project; two large murals entitled "Indian Legends"; many landscapes. Represented in White House collection; Woman's Club of Cleveland; University of Pennsylvania, and Bryn Athyn Library. Has exhibited in San Francisco and Los Angeles.

MECHAU, FRANK A., New Fine Arts Center Building
COLORADO SPRINGS, COLORADO

Selected to design murals for the Colorado Springs Post Office. Later won competition for murals in the Post Office Department Building, Washington, D. C.

1904, BORN, January 26, Wakeeney, Kansas. Studied at Denver University; Denver Art Academy; Chicago Art Institute. Illustrated "Myhrinne and Konallis" by Richard Aldington. 1929—Studied abroad. Exhibited with Surindependents and Artistes Americains Modernes, Paris; and at Denver Museum; Colorado Springs Regional Exhibition; Whitney Museum, New York. Work includes mural "Horses at Night" for Fine Arts Department, Denver Public Li brary, under Public Works of Art Project. 1933—Won Guggenheim Fellowship to paint in Rocky Mountain region; extended in 1935.

MILLMAN, EDWARD,
118 Pearson Street
CHICAGO, ILLINOIS

Winner of competition for mural in the Moline, Illinois, Post Office.

1907, BORN, January 1, Chicago, Illinois. Awarded scholarship, Chicago Art Institute, while still in grade school. Worked in studios in Chicago; studied at Art Institute night classes. Employed on Art Staff, Chicago Evening American; Art Director, Chicagoan Magazine, number of years. Painted and studied fresco in Mexico, 1934-1935. Held one-man show in Mexico City. Exhibited at Chicago Art Institute. Work includes mural for Century of Progress Exposition, Chicago; murals for Glencoe, Illinois, Central School, under Public Works of Art Project; and a fresco now being designed for the City of Chicago. Member, Chicago Society of Artists; also member of the Executive Board, Artists' Union, Chicago.

MOFFETT, ROSS,
PROVINCETOWN, MASSACHUSETTS

Winner of competition for mural in the Holyoke, Massachusetts, Post Office.

1888, BORN, Clearfield, Iowa. Studied at Chicago Art Institute and Art Students' League; pupil of Charles Hawthorne. Work includes mural in Town Hall, Provincetown. Represented in Pennsylvania Academy of Fine Arts; Corcoran Gallery, Washington, D. C.; Whitney Museum of American Art, New York; Buffalo Museum; Speed Museum, Louisville; University Gallery, Lincoln, Nebraska. Awards: Chicago Art Institute, 1918—Harris Silver Medal; Carnegie Institute, 1921—Honorable Mention; National Academy of Design, 1921—First Hallgarten Prize; Chicago Art Institute, 1927—French Gold Medal.

MOPOPE, STEPHEN,
FORT COBB, OKLAHOMA

Appointed to design murals for the Anadarko, Oklahoma, Post Office, as result of quality of sketches submitted in competition for decoration of the Wichita, Kansas, Post Office.

1900, BORN, August 14, Fort Cobb, Oklahoma, of Indian parentage. As a boy he watched his great uncles Hannqueah (Silver Horn) and Hobab (Hill Side) paint buckskins, tom toms, and ceremonial clothes. Drew Indians and horses, also shields and other symbols. Educated at St. Patrick's Mission, near Anadarko. Pupil of Professor O. B. Jacobson and Edith Makeir, University of Oklahoma Art School. Has exhibited in almost all Middle and South Western Universities and Museums; also New York, Honolulu, and Prague. Work includes murals for Federal Building, Muskogee, Oklahoma; N. E. State Teachers College, Tahlequah, Oklahoma; U. S. Field Artillery Museum, Fort Sill, Oklahoma; N. W. State Teachers College, Weatherford, Oklahoma; St. Patrick's Mission, Anadarko; University of Oklahoma; Anadarko High School and First National Bank.

MORA, F. LUIS,
GAYLORDSVILLE, CONNECTICUT

Appointed to design mural for the Catasauqua, Pennsylvania, Post Office, as result of quality of sketches submitted in National Competition for decoration of the Post Office Department Building, Washington, D. C.

1874, BORN, July 27, Montevideo, Uruguay, South America. Pupil of his father, Domingo Mora, Spanish sculptor; Benson and Tarbell, Museum of Fine Arts, Boston; Mowbray, Art Students' League, New York. Illustrated books and magazines. Taught painting and drawing, Chase School and Art Students' League, New York, for many years. Member, National Academy of Design; Architectural League; Water Color Society; Society of American Etchers. Has exhibited in many exhibitions throughout country. Work includes large mural in Reading Room, Lynn, Massachusetts, Public Library; decoration for Orpheum Theatre, Los Angeles, California; mural for Boys' Club, Pittsfield, Massachusetts; decorative panel for Red Cross Headquarters, Washington, D. C.; portrait of Warren G. Harding for White House, John Joy Edson for Chamber of Commerce, Washington, D. C.; also small murals for private residences. Executed porcelain groups, using American Indian as subject matter; worked in sculpture. Awards: Sears Prize, Boston, Rothschild Prize, New York, while a student; Philadelphia Art Club, 1901—Gold Medal; National Academy of Design, 1905—1st Hallgarten Prize; Beal Prize, Water Color, 1907; Evans Prize, New York, 1908; Shaw Prize, Salmagundi Club, 1910; International Exhibition, Buenos Aires, 1910—Silver Medal; San Francisco Exposition, 1915—Gold Medals; National Academy, New York, 1930—Carnegie Prize.

MORTELLITO, DOMENICO,
207 East 49th Street
NEW YORK CITY

Selected to design murals for the Port Chester, New York, Post Office, and linoleum panels for the P.W.A. Harlem Housing Project, New York City.

1906, BORN, Newark, New Jersey. 1923 to 1926—Attended Pratt Institute, Brooklyn. Worked in decorating firm, reproducing period designs, experimenting in painting and decoration for public buildings and private residences. Studied pigments with chemist. Worked under Public Works of Art Project. Has exhibited in Architectural League; Corcoran Gallery, Washington, D. C.; Newark Museum. Work includes frieze for Morgan Library Annex; murals in Capitol Theatre, Atlanta, Georgia; Woolsey Hall Auditorium, New Haven; St. Joseph's Chapel, Brentwood, Long Island; Newark Court House; Rialto Theatre, Atlanta, Georgia. Has decorated screens which are owned by a number of private collectors.

MOZLEY, LOREN,
TAOS, NEW MEXICO

Selected to design mural for the Albuquerque, New Mexico, Post Office.

1905, BORN, October 2, Brookport, Illinois. Studied at University of New Mexico; in Paris, independently and worked at various academies and sketch classes. Early invaluable assistance from Arnold Ronnebeck, Andrew Dasburg, John Marin. Has followed various pursuits, including Indian trader, lumber camp merchant, museum curator, and lithographer. Represented in private collections. Exhibited largely in local group exhibitions in New Mexico.

NEFF, EARL J.,   20871 Northwood Avenue
FAIRVIEW VILLAGE, OHIO

Selected to design murals for the P.W.A. Whiskey Island Housing Project, Cleveland, Ohio.

1902, BORN, April 4, Cleveland, Ohio. Has illustrated a number of children's books. Worked in creative department of lithograph plant. Free lance work in commercial art and book illustration, for thirteen years. Taught at Lakewood Branch, Cleveland School of Art, one year. Has exhibited annually at Cleveland Museum of Art. Work includes murals in Cleveland Public Library, based on Hans Christian Andersen stories for children.

OAKMAN, ARTHUR W.,   480 Boylston Street
BOSTON, MASSACHUSETTS

Selected to design mural for the P.W.A. Old Harbor Village Housing Project, Boston, Massachusetts.

1910, BORN, May 8, Neponset, Massachusetts. Won scholarship at age of thirteen, enabling him to study at Museum of Fine Arts, Boston; graduated from Designers Art School, Boston, course in drawing and painting as applied to decoration and mural design; night sessions at Massachusetts Normal Art School. Work owned by Phillips Memorial Art Gallery, Washington, D. C., and private collectors.

OLSON, T. FRANK,

Winner of competition for mural in the Jeannette, Pennsylvania, Post Office.

1891, BORN, Norway. Died Pittsburgh, Pennsylvania, September 9, 1935. Studied art in Norway, New York and Pittsburgh. Lived in Pittsburgh ten years, working as free lance artist, and painted several murals there.

PALMER, WILLIAM C.,   220 West 16th Street
NEW YORK CITY

Winner of competition for murals in the Post Office Department Building, Washington, D. C.

1906, BORN, January 20, Des Moines, Iowa. Studied at Art Students' League, New York, under Boardman Robinson and Kenneth Hayes Miller. 1927—Studied fresco abroad under M. Baudoin, Ecole des Beaux Arts, Fontainebleau. Executed mural for Queens General Hospital, New York, under Public Works of Art Project. Has held one-man shows in New York, Washington, and other parts of the country. Member, Art Students' League; Secretary, National Society of Mural Painters. Work owned by Whitney Museum of American Art, New York, and private collectors.

PEIXOTTO, ERNEST,   137 East 66th Street
NEW YORK CITY

Selected to design murals for the Oyster Bay, New York, Post Office.

1869, BORN, October 1, San Francisco, California. Studied abroad. 1918—Official artist, A.E.F.; Director, Atelier of Painting, A.E.F. Art Training Center, Bellevue, France. Lectures on mural painting, trends in painting. 1919 to 1926—Director, Department of Mural Painting, Beaux Arts Institute, New York. Author of "By Italian Seas," "Our Hispanic Southwest," "Romantic California," "The American Front." Associate National Academy of Design; Member, Society of Mural Painters (President); New York Architectural League; Society of Illustrators; American Institute of Architects (Honorary); Beaux Arts Institute (Honorary); American Federation of Arts; Société des Artistes Francais. Represented in National Gallery, Washington, D. C.; Hispanic Society of America. Work includes murals in Seaman's Bank, Bank of New York and Embassy Club, New York City; illustrations for Roosevelt's "Life of Cromwell" and "Wanderings" by Clayton Hamilton. Awards: Paris Salon, Chevalier of Legion of Honor, 1921—Honorable Mention; Officer, 1924. Member of National Jury.

PICKEN, GEORGE,   518 East 85th Street
NEW YORK CITY

Appointed to design murals for the Hudson Falls, New York, Post Office, as result of quality of sketches submitted in competition for decoration of the Pittsburgh, Pennsylvania, Post Office and Court House.

1898, BORN, October 26, New York City. Studied at Art Students' League, New York. Served in Medical Department, U. S. Army, during World War. Sergeant, Evacuation Hospital No. 15, A.E.F.; in St. Mihiel and Meuse-Argonne drives; with Army of Occupation in Coblentz, Antwerp, and Belgium. 1922—Studied and exhibited abroad. Instructor in etching, lithography and composition, Art Students' League. Work includes mural for St. Ambrose Church, Brooklyn, New York. Author, "Tools and Materials—Lithography," American Magazine of Art, December, 1934. Member, Society of Painters, Sculptors and Gravers; Salons of America; Artists' Congress. Has exhibited in Carnegie International, Chicago Art Institute, Pennsylvania Academy, Brooklyn Museum, Addison Gallery; one-man shows in various New York galleries. Represented in Whitney Museum of American Art; Rockefeller Collection, Dartmouth College; New York Public Library; and many private collections.

POOR, HENRY VARNUM,
NEW CITY, NEW YORK

Appointed to design murals for the Department of Justice Building, Washington, D. C.

1888, BORN, Chapman, Kansas. Attended Kansas City public schools and Stanford University. Worked summers in wheat fields and lumber camps of West and Northwest. Pupil of Walter Sickert, London; Julian's Academy, Paris. Taught drawing and painting, Stanford University and California School of Fine Arts. Drafted into Army during World War; did portraits of fellow soldiers; promoted to "regimental artist." 1920—First one-man show at a New York gallery. Studied book on pottery and worked in a friend's kiln. 1921—Exhibited pottery at a New York gallery. Has carried out ceramic decorations. Built own house. Represented in Metropolitan Museum, Whitney Museum of American Art.

PUCCINELLI, DOROTHY, 15 Hotaling Place
SAN FRANCISCO, CALIFORNIA

Winner of competition for mural in the Merced, California, Post Office.

1901, BORN, December, San Antonio, Texas. Pupil of Rudolph Schaeffer and Beniamino Bufano; California School of Fine Arts. Worked as illustrator and interior decorator. Member, San Francisco Art Association; San Francisco Society of Women Artists; San Francisco Society of Mural Painters, etc. Has held one-man shows, Art Center, San Francisco; California Palace of Legion of Honor. Work includes mural for the Fleischhacker Memorial Mothers House, under Public Works of Art Project; murals for hotels and private residences, San Francisco. Represented in Palace of Legion of Honor, San Francisco Museum of Art, and private collections. Award: San Francisco Society of Women Artists, 1932—First Prize.

REDMOND, JAMES, 221½ South Spring Street
LOS ANGELES, CALIFORNIA

Selected to design murals for the Compton, California, Post Office.

1901, BORN, September 14, Grand Rapids, Michigan. Pupil of McDonald Wright. Work includes murals for Phineas Banning Junior High School, Wilmington, California; Thomas Starr King Junior High School, Los Angeles, under Public Works of Art Project. Represented in San Diego Museum and private collections.

REINDEL, EDNA, 21 University Place
NEW YORK CITY

Selected to design murals for the P.W.A., Stamford, Connecticut, Housing Project.

Born Detroit, Michigan. Studied at Pratt Institute, Brooklyn. Illustrated books. 1927—Won Tiffany Foundation Fellowship for painting. 1933—Worked under Public Works of Art Project. Has exhibited at Whitney Museum of American Art, Corcoran Gallery, Albright Art Museum, Worcester Museum, Cincinnati Museum, Chicago Art Institute. One-man shows in various cities.

RHODES, DAN, 1741 8th Avenue
FORT DODGE, IOWA

Appointed to design mural for the Glen Ellyn, Illinois, Post Office, as result of quality of sketches submitted in National Competition for decoration of the Department of Justice Building, Washington, D.C.

1911, BORN, Fort Dodge, Iowa. University of Chicago, Ph.B., 1933. Studied at Chicago Art Institute; Art Students' League, under John Steuart

Curry; pupil of Grant Wood. Work includes mural in Navy Department Building, Washington, D. C., under Public Works of Art Project. Taught in Blanden Gallery, Fort Dodge.

RISEMAN, WILLIAM, 91 Court Road
WINTHROP, MASSACHUSETTS

Winner of competition for mural in the Lynn, Massachusetts, Post Office.

1910, BORN, Boston, Massachusetts. 1933—B.F.A., Yale School of Fine Arts. Work includes decorations for Park Central, St. Moritz and Montclair Hotels, New York; murals in La Fayette Hotel, Portland, Maine; Mon Paris, New York; Hotel Brunswick, Boston; La Fayette Hotel, Boston. Won scholarships at Yale for excellence in painting, and awards from Beaux Arts Institute of New York for mural design.

ROBINSON, BOARDMAN, 721 North Cascade Avenue
COLORADO SPRINGS, COLORADO

Appointed to design murals for the Department of Justice Building, Washington, D. C.

1876, BORN, September 6, Somerset, Nova Scotia. Studied at Massachusetts School of Art, Boston, and various Paris ateliers. Worked in stained glass, San Francisco. Did magazine illustration and newspaper cartooning, New York Morning Telegraph, New York Tribune, The Masses and The Liberator. Went to Serbia and Russia as artist-correspondent with John Reed for Metropolitan Magazine. 1919 to 1930—Taught at Art Students' League, New York. Illustrated "The War in Eastern Europe" by John Reed; "Brothers Karamazov" and "The Idiot" by Dostoyevsky. Work includes ten mural panels for Kaufmann Department Store, Pittsburgh; mural for Rockefeller Center, New York; paintings and drawings in various museums, including Metropolitan, New York. Art Instructor, Fountain Valley School for Boys, Colorado Springs; Art Director, Colorado Springs Fine Arts Center, Colorado Springs.

ROMANELLI, FRANK, 1301 West Avenue
BUFFALO, NEW YORK

Selected to design murals for the Nurses' Home, Buffalo, New York, Marine Hospital.

1909, BORN, February 20, Torenza, Italy. Parents skilled in crafts. Studied at Albright School of Fine Arts, Buffalo; architecture at Atelier Rectagon. Worked as factory hand, blacksmith, and followed other pursuits to support large family; dissected bodies and made anatomical drawings for Buffalo City Hospital, now in permanent reference library of the hospital. Work includes miniature sculptures for Hall of Primitive Man, Museum of Science, Buffalo; stone frieze for Library, State Teachers College, Buffalo, under Public Works of Art Project, carved by hand. Member, Artists' Cooperative, Buffalo Society of Artists, Pateran Society. Has exhibited locally. Awards: Albright School of Fine Arts—Honorable Mention and Carey Award.

ROMANO, UMBERTO,   67 West Street
                          WORCESTER, MASSACHUSETTS

*Appointed to design murals for the Springfield, Massachusetts,
Post Office, as result of quality of sketches submitted in competition
for decoration of the Lynn, Massachusetts, Post Office.*

1905, BORN, February 26, Italy. 1913—Came to the United States. Took night courses in art while at school. Studied at National Academy of Design, New York, and in art centers abroad. Has exhibited in leading museums and galleries in the United States. Represented in Rhode Island School of Design; Worcester Art Museum; Springfield Museum of Fine Arts; Smith College Museum; Fogg Museum; and private collections. Instructor in Advanced Drawing and Figure Painting, Worcester Art Museum School. Awards: National Academy of Design, 1926—Suydam Silver Medal; Tiffany Foundation Fellowship, 1926; Pulitzer Traveling Scholarship, 1926; Chicago Art Institute, 1928—Honorable Mention; Springfield Art League.

ROSEN, CHARLES,

                               WOODSTOCK, NEW YORK

Selected to design murals for the Beacon, New York, Post Office.

1878, BORN, Pennsylvania. Studied at National Academy of Design; New York School of Art, under Chase, Du Mond, Henri. Primarily interested in landscape, but has done number of portraits, some of which are hanging at West Point Military Academy. Represented in St. Louis Museum; Philadelphia Art Gallery; Delgado Museum, New Orleans; Minneapolis Art Gallery; Butler Museum, Youngstown, Ohio; Whitney Museum of American Art; Michigan University; Duluth Art Society. Awards: National Academy of Design—Inness Gold Medal and First Altman Prize; Pennsylvania Academy—Sesnan Gold Medal; Carnegie Institute—Honorable Mention.

ROUSSEFF, W. VLADIMIR,   615 East Oakwood Boulevard
                                   CHICAGO, ILLINOIS

Appointed to design murals for the Iron Mountain, Michigan, Post Office, as result of quality of sketches submitted in National Competition for decoration of the Post Office Department Building, Washington, D.C.

1890, BORN, May 24, Silistria, Bulgaria. Studied at Chicago Art Institute; pupil of Albert H. Krehbiel; Randall Davey. Work includes seven panels for Nichols Intermediate School, Evanston, Illinois, under Public Works of Art Project. Represented in Municipal Art League, Chicago; Chicago Art Institute Permanent Collection; and various private collections. Awards: Chicago Art Institute: 1919—Art Students' League Prize, 1926—Frank Prize, 1929—Logan Prize.

ROWE, WILLIAM B.,   715 Parkside Avenue
                                    BUFFALO, NEW YORK

Winner of competition for murals in the Buffalo, New York, Marine Hospital.

1910, BORN, May 25, Chicago, Illinois. Studied at Cornell University; pupil of Walter King Stone. Executed murals for Bennett High School,

Buffalo, under Public Works of Art Project. Has exhibited locally. Member, Pateran Art Society; Buffalo Society of Artists; Decorative Arts Guild; Artists Cooperative Group. Work owned in private collections. Awards: Honorable Mention in architectural competition; Janis Prize for Sculpture, Buffalo Society of Artists.

SAMPLE, PAUL,   676 La Loma Road
                                    PASADENA, CALIFORNIA

Appointed to design murals for the Redondo Beach, California, Post Office, as result of quality of sketches submitted in National Competition for decoration of the Post Office Department Building, Washington, D. C.

1896, BORN, September 14, Louisville, Kentucky. Graduate Dartmouth College, 1921. Served overseas in Navy during World War. Self-taught. Associate Professor of Fine Arts, University of Southern California. Work owned by Springfield, Massachusetts, Museum; Canajoharie, New York, Museum; Wood Art Museum, Montpelier, Vermont; West Museum, Swarthmore College; Foundation of Western Art, Los Angeles; University of Southern California; Los Angeles Board of Education. Has won several awards and exhibited in many national exhibitions. Los Angeles Museum, 1930—First Prize; California Arts Club—Mabury Prize; Pasadena Art Institute, 1932—First Prize; California State Fair—First Prize; National Academy of Design—Isidor Gold Medal; Santa Cruz Art League, 1933—First Prize; Carnegie Institute, 1936—Honorable Mention.

SARISKY, MICHAEL,   11225 Parkview Avenue
                                    CLEVELAND, OHIO

Winner competition for mural, Barnesville, Ohio, Post Office.

1906, BORN, September 24. Pupil of Henry George Keller, Cleveland School of Art; John Huntington Institute; Henry Tonks, Slade School, London. Instructor in Figure Drawing, Cleveland School of Art, for four years. Work includes mural for Rocky River Masonic Temple; two murals for Cleveland Auditorium, under Public Works of Art Project. Has exhibited at Dayton Museum, and in traveling exhibits of the Cleveland Museum. Awards: Gottwald Traveling Scholarship, 1928; Slade Prize, London, 1929; Prix de Rome Competition, 1931-1932, Second; Cleveland Museum, Figure Composition Prize and also Portrait Prizes.

SCHEUCH, HARRY W.,   1204 Wood Street
                                  WILKINSBURG, PENNSYLVANIA

Appointed to design mural for the Scottdale, Pennsylvania, Post Office, as result of quality of sketches submitted in competition for Pittsburgh, Pennsylvania, Post Office and Court House decorations.

1907, BORN, April 6, Elizabeth, New Jersey. Studied at Carnegie Institute of Technology, College of Fine Arts; pupil of Giovanni Romagnola. Member, Associated Artists of Pittsburgh. Worked under Public Works of Art Project. Has exhibited in Carnegie Institute. Represented in Pennsylvania State College; "100 Friends of Pittsburgh Art."

SCHWARTZ, WILLIAM S.,   29 East Ohio Street
                                         CHICAGO, ILLINOIS

Winner of competition for Fairfield, Illinois, Post Office mural.

1896, BORN, February 23, Russia. Studied at Vilna Art Academy, Russia; Chicago Art Institute. Work includes murals for Century of Progress Exposition, Chicago, and Cook County Nurses' Home. Has exhibited in National Gallery, Ottawa; Canada Gallery of Art, Toronto; many museums and galleries in the United States; and has held several one-man shows. Work owned by Chicago Public School; University of Nebraska; University of Missouri; University of Wisconsin; Cincinnati Public Library; Public Art Gallery, Dallas, Texas; Glencoe Public Library; Barrington Public Library. Awards: Detroit, 1925—First Kahn Prize; 1926—First Temple Beth El Sisterhood Prize; Chicago Art Institute, 1927—Homes Prize; 1929—Kohnstamm Prize; 1930—Shafer Prize; 1936—Clyde M. Carr Prize.

SCHWEINSBURG, ROLAND A.,   2323 Belmont Avenue
                                         YOUNGSTOWN, OHIO

Selected to design mural for the East Liverpool, Ohio, Post Office.

1898, BORN, July 27, Ellwood City, Pennsylvania. Father, steel mill worker. Served as apprentice. Pupil of Henry Keller, Herman Matzen, Paul Travis, Otto F. Ege, Frank Wilcox, William Eastman, Glenn Shaw, Henry Turner Bailey, at the Cleveland Art School. Free lance work in Cleveland. Designed interiors. Four years work as advertising and newspaper artist. Work includes five murals for Reuben McMillan Public Library, under Public Works of Art Project. 1932 to 1935—President, Mahoning Society of Painters.

SEEDS, ELISE,   1547 Elevado Street
                                         LOS ANGELES, CALIFORNIA

Appointed to design mural for the Oceanside, California, Post Office, as result of quality of sketches submitted in competition for decoration of the Beverly Hills, California, Post Office.

1904, BORN, Philadelphia, Pennsylvania. Attended Pennsylvania Academy of Fine Arts for two years, receiving criticisms from Daniel Garber, Hugh Breckinridge, and Arthur Carles. Has given dance recitals and played in theatrical companies; some experience in stage design. Chief cartoonist for American Sketch, 1929. Lithographs included in Fifty Prints of Year, 1934-1935. Work includes two murals for the Los Angeles Museum, under Public Works of Art Project.

SHAW, GLENN,   15316 Lake Avenue
                                         LAKEWOOD, CLEVELAND, OHIO

Appointed to design murals for the Canton, Ohio, Post Office, as result of quality of sketches submitted in competition for decoration of the Cleveland, Ohio, Post Office.

1891, BORN, February 6, Olmsted Falls, Ohio. Studied at Cleveland School of Art; pupil of Henry Keller and Charles Hawthorne. Studied abroad. Instructor in Figure and Costume Painting, Cleveland School of Art; Instructor in Graphic Design, John Huntington Polytechnic Institute, Cleveland. Work includes murals for Central National Bank, Cleveland; Old National Bank, Lima, Ohio; lunettes and ceiling decoration for Lincoln National Bank, Fort Wayne, Indiana; mural for Federal Reserve Bank, Pittsburgh; two historic panels for Lakewood, Ohio, High School; decorative panel for Statler Hotel, Cleveland; two decorative panels for Statler Hotel, Buffalo. Represented in Cleveland Museum of Art and private collections.

SHORE, HENRIETTA,
                                         CARMEL-BY-THE-SEA, CALIFORNIA

Selected to design murals for the Santa Cruz, California, Post Office.

Born Toronto, Canada. Studied at New York School of Art; Art Students' League, New York; Heatherley Art School, London. Became American citizen, 1921. One of Founders, New York Society of Women Artists and Los Angeles Modern Art Society. 1923—Retrospective exhibition of work shown at Worcester Art Museum, Minnesota State Fair, California Palace of Legion of Honor, and M. H. de Young Memorial Museum, San Francisco. Represented in Library of Congress; National Gallery of Art, Ottawa, Canada; Gallery of Fine Arts, San Diego, California; University of Washington, Seattle. Winner of several awards in painting and the graphic arts.

SILVETTE, DAVID,   901 West Grace Street
                                         RICHMOND, VIRGINIA

Winner mural competition New Bern, North Carolina, Court House.

1909, BORN, May 28. Pupil of E. M. Silvette (Father); Cecilia Beaux; Charles Hawthorne. Has exhibited extensively and done number of portrait commissions, including group portrait for Virginia State Capitol. Represented in Corcoran Gallery, Washington, D. C., and Richmond Academy of Arts. Awards: Richmond Academy, 1930—Portrait Prize; Corcoran Gallery, 1932—Third Prize. One-man exhibition, Brooklyn Museum, at the age of twenty-three.

SMITH, JACOB GETLAR,   63 East 57th Street
                                         NEW YORK CITY

Selected to design murals for the Nyack, New York, Post Office.

1898, BORN, February 3, New York City. Studied at National Academy of Design and independently abroad. Has exhibited at Carnegie International; Chicago Art Institute; Century of Progress Exposition; Baltimore Pan-American; Whitney Museum of American Art; St. Louis Art Museum; National Gallery of Canada; Corcoran Gallery; Pennsylvania Academy; First Municipal Art Show, New York; California Palace of Legion of Honor, San Francisco. Represented in Whitney Museum of American Art, and private collections. Awards: Chicago Art Institute, 1927—Honorable Mention in Figure Painting; Guggenheim Fellowship, 1929; Chicago Art Institute, 1930—Logan Prize. Has held four one-man shows in New York.

STERNBERG, HARRY, 333 West 18th Street
NEW YORK CITY

Appointed to design mural for the Sellersville, Pennsylvania, Post Office, as result of quality of sketches submitted in National Competition for decoration of the Justice Department Building, Washington, D. C.

1904, BORN, July 19. Studied at Art Students' League; pupil of George Bridgman and Harry Wickey. 1932 and 1934—One-man shows in a New York gallery. Instructor in Etching and Lithography, Art Students' League. Represented in Whitney Museum of American Art; New York Public Library; Newark Public Library; Ohio University; Addison Museum, Andover, Massachusetts; Cleveland Museum; Brooklyn Museum; Victoria and Albert Museum, London; Bibliothèque Nationale, Paris, Fine Prints of the Year, 1931, 1933, 1934.

STERNE, MAURICE, 970 Chestnut Street
SAN FRANCISCO, CALIFORNIA

Appointed to design murals for the Library of the Justice Department Building, Washington, D. C.

1877, BORN, Libau, Russia. Came to New York, 1899. Studied at National Academy of Design and other schools in New York. Traveled extensively in Europe; special study of people of Bali. Member, Society of Painters, Sculptors and Gravers. Represented in Carnegie Institute, Pittsburgh; Rhode Island School of Design; Metropolitan Museum; Boston Museum of Fine Arts; Detroit Museum; Harrison Gallery; Los Angeles Museum; Corcoran Gallery, Washington; Cleveland Museum of Arts; San Diego Fine Arts Gallery; Kaiser Friederich Museum, Berlin; Cologne Museum; Tate Gallery, London. Monument, "The Early New England Settlers," Worcester, Massachusetts. Awards: Chicago Art Institute, 1928—Logan Prize; Corcoran Gallery, 1930—First Clark Prize and Corcoran Gold Medal.

STEVENS, W. LESTER, 59 Pine Street
SPRINGFIELD, MASSACHUSETTS

Selected to design mural for the Dedham, Massachusetts, Post Office.
Pupil of Parker S. Perkins, Boston Museum School. Member, Associate National Academy of Design; Rockport Art Association; Springfield, Massachusetts, Art League; New Haven Paint and Clay Club; North Shore Art Association; Guild of Boston Artists. Awards: Corcoran Gallery—Fourth Clark Prize; Connecticut Academy of Fine Arts—Gedney Bunce Prize; National Academy of Design, 1927—Second Altman Prize; American Water Color Society—Delano Prize; New Haven Print and Clay Club—Mansfield Prize and Club Prize; Springville, Utah—Special Award of Honor; Springfield Art League—Patrons' Prize.

TABOR, ROBERT,
INDEPENDENCE, IOWA

Winner of competition for mural in the Independence, Iowa, Post Office.
1882, BORN, February 12, Independence, Iowa. Studied sketching at Cedar Rapids, Iowa. Worked under Public Works of Art Project. Works include portraits, easel pictures, murals for a hotel and a club in Des Moines, Iowa. Has exhibited at Iowa State Fair, receiving Fourth Award in 1934. Represented in White House collection.

THOMPSON, LORIN, JR., 511 Jeannette Street
WILKINSBURG, PENNSYLVANIA

Appointed to design murals for the Altoona, Pennsylvania, Post Office, as result of quality of sketches submitted in competition for Pittsburgh, Pennsylvania, Post Office and Court House decoration.

1911, BORN, March 19, Pittsburgh, Pennsylvania. Pupil of Alexander J. Kostellow, Carnegie Institute of Technology College of Fine Arts. In charge of art education at a local art center. Work includes murals for the Somerset, Pennsylvania, High School, under Public Works of Art Project; murals on aluminum for Aluminum Company of America exhibit at Annual Science Exhibition, American Association for the Advancement of Science. Has exhibited at Chicago Art Institute; Iowa State University; William R. Nelson Gallery of Art, Kansas City; Minneapolis Institute. Is in charge of art education at a local educational center.

TURZAK, CHARLES, 1265 Foster Avenue
CHICAGO, ILLINOIS

Selected to design murals for the Chicago, Illinois, Post Office.

1899, BORN, August 20, Streator, Illinois. Studied at Chicago Art Institute, 1920 to 1924, and since then independently. Works in water color, oil and woodcut. Work includes biographies of Abraham Lincoln and Benjamin Franklin which are profusely illustrated with woodcuts, with text by Florence Turzak; and a series of woodcuts, "Chicago Moods" and "History of Illinois," under Public Works of Art Project.

VAN VEEN, STUYVESANT, 24 West 96th Street
NEW YORK CITY

Winner of competition for mural in the Pittsburgh, Pennsylvania Post Office and Court House.

1910, BORN, September 12, New York City. Pupil of and later assistant to David Karfunkle; studied under Barber, Harding, Pearson, Pennsylvania Academy of Fine Arts Summer School; student of Thomas Benton, Art Students' League; worked in New York Industrial School of Art and National Academy of Design School. Taught at John Reed Art School. Has done portraits, landscape, water colors, etchings, lithographs, illustration and textile design. Illustrating and collaborating on book on Anthropology. Research Associate, Department of Anthropology, Columbia University. Worked under Public Works of Art Project. Member, Society of Mural Painters, Artists' Union. Has exhibited extensively.

WARD, CHARLES W.,   449 South Olden Avenue
                                            TRENTON, NEW JERSEY

Selected to design murals for the Trenton, New Jersey, Post Office.

1900, B O R N , January 24, Trenton, New Jersey. Pupil of George Harding, Pennsylvania Academy of Fine Arts. Won Lea Award for draughtsmanship; Cresson Traveling Scholarship. Studied abroad, paying particular attention to church paintings and frescoes by early Italian painters. Has held one-man shows in Raleigh, North Carolina; Trenton, New Jersey; New York City; Scranton, Pennsylvania. Work owned by Scranton Museum; Pennsylvania Museum, and private collectors. Executed industrial mural for Trenton Post Office, under Public Works of Art Project.

WESSEL, HERMAN H.,   2152 Alpine Place
                                            CINCINNATI, OHIO

Winner of competition for mural in the Springfield, Ohio, Post Office.

1878, B O R N , Vincennes, Indiana. Studied at Cincinnati Art Academy; Colarossi's and Julian Academy, Paris. Pupil of Duveneck. Member of Faculty, Cincinnati Art Academy. Work includes murals in Federal Branch Bank, Cincinnati; Court House, Portsmouth, Ohio; State Office Building, Columbus, Ohio. Has exhibited extensively. Awards: South Western Artists, 1915—Fine Arts Prize; Atlanta, 1920— First Prize; Columbus, 1932—First Portrait Prize

WESTON, HAROLD,
                                            ST. HUBERT'S, ESSEX COUNTY, NEW YORK

Appointed to design murals for the Treasury Department Procurement Division Building, Washington, D. C., as result of quality of sketches submitted in competition for decoration of the Philadelphia, Pennsylvania, Custom House and Appraisers' Stores.

1894, B O R N , February 14, Merion, Pennsylvania. Harvard College, 1916; studied under Denman Ross. Worked for short periods under Hamilton Easter Field, Homer Boss, Henry McCarter, William Schumacher. For three years attached to British Army, Y.M.C.A., during World War. 1917—Founded Baghdad Art Club. 1918—Sent to Persia to sketch for London War Museums. Has held one-man exhibitions in New York, Washington, Philadelphia, Rochester, Cleveland, Chicago, St. Louis, Louisville, Paris, Baghdad. Represented in London War Museum; Rochester Memorial Art Gallery; Pennsylvania Academy of Fine Arts; Phillips Memorial Gallery, Washington; Yale Museum of Fine Arts; Butler Gallery, Columbia University; and a large number of private collections.

WHITE, FRANCIS ROBERT,   The Little Gallery
                                            CEDAR RAPIDS, IOWA

Appointed to design murals for the Cedar Rapids, Iowa, Post Office and Court House, as result of quality of sketches submitted in National Competition for decoration of the Post Office Department Building, Washington, D. C.

1907, B O R N , April 19, Oskaloosa, Iowa. Studied at Pennsylvania Academy of Fine Arts; Art Students' League (night school), under John Sloan, John Steuart Curry, Harry Wickey. Worked and studied abroad independently. Executed two murals in Philadelphia; apprenticed in art glass studio, Wilkes-Barre, Pennsylvania; designed and executed window. Worked under Public Works of Art Project, Chicago; in C.C.C. camp, Cody, Wyoming. Member, Cooperative Mural Painters. Exhibited in Little Gallery, Cedar Rapids; Corcoran Gallery; Museum of Modern Art, New York. Work owned by Whitney Museum, New York. Award: Guggenheim Scholarship, 1930-1931.

WHITE, WILLIAM D.,   Box 243-B, Marsh Road
                                            WILMINGTON, DELAWARE

Selected to design murals for the Dover, Delaware, Post Office.

1896, B O R N , July 22, Wilmington, Delaware. Pupil of Emil Carlsen, Philip Hale, Hugh Breckenridge, Daniel Garber, Cecilia Beaux, Joseph Pearson, Henry McCarter—Pennsylvania Academy of Fine Arts. Commissioned by power company to paint miners in anthracite coal fields; has carried out various other commissions for mining and engineering companies. Represented in Corcoran Gallery of Art, Washington, D. C.; Pennsylvania Museum of Art; Wilmington Society of Fine Arts.

ZOELLNER, RICHARD,   1 Filson Place, Mount Adams
                                            CINCINNATI, OHIO

Winner of competition for mural in the Portsmouth, Ohio, Post Office, and selected to design murals for the Hamilton, Ohio, Post Office.

1908, B O R N , June 30, Portsmouth, Ohio. Pupil of H. H. Wessel, John Weiss, and William Hentschel, Cincinnati Art Academy. Won two scholarships at Academy and a scholarship later from the Tiffany Foundation. Did free lance work as student and taught drawing and painting in private classes. Instructor in Color Design, Children's Class, Cincinnati Art Museum. Worked under Public Works of Art Project, executing four panels showing development of mails for the Cincinnati Post Office. Has exhibited at Cincinnati Annual Exhibition of American Art; College Art "Young Artists' Show; Chicago International Water Color Exhibition.

171